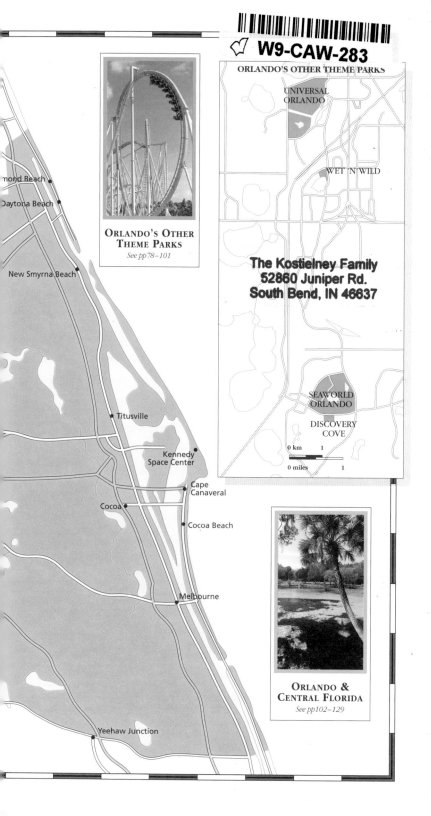

W9-CAW-283

ORLANDO'S OTHER THEME PARKS

UNIVERSAL
ORLANDO

WET 'N WILD

SEAWORLD
ORLANDO

DISCOVERY
COVE

0 km   1

0 miles   1

The Kostielney Family
52860 Juniper Rd.
South Bend, IN 46637

mond Beach
Daytona Beach

New Smyrna Beach

**ORLANDO'S OTHER
THEME PARKS**
See pp78–101

Titusville

Kennedy
Space Center

Cape
Canaveral

Cocoa

Cocoa Beach

Melbourne

Yeehaw Junction

**ORLANDO &
CENTRAL FLORIDA**
See pp102–129

EYEWITNESS TRAVEL GUIDES

WALT DISNEY
WORLD® RESORT
& ORLANDO

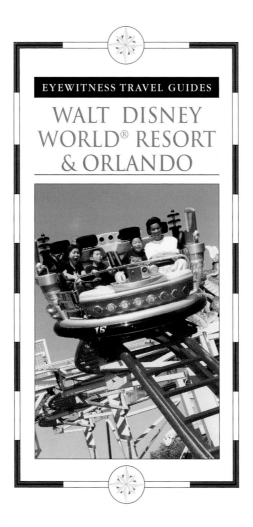

EYEWITNESS TRAVEL GUIDES

WALT DISNEY WORLD®
RESORT & ORLANDO

Epcot

DK

LONDON, NEW YORK,
MELBOURNE, MUNICH AND DELHI
www.dk.com

Managing Editor Aruna Ghose
Art Editor Benu Joshi
Senior Editor Rimli Borooah
Editor Shahnaaz Bakshi
Designer Kavita Saha
Picture Researcher Taiyaba Khatoon
Cartographer Suresh Kumar
DTP Coordinator Shailesh Sharma
DTP Designer Vinod Harish

Main Contributors
Phyllis and Arvin Steinberg, Joseph Hayes, Charles Martin

Consultant
Richard Grula

Reproduced by Colourscan (Singapore)
Printed and bound in China by L. Rex Printing Co. Ltd

First American Edition 2005
00 01 02 03 04 05 10 9 8 7 6 5 4 3 2 1

Published in the United States by
DK Publishing, Inc., 375 Hudson Street,
New York, New York 10014

Copyright © 2005 Dorling Kindersley Limited
London
A Penguin Company

Published in Great Britain by Dorling Kindersley Limited.

A Cataloging in Publication record is available from the
Library of Congress.

ISSN 1542 1554

ISBN 0 7566 0528 8

This book makes reference to various trademarks, marks and registered
marks owned by the Disney Company and Disney Enterprises, Inc.

**A ride at Universal Orlando's
Islands of Adventure (see pp96–7)**

CONTENTS

INTRODUCING
WALT DISNEY
WORLD® RESORT
& ORLANDO

**Dolphins performing at a show
at SeaWorld (see pp82–5)**

◁ **Spectacular fireworks above Cinderella's Castle at Magic Kingdom®, Walt Disney World® Resort**

Primeval Whirl®, at Disney's Animal Kingdom® *(see pp64–7)*

Stone crab claws,
a popular appetizer

SURVIVAL GUIDE

WALT DISNEY WORLD® RESORT & CENTRAL FLORIDA AREA BY AREA

Highway patrol insignia

TRAVELERS' NEEDS

A boardwalk trail at Blue Spring State Park *(see p116)*

Space shuttle launch pad *(see pp20–1)*

INTRODUCING WALT DISNEY WORLD® RESORT & ORLANDO

O.129—A. C. L. Railway Station, Orlando, Fla.
"The City Beautiful"

Putting Central Florida on the Map

AT THE APPROXIMATE geographic center of Florida, the Greater Orlando area covers around 2,850 sq miles (7,380 sq km). Flanked by beaches, peppered with lakes, and blessed with exceptional weather, the area's 1.8 million residents play host to over 46 million visitors a year. Walt Disney World® Resort and the region's other theme parks are the top attractions for the majority of vacationers. A sizeable number also visit the surrounding Central Florida area – including the beaches on the east, Ocala National Forest to the north, and the Kennedy Space Center on the Space Coast, named for its heavy concentration of space and defense industries.

The state seal of Florida

Fireworks in Walt Disney World® Resort's Magic Kingdom®

◁ Fun and frolic in the waters and sands of Discovery Cove

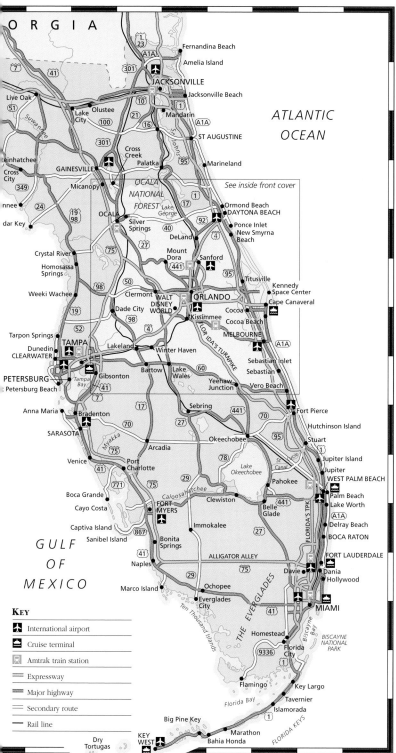

ORGIA

ATLANTIC OCEAN

Fernandina Beach
Amelia Island

JACKSONVILLE
Jacksonville Beach
Mandarin
ST AUGUSTINE
Marineland

Live Oak
Lake City
Olustee
Cross Creek
Palatka

einhatchee
Cross City
GAINESVILLE
Micanopy
nnee
dar Key

OCALA NATIONAL FOREST
Lake George

See inside front cover

Ormond Beach
DAYTONA BEACH
Ponce Inlet
New Smyrna Beach

OCALA
Silver Springs
DeLand

Crystal River
Homosassa Springs
Weeki Wachee

Mount Dora
Sanford

Titusville
Kennedy Space Center
Cape Canaveral

Clermont
Dade City
WALT DISNEY WORLD
ORLANDO
Kissimmee
Cocoa
Cocoa Beach

MELBOURNE

Tarpon Springs
Dunedin
CLEARWATER
TAMPA
Lakeland
Winter Haven
Bartow
Lake Wales

Sebastian Inlet
Sebastian
Vero Beach

PETERSBURG
Petersburg Beach
Gibsonton
Tampa Bay

Yeehaw Junction

Fort Pierce
Hutchinson Island

Anna Maria
Bradenton
SARASOTA

Sebring

Stuart

Venice
Port Charlotte
Arcadia

Okeechobee
Lake Okeechobee

Jupiter Island
Jupiter
WEST PALM BEACH
Palm Beach
Lake Worth

Boca Grande
Cayo Costa
Captiva Island
Sanibel Island

FORT MYERS
Clewiston
Belle Glade
Pahokee

Delray Beach
BOCA RATON

GULF OF MEXICO

Bonita Springs
Naples

Immokalee
ALLIGATOR ALLEY

FORT LAUDERDALE
Davie
Dania
Hollywood

Marco Island
Ochopee
Everglades City

THE EVERGLADES

MIAMI

Homestead
Florida City
BISCAYNE NATIONAL PARK

Ten Thousand Islands

Flamingo
Key Largo
Tavernier
Islamorada

Florida Bay

Big Pine Key
KEY WEST
Marathon
Bahia Honda

FLORIDA KEYS

Dry Tortugas

KEY

- ✈ International airport
- ⚓ Cruise terminal
- 🚉 Amtrak train station
- Expressway
- Major highway
- Secondary route
- Rail line

A PORTRAIT OF
CENTRAL FLORIDA

SUN-DRENCHED BEACHES *with aquamarine waters and the never-ending amusement offered by its theme parks make Central Florida the ultimate family vacation destination. Adding to the mix are scenic nature preserves, unique cultural and historic attractions, fantastic shopping, and evening entertainment options.*

In the last 50 years, Orlando and Central Florida have witnessed a spurt of development unmatched by any other region of the state. The initial fillip to this primarily agricultural community was provided by the increased employment opportunities associated with the space program at Cape Canaveral.

Juan Ponce de Leon

Then Walt Disney World arrived on the scene, opening its first theme park – Magic Kingdom – in 1971. The rest, as they say, is history.

HISTORY

The first Europeans to set foot on the Florida peninsula were Spanish explorers who sighted land between Cape Canaveral and the Matanzas Inlet in 1513. On April 2, 1513, Ponce de Leon claimed the territory for King Phillip of Spain and named it La Florida – the Place of Flowers. Spain, France, and England ruled the region in turns. The 20-year British rule, from 1763 to 1783, is notable for the growth of a flourishing plantation economy: the Daytona Beach area, for instance, successfully produced cotton, sugarcane, rice, and indigo. In 1821, Florida was finally ceded to the United States by Spain. The plantation system soon entered the Industrial Revolution, with the application of steam power to sugar and rum processing: the first steam-operated mill was at the Dummett Plantation in Ormond Beach.

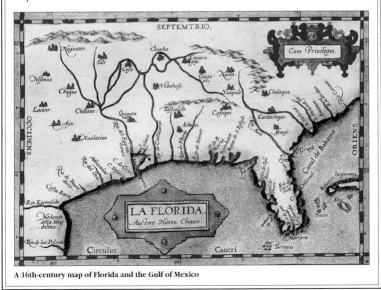

A 16th-century map of Florida and the Gulf of Mexico

◁ **A lifeguard sits on duty at Daytona Beach, one of the country's most popular beaches**

Attempts by the Americans to remove the Seminole Indians, who had settled in the area in the 17th century, continued for decades. Central Florida's plantation economy suffered major losses when the Seminole Indians destroyed many plantations and sugar mills during the seven-year Second Seminole War, which ended in 1842. Orlando was born during this period, developing around an Army post, Fort Gatlin.

With ample land available for grazing, Central Florida fostered a thriving cattle industry. By the early 1860s, cattle and cotton were the mainstays of the region's economy. The Civil War, however, sounded the death knell of the cotton industry by taking away much of its workforce. Then came a hurricane in 1871, which wiped out the whole crop. Farmers turned to citrus, which was easier to grow than cotton. The region's citrus indutry grew by leaps and bounds, helped along by developments such as the extension of the South Florida Railroad into Central Florida in 1880. Freezing weather in 1894–95 hit Central Florida's citrus

Oranges, Central Florida's juiciest crop

industry very hard, but it recovered and continued on course to make the region one of the world's leading producers of citrus fruit.

During the hard freezes, an innovative citrus grower, John B. Steinmentz, converted his citrus packing house into a skating rink, built a bathhouse and picnic area, and created a toboggan slide that led into a spring. Thus was set up the region's first entertainment complex, a precursor of things to come.

With the advent of electricity in 1900, telephones in 1901, and the first cars in 1903, Central Florida entered the 20th century. The Orlando Municipal Airport opened in 1928. A major turning point was in 1955, when the NASA space program was launched at Cape Canaveral near Orlando. The Glenn L. Martin Company set up a missile factory south of the city in 1956, and became the area's largest employer before Walt Disney arrived.

The success of Disney's Magic Kingdom led to a proliferation of theme parks. SeaWorld Orlando opened in 1973, while Walt Disney World continued to expand with the setting up of Epcot, Disney-MGM Studios, and Animal Kingdom. In 1977, Wet 'n Wild, the world's first water park, opened with a splash. In 1990, Universal Orlando entered the arena with Universal Studios Florida, followed a few years later by Universal CityWalk and Islands of Adventure. Discovery Cove in 2000. This wealth of entertainment options has earned Orlando the title of "Theme Park Capital of the World," and has firmly entrenched it as one of the world's topmost vacation spots.

BEYOND THE THEME PARKS

Central Florida's tourist appeal is not limited to its theme parks. The great outdoors beckons along the East Coast and the forests and waterways of the interior. Pristine beaches, lush state and county parks, and natural sanctuaries are all within easy reach of the highways and at times run parallel to

A dizzying thrill ride at SeaWorld® Orlando

A Disney Cruise Line® ship at a gleaming terminal in Port Canaveral

them, making driving in the area an enjoyable experience. Another way to enjoy the region's natural beauty is to board a seaplane from Orlando: rides and tours take passengers from the water to the air for amazing sightings of alligators, eagles, deer, and other wildlife in their natural habitat.

Outdoor activities are available in plenty, from biking, hiking, and golfing to swimming, angling, boating, and most other watersports. Additionally, outstanding professional sports bring tourists to the region in droves. The cruise industry is also flourishing, with Port Canaveral, the world's second largest multi-day cruise port, just 45 minutes east of Orlando. Thousands of visitors take the Disney Cruise Line ships and other luxury cruises from this port to destinations around the world.

A Florida Film Festival poster

Along the Space Coast is the Kennedy Space Center, home to NASA. Opened to the public in 1996, it now attracts more than 2 million visitors each year to see shuttles launched into space and to explore its workings and technology.

Farther north up the Space Coast is Daytona Beach, synonymous with car racing. From 1903 to 1935, all of the world's land speed records were set here. Stock cars began racing at Ormond Beach in 1936, and the first Daytona 200 motorcycle race took place there the following year. In 1959 Daytona International Speedway opened, and racing on the beach was abandoned. The speedway hosts numerous sports car, motorcycle, and go-karting races, attracting racing aficionados from all over the world.

Apart from the big theme parks, Central Florida offers countless smaller entertainment venues, ranging from the old-fashioned to the ultra-glitzy. Trendy nightspots, dinner shows, rodeos, fine dining, and a surfeit of shopping options add to the Orlando area's charm. There is plenty of cultural activity as well, with art and history museums dotting the area, and a highly active theater, opera, ballet, film, and live concert scene.

Central Florida's weather plays no small role in the region's appeal. Many people think of the area as a place where the sun always shines and the temperatures are warm, but this is not always so and there are days and

Shuttle launch at Kennedy Space Center

Glittering high-rises reflected in the placid waters of Lake Eola in Downtown Orlando

evenings in December, January, and February when it can get extremely cold. However, this in no way detracts from Central Florida's status as a year-round destination.

ECONOMY & TOURISM

For most of its history, the main source of revenue of the region – and the entire state – has been agriculture. Improved communications and transportation have kept the citrus and cattle industries buoyant. The area along the Kissimmee River is Florida's principal cattle ranching country, and the town of Kissimmee is known as the state's "Cow Capital." The region has contributed hugely to making Florida second only to Kentucky in the raising of beef cattle in the Southeastern states. Central Florida also continues to be the state's major supplier of citrus fruits; here, fruit trees stretch as far as the eye can see. The high-tech

Tourists riding a trail at a resort in Orlando

industry has also become a significant factor in the region's economy.

However, it is tourism that is now the mainstay of the economy of Central Florida. Theme parks dominate the region's tourism industry, but Orlando has also emerged as one of the country's leaders in the meetings and conventions industry. The city's Orange County Convention Center is one of the country's largest. The broader Orlando area has more than 110,000 hotel rooms, testifying to the huge numbers of visitors drawn by its many entertainment and business opportunities. Today, tourism is the largest employer in Metropolitan Orlando, accounting for around 27 percent of the jobs.

PEOPLE & CULTURE

The state "where everyone is from somewhere else," Florida has always been a mix of cultures and nationalities. The Seminole Indians, who arrived in the 17th century, now live mostly on reservations. The best candidates for the title of "true Floridian" are probably the Cracker farmers, whose ancestors settled in Central Florida and its environs in the 1800s; their name comes perhaps from the cracking of their cattle whips or the cracking of corn to make grits. However, visitors rarely encounter a Cracker in Orlando or the nearby heavily populated areas.

North Americans have poured into Florida since World War II; the 20th most populous state in the US in 1950, Florida is now ranked fourth. The largest single group to move south has been the retirees, for whom Florida's climate and leisurely lifestyle hold great appeal after a life of hard work. They take full advantage of Central Florida's abundance of recreational and cultural opportunities. Many seniors can be seen playing a round of golf, fishing, or browsing around the state-of-the-art shopping malls. An increasing number of new arrivals are young people who see Central Florida as a land of opportunity because of its booming tourism industry. They find it easy to get jobs as tour guides, hotel staff, theme park workers, and numerous other posts related to the thriving tourist-oriented economy.

Zora Neale Hurston, leading writer of her time

From 1959 on, there has also been massive immigration from Latin America. There are many Mexican farm-workers as well as a large Cuban population in Florida. Many businesses in Central Florida hire employees who speak Spanish in addition to English because of the numerous residents and vacationers from Latin American countries. This ethnic diversity is celebrated in the local food, which features genuine re-creations of Caribbean and other ethnic dishes. Several exciting and innovative dishes have also originated in the region as a result of the craze for cross-cultural cuisine.

The diversity of Central Florida's people is also celebrated in many festivals held throughout the year, such as the Native American Festival in November in Silver Springs, the Epcot International Food and Wine Festival in October and November, and the Kissimmee Bluegrass Festival in March. Another significant cultural event is held in Eatonville, the oldest incorporated African-American community in the US. This festival is named for its native daughter Zora Neale Hurston (1891–1960), a well-known novelist, folk-lorist, and anthropologist.

Relaxed and laidback are the words that best describe the people of Central Florida. It is also the area's dress code: rarely will visitors come across a place that requires them to wear a jacket and a tie. People are often seen in the fanciest of restaurants in blue jeans and tennis shoes. Central Florida is a place where tourists can ask a native for directions, and get a friendly smile and an answer, no matter how complicated the question. Folk here are rarely in a rush to get anywhere. They came to Central Florida to escape the harsh winters in the north and elsewhere. They are here to relax and have fun, and they are quite proficient at it.

A cabin owner fishes from his front porch at the Wekiva River Corridor near Orlando

Theme Parks

THE ATTRACTIONS AT Walt Disney World, Universal Orlando, SeaWorld, Discovery Cove, and Wet 'n' Wild give a whole new meaning to the word "fun." There is something for everyone, young and old, at these amazing theme parks. On offer are the high-voltage excitement of rides – including roller coasters as well as simulator and flume rides – the thrill of animal encounters and Space Age attractions, the magic of fairy-tales and the movies, the visual extravaganza of parades and fireworks, and much more, with one theme park usually specializing, or scoring over the others, in a particular area.

Fireworks
Dazzling displays against the superb setting of Cinderella's Castle make the fireworks at Magic Kingdom difficult to beat.

Kid's rides at their best are to be found at Magic Kingdom's Fantasyland. Most of them are based on classic Disney films.

Parades
Magic Kingdom has the biggest and best parades, along Main Street, in the afternoons and evenings. Spectacular affairs, they feature grandiose floats, with colorfully clad Disney characters and special effects.

Science attractions at Epcot's Future World win hands-down. One of the most popular is the simulated adventure Mission: SPACE, designed with the help of professional astronauts.

Lake Tibet

Lake Mabel

Lak Shee

WINTER GARDEN-VINELAND ROAD

Magic Kingdom® Park
(See pp34–41)

Bay Lake

WALT DISNEY WORLD® RESORT

WORLD DRIVE

EPCOT CENTER DRIVE

Epcot®
(See pp42–53)

Downtown Disney®
(See pp74–

Disney's Animal Kingdom®
(See pp64–7)

Disney-MGM Studios
(See pp54–63)

Blizzard Beach
(See p70)

Typhoon Lagoo
(See p71)

424

Disney's Wide World of Sports®
(See p178)

4

Wildlife
Real and mythical animals crowd the best theme park in which to view wildlife, Animal Kingdom. Glimpse hippos, giraffes, and zebras on a jeep ride through a re-created African landscape on Kilimanjaro Safaris.

Sports
With facilities for more than 30 sports – including baseball, basketball, tennis, and much more – Disney's Wide World of Sports overshadows all other sports venues at theme parks.

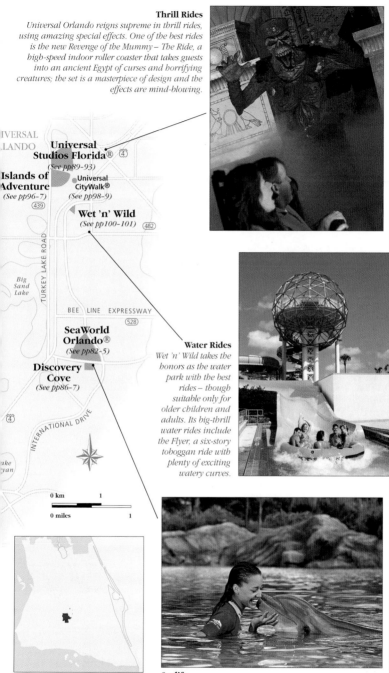

Thrill Rides
Universal Orlando reigns supreme in thrill rides, using amazing special effects. One of the best rides is the new Revenge of the Mummy – The Ride, a high-speed indoor roller coaster that takes guests into an ancient Egypt of curses and horrifying creatures; the set is a masterpiece of design and the effects are mind-blowing.

IVERSAL
LANDO   **Universal Studios Florida**® ④
(See pp89–93)

Islands of Adventure
(See pp96–7)
(439)

Universal CityWalk®
(See pp98–9)

Wet 'n' Wild
(See pp100–101)   (482)

TURKEY LAKE ROAD

Big Sand Lake

BEE LINE EXPRESSWAY
(528)

SeaWorld Orlando®
(See pp82–5)

Discovery Cove
(See pp86–7)

④

INTERNATIONAL DRIVE

ake
yan

0 km   1

0 miles   1

Water Rides
Wet 'n' Wild takes the honors as the water park with the best rides – though suitable only for older children and adults. Its big-thrill water rides include the Flyer, a six-story toboggan ride with plenty of exciting watery curves.

LOCATOR MAP

■ *Area covered*

Sealife
SeaWorld is the park for those who want close encounters with sea creatures. See incredible live shows with highly trained dolphins, whales, sea otters, penguins, and more.

Wildlife & Natural Habitats

Cᴇɴᴛʀᴀʟ ꜰʟᴏʀɪᴅᴀ'ꜱ ɢʀᴇᴀᴛ variety of habitats and wildlife is due to the meeting of temperate and subtropical climates in many areas, complemented by its humidity, sandy soils, low elevation, and proximity to the water. An amazing diversity of habitats is found within several wildlife preserves, such as Merritt Island National Wildlife Refuge, and numerous state and county parks. Native flora in Central Florida ranges from longleaf and slash pines to various palms and cypress trees, while the region is home to more than 4,000 species of wildlife – from alligators and loggerhead sea turtles to brown pelicans and red-bellied woodpeckers.

Oranges
This introduced plant has thrived in Central Florida. The state's citrus industry supplies the bulk of the nation's crop.

Sᴄʀᴜʙꜱ & Sᴀɴᴅʜɪʟʟꜱ

Called "Florida's Ancient Islands," the ridges of Central Florida were formed along the backbone of peninsular Florida millions of years ago when ocean levels were much higher than they are today. The sandy, porous soils of the ridges are home to two types of high and dry plant communities – scrubs and sandhills. Several species of plants and animals unique to Central Florida are found in this habitat.

Pɪɴᴇ Fʟᴀᴛᴡᴏᴏᴅꜱ

Pine flatwoods are the most common plant community in Central Florida. Dominated by an overstory of pines, the subcanopy of flatwoods is comprised mainly of saw palmetto shrubs, but there may be 50 to 75 different plant species per acre. Pine flatwoods are often interspersed with swamps and other habitats, and thrive when periodically swept by fire. The plants and animals here have adapted to survive the difficult conditions.

Scrub oaks are generally less than 10 ft (3 m) in height. These hardy plants produce plentiful acorns for the region's fauna.

The bobcat has a distinctive short tail with a dark tip, facial ruff, and spotted coat, and hunts by both day and night.

The gopher tortoise, the only type found in Florida, has a large, thick shell and heavily scaled legs.

Palmetto is one of the most widespread plants in Florida. The saw palmetto variety is harvested and used for medicinal purposes.

PROTECTING THE SEA TURTLE

At Marine Science Center, Ponce Inlet

From May through October, the East Coast beaches of Central Florida are host to three species of sea turtles – green, loggerhead, and leatherback turtles. These magnificent animals emerge from the surf at night to lay their eggs in nests, dug into the dry sand, then return to the sea. Two months later, about 100 baby turtles emerge from each of these nests and crawl to the ocean. To protect these gentle creatures, beach driving, parking, and lighting on beachfront properties are regulated. Avoid walking or cycling in places posted as nesting areas, and never disturb the protective screening over turtle nests.

Loggerhead turtle hatchlings heading to sea

FRESHWATER MARSHES & SWAMPS

Freshwater marshes and swamps are usually inundated with water throughout or during a portion of the year. Such wetlands once comprised about 50 percent of the land area in Central Florida. Freshwater swamps are dominated by cypress or bay trees, while marshes tend to be open, vegetated mostly by rushes and sedges. They are rich in bird life, such as varieties of herons, storks, and warblers.

RIVERS

The floodplain – the low land along either bank that is periodically flooded – of a Central Florida river contains forests of water-tolerant trees or low marshes. Some rivers "bubble up" from natural free-flowing springs while others start slowly as small streams. As rivers make their way toward the sea, they form brackish estuaries that support saltwater fish and wildlife.

Pitcher plants grow in acidic, saturated soil. The species found in Central Florida is called Sarracenia minor, *and has gracefully curved yellow flowers.*

Bald cypress, one of the largest trees in North America, is a long-lived wetland species, known for its "knees" – projections from its submerged roots – and buttressed trunk.

The great blue heron is gray-blue, and has a white head with a black stripe above the eye. This big, long-legged, yellow-billed wader usually holds its neck in an "S" curve.

The bald eagle, an endangered species found by the ocean, lakes, and rivers, has a distinctive white head and tail and a dark brown body. Its wings span 7 ft (2 m).

The Space Shuttle

Shuttle mission insignia

THE SPACE COAST'S Kennedy Space Center is NASA's launch headquarters and the home of the space shuttle program. The program was begun in the late 1970s, by which time the cost of sending astronauts into space had become too much for the American space budget; hundreds of millions of dollars were spent lifting the Apollo missions into space, with little more than a scorched command module ever returning to earth. It was time to develop a reusable spacecraft made for years of service, whose main cost after production would lie in maintenance. The answer was the space shuttle – *Columbia* was launched into space on April 12, 1981.

***When in orbit**, the shuttle's cargo doors are opened. The Hubble telescope was one of its payloads.*

***The flight deck** of the shuttle is extremely complex – even more so than the shuttle itself, which is built along the lines of an aircraft. You can get some idea of how the shuttle is navigated at the Launch Status Center (see p127).*

Tracks enable the tower to be moved away before liftoff.

***The Crawlerway** is a double pathway, 100 ft (30 m) wide. It has been specially designed to withstand the weight of the shuttle as it is taken to the launch pad by gigantic crawlers. The rock surface overlies a layer of asphalt and a 7-ft (2-m) bed of crushed stone.*

The Crawler backs away once the shuttle is in place.

SHUTTLE CYCLE

The Space Shuttle has three principal elements: the main orbiter spacecraft (with its three engines), an external tank of liquid hydrogen and oxygen fuel, and two solid-fuel booster rockets, which provide the extra thrust needed for liftoff. Like earlier rockets, the shuttle reaches orbit in stages.

1. Prelaunch
The external tank and rocket boosters are fitted to the orbiter in the Vehicle Assembly Building. Then it is moved to the launch pad.

2. Launch
After a final check, the shuttle blasts off, using its own three engines and its two booster rockets.

The service tower gives access for fueling and cargo installation.

The access arm is a corridor through which the astronauts board the shuttle.

Orbiter

Solid Rocket Booster

The flame trench channels the burning gases away from the vehicle.

THE SHUTTLE LAUNCHES

Since the shuttle's maiden voyage in 1981, there have been many missions shared between the *Columbia, Challenger, Discovery, Atlantis,* and *Endeavour* vehicles. The program was severely crippled when *Challenger* exploded shortly after liftoff in 1986, and again when *Columbia* disintegrated on re-entry in 2003. Regular launches will be held again when the safety of the other shuttles is assured. You need a ticket to view the launches at the Space Center. Free viewing sites are available on US 1 at Titusville and A1A at Cocoa Beach and Cape Canaveral.

Shuttle clearing the launch tower

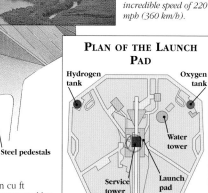

For landing *back on Earth, the shuttle re-enters the atmosphere and begins to glide with its engines off. It heads toward the Space Center and proceeds to land on the runway at an incredible speed of 220 mph (360 km/h).*

Vent for spent gases

Steel pedestals

PLAN OF THE LAUNCH PAD

Hydrogen tank

Oxygen tank

Water tower

Service tower

Launch pad

Crawlerway

SHUTTLE LAUNCH

The launch pad is made of 2 million cu ft (56,000 cu m) of reinforced concrete, supported by six steel pedestals. The flame trench is flooded with cooling water when the engines ignite, producing an immense cloud of steam.

3. Separation
Two minutes later, the boosters separate and are parachuted back to earth. At eight minutes, the external tank detaches.

4. Orbital Operations
Using its own engines, the shuttle maneuvers itself into orbit and begins its operations. The mission may last between 7 and 18 days, flying at an altitude of 115–690 miles (185–1,110 km).

5. Re-entry
The shuttle re-enters the atmosphere backward, using its engines to decelerate. It turns nose-first as it descends into the stratosphere and uses parachutes to stop.

CENTRAL FLORIDA THROUGH THE YEAR

ONE OF Central Florida's biggest attractions is its year-round mild weather. The region's climate has long been its top drawing card for tourists and residents. The average annual temperature is a comfortable 72.4°F (22.4°C) and the average rainfall is 50 in (1,270 mm), keeping the area green with flowering plants and trees year-round. The busiest time in the Orlando area is from November to December, when tourists come in

Livestock show, Central Florida Fair

huge numbers to enjoy the mild winters. Summer can be somewhat hot, but Orlando's theme parks still attract families with kids on school vacations, with some hotels offering special summer rates for families, including free transportation to the theme parks. Whatever time of year you visit, you will encounter an entertaining festival of some kind. For a complete schedule of festivals, contact the local tourist offices.

Motorcyclists show off their bikes during Bike Week, Daytona Beach

SPRING

STARTING IN late February, students from all over the US head for Florida's coastal resorts, such as the Daytona Beach area, for the spring break. For the next six weeks these areas are bursting, putting pressure on accommodations. Baseball training is also a big attraction in Central Florida in spring.

MARCH

Orlando Bike Week *(first weekend)*. Harley enthusiasts throughout the globe eagerly anticipate this annual event, headquartered at the Orlando Historic Factory dealership.
Bike Week *(first weekend)*, Daytona Beach. A huge and popular motorcycle event brimming with shows, concerts, and exhibits.

Kissimmee Bluegrass Festival *(first weekend)*. Features music styles ranging from bluegrass and Creole to Texas swing.
Central Florida Fair *(early Mar)*, Orlando. This large fair features more than 90 rides and exhibits.
SeaWorld, Bud & BBQ Fest *(early Mar)*, Orlando. Two weekends of fun, food, and racing at this park-wide event.
Annual Winter Park Sidewalk Arts Festival *(mid-Mar)*, Orlando. The most prestigious outdoor fine arts festival in Southeastern USA, this features three days of art, food, music, children's activities, and jazz.
Antique Boat Festival *(late Mar)*, Mount Dora. Display of more than 150 classic and historic boats.

Annual Downtown Antique Fair *(late Mar)*, Mount Dora. Treasures on display in downtown streets.
Florida Film Festival *(late Mar)*, Orlando. Ranked among the best film festivals in the world, this features more than 100 films, documentaries, and shorts from around the globe.
Orlando-UCF Shakespeare Festival *(Mar–May)*, Lake Eola Park. Outdoor productions at Walt Disney Amphitheater *(see p107)*.

APRIL

Spring Fiesta in the Park *(Apr)*, Orlando. Booths full of regional arts and crafts line the shores of Lake Eola.
Epcot Flower & Garden Festival *(Apr–Jun)*. Epcot blooms with elaborate gardens and topiary displays. You can attend gardening workshops.
Kissimmee Jazz Fest *(early Apr)*. This jazz concert held at the Kissimmee Lakefront includes entertainment from local high school performers to top jazz artists, as well as crafts and good food.
Maitland Arts & Fine Crafts Festival *(mid-Apr)*. The juried arts and fine crafts show highlights original artwork by the finest craftsmen in Southeast USA.

FLORIDA FILM FESTIVAL

Florida Film Festival logo

Boats on display at the Antique Boat Festival, Mount Dora

Annual Taste of Winter Park *(mid-Apr)*. Sample cuisine from local restaurants.
Black College Reunion *(mid-Apr)*, Daytona Beach. Thousands of students and alumni of black colleges and universities come together for this reunion.
Festival of Exotic Cars *(mid-Apr)*, Mount Dora. More than 150 rare and exotic cars can be seen on the downtown streets.
Festival of Music & Literature *(mid-Apr)*. Mount Dora. Outstanding artistic programs in music, literature, and other genres.
Indian River Festival *(mid-Apr)*, Titusville. Live music, carnival rides, food, arts, crafts, and antiques are some of the highlights here.
Cracker Day *(late Apr)*, DeLand (near Daytona Beach). Celebration of Florida heritage with games for the entire family. Features a cattleman's barbecue.

MAY

Viva La Musica *(mid-May)*, SeaWorld Orlando. Two spicy weekend fiestas of Latino music, dance, culture, and great food.
Orlando International Fringe Festival *(mid-May)*. The 10-day festival of theatrical performances showcases original works; premiere performances; and first-class improvisational comedy, musicals, drama, mime, and dance in 500 shows by performers from around the world.

SUMMER

Many families head to Orlando for the summer season and for good reason. The hotel rates are discounted for families and the theme parks stay open for a longer period, giving tourists more time to enjoy the attractions. The big summer holiday is of course Independence Day on July 4, which is celebrated with fireworks, parades, and picnics.

JUNE

Suncoast Gun & Knife Show *(mid-Jun)*, DeLand. Features a large collection of antique firearms and supplies, hunting rifles, collectibles, and more, at the Volusia County Fairgrounds.
Fiesta San Juan en Wet 'n' Wild *(late Jun)*. Wet 'n' Wild celebrates Latin culture in this fiesta of dancing, music, competitions, Latin food, and local Latin entertainment.

JULY

Lake Eola Picnic in the Park *(early Jul)*, Orlando. Celebrate the Fourth of July at this Downtown Orlando tradition with games and entertainment. Fireworks wrap up the show at 9pm.
Pepsi 400 *(early Jul)*, Daytona Beach. NASCAR racing on Daytona International Speedway during the Independence weekend. Other activities include concerts and beach parties.
Christmas in July Craft Fair *(mid-Jul)*, Lakeland. Shop from local vendors for beautiful handmade gifts for family and friends.
Florida International Festival *(mid-Jul)*, Daytona Beach. This multi-day event features performances by ensembles such as the London Symphony Orchestra.

AUGUST

Ocala Shrine Club Rodeo *(mid-Aug)*. Cow-roping, steer-riding, and more, are on offer at this action-packed annual attraction, held at the Livestock Pavilion.
Ocala Sturgis Rally & Bike Show *(mid-Aug)*. Field events are open to spectators.
International Food Festival *(mid-Aug)*, Auburndale (near Lakeland). On offer at "A Taste of Auburndale" are delicacies from local restaurants and lots of entertainment options.

A contest at Fiesta San Juan en Wet 'n' Wild

Flamenco dancer at the Viva La Musica, SeaWorld® Orlando

FALL

THE THEME PARKS are less crowded in the fall and the temperatures are cooler, making this an ideal time to visit Central Florida. Halloween is the big fall holiday in Orlando, with several theme parks offering special celebrations. Thanksgiving is the other major holiday. Fall is the best time for birdwatching and visiting the region's wildlife preserves.

SEPTEMBER

Viva La Musica *(mid-Sep)*, SeaWorld Orlando. A celebration of Hispanic food and culture during Hispanic Heritage Month. Live performances by hot Latino bands.
Lake Mirror Classic Auto Festival *(mid-Sep)*, Lakeland. All types of classic automobiles on display.

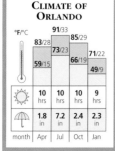

CLIMATE OF ORLANDO

°F/°C	Apr	Jul	Oct	Jan
	83/28	91/33 / 85/29	73/23 / 71/22	66/19
	59/15			49/9
☀ hrs	10	10	10	9
☂ in	1.8	7.2	2.4	2.3
month	Apr	Jul	Oct	Jan

OCTOBER

Epcot International Food & Wine Festival *(Oct–Nov)*. The temptation to dine your way around World Showcase is intensified by cooking demonstrations, samples of exotic dishes, and international wines and desserts.
Bicycle Festival *(second weekend)*. Mount Dora. Attracting 1,500 cyclists, this is Florida's oldest and largest bicycling event.
Biketoberfest *(third weekend)*, Daytona Beach. International motorcycle show, demonstrations, and concerts.
Craft Fair *(fourth weekend)*, Mount Dora. More than 350 craftspeople and 250,000 visitors come from all over the nation for this fair.

NOVEMBER

Fall Fiesta in the Park *(first weekend)*, Downtown Orlando. Enjoy 550 booths full of regional arts and crafts along Lake Eola. One of the top five outdoor arts and crafts shows in Florida.
Plant & Garden Fair *(first weekend)*, Mount Dora. More than 10,000 rare and exotic plants and accessories displayed at the lakefront at Simpson's in Mount Dora.
Halifax Art Festival *(early Nov)*, Daytona Beach. This annual festival features the works of more than 250 artists, plus live entertainment.
Native American Festival *(early Nov)*, Silver Springs. A celebration of Native American culture, arts, crafts, and entertainment.
Annual Orlando Beer Festival *(mid-Nov)*. An impressive assortment of beers at this festival, sponsored by Universal CityWalk. Enjoy ales, lagers, pilsners, stouts, and barley wines.
ABC Super Soap Weekend *(mid-Nov)*, Disney MGM Studios. In the world's biggest soap fan event,

actors from the ABC daytime soap operas such as *Port Charles* and *General Hospital* visit the studios, affording autograph and photo opportunities.
Festival of the Masters *(mid-Nov)*, Downtown Disney. More than 200 artists participate in this three-day festival of the fine arts. Music and food round out the activities.
Annual Championship Ocala Scottish Games & Irish Fest *(mid-Nov)*. Grand parade, games, food, and entertainment.
Birding & Wildlife Festival *(mid-Nov)*, Titusville. This festival features birding trips, wildlife seminars, workshops, an art competition, and paddling adventures.
Daytona Turkey Run *(late Nov)*. Car show and swap meet on the Thanksgiving weekend at the Daytona International Speedway.
Birthplace of Speed Celebration *(late Nov)*, Ormond Beach. Gaslight parade of antique cars, as well as a car show.
Light Up Mount Dora *(Nov 28)*. Close to two million sparkling lights switch on in celebration of the holiday season. Festivities include singing by the community choir, ballet, and other entertainment, at Donnelly Park.

PUBLIC HOLIDAYS

New Year (Jan 1)
Martin Luther King Day (3rd Mon, Jan)
Presidents' Day (3rd Mon, Feb)
Memorial Day (last Mon, May)
Independence Day (Jul 4)
Labor Day (1st Mon, Sep)
Columbus Day (2nd Mon, Oct)
Election Day (1st Tue, Nov)
Halloween (Oct 31)
Veterans Day (Nov 11)
Thanksgiving (4th Thu, Nov)
Christmas Day (Dec 25)

Zora Neale Hurston Festival of Arts & Humanities, Orlando

WINTER

THE CROWDS multiply in winter as the flood of "snowbirds" from the north intensifies. The celebrities arrive too, some to relax, others to perform during the region's busiest entertainment season. The parks are all aglow with Christmas lights and festivities – there are special Christmas parades and parties. Magic Kingdom is at its most colorful.

DECEMBER

Mickey's Very Merry Christmas Party *(all month)*, Magic Kingdom. Evening of seasonal fun complete with snow and enchanting parades with a Christmas theme.
Festival of Trees *(early Dec)*, Ocala. Decorated trees and lovely wreaths are displayed at the Appleton Museum of Art, along with crafts and decorations created by local artisans, which are for sale.
Festival of Lights *(mid-Dec)*, Silver Springs. Follow millions of sparkling lights through a maze of illuminated gardens, twinkling topiaries, and dozens of holiday scenes. A holiday buffet is on offer.

JANUARY

Renninger's Antique Extravaganza *(third weekend, Jan, Feb & Nov)*, Mount Dora. An antique lover's dream, this event held at Renninger's Twin Markets has more than 1,500 dealers selling their wares.
Zora Neale Hurston Festival of Arts & Humanities *(late Jan)*, Orlando. This festival at Eatonville highlights the life and works of America's most celebrated collectors and interpreters of Southern rural African-American culture. Features art exhibits, theatrical performances, and educational programs.

FEBRUARY

Mount Dora Arts Festival *(first weekend)*. Celebrated on the streets of Mount Dora since 1977, this festival showcases the works of more than 300 juried artists. Artists compete for awards in painting, printmaking, photography, jewelry, sculpture, and a variety of other categories. Live entertainment, children's activities, and food are also part of the festivities.
Speedweeks *(first three weeks)* Daytona. Daytona International Speedway becomes the World Center of Racing during three weeks in February. Action kicks off with the Rolex 24 Hours at Daytona, followed by events leading up to the Daytona 500.
ArtsFest *(mid-Feb)*, Orlando. Showcases Central Florida's best in arts and culture, with more than 50 planned events, which range from symphony and ballet performances to art exhibits and lessons in Central Florida's history.
Mardi Gras at Universal Orlando *(mid-Feb–mid-Mar)*. Music and pageantry, colorful costumes, parades, food, and high-energy excitement at this annual Mardi Gras celebration at Universal.

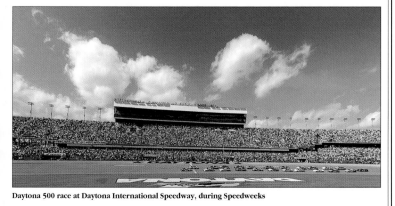
Daytona 500 race at Daytona International Speedway, during Speedweeks

Moss-covered oaks in Lake Kissimmee State Park ▷

WALT DISNEY WORLD® RESORT & CENTRAL FLORIDA AREA BY AREA

WALT DISNEY WORLD® RESORT

THE LARGEST ENTERTAINMENT *complex on earth, Walt Disney World® Resort sprawls across 47 sq miles (121 sq km), encompassing four theme parks renowned for their imaginative and state-of-the-art attractions. Two water parks, a sports complex, a cruise ship line, and a range of hotels, restaurants, nightclubs, golf courses, and shops combine to make it the complete vacation experience.*

Unless you're a cynic, Walt Disney World will amaze you. Peerless in its creativity and attention to detail, the resort offers a respite from the real world and takes you on a trip into a realm of fantasy and wonder.

Disney's first theme park, Magic Kingdom, opened in 1971. Consisting of seven "Lands," it remains one of the most popular theme parks of all time. In 1982, the ever-evolving Disney set up the 300-acre (120-ha) Epcot, an international and futuristic showplace, which focuses on discoveries and scientific achievements, and also provides an insight into the cultures of 11 nations across the world.

Disney-MGM Studios followed in 1989. The smallest of the four parks, it celebrates films and television in its shows and rides. Disney's Animal Kingdom, the newest park, covers 500 acres (200 ha) of jungles and savanna featuring exotic creatures, safaris, and trails. Then there are the water parks, Typhoon Lagoon and Blizzard Beach, with their ingenious landscaping and some thoroughly enjoyable rides. Downtown Disney amalgamates nightclubs, shows, restaurants, and shops into a vibrant entertainment area that pulsates at night.

The possibilities at Disney seem endless. Its cruise line offers two luxury ships with various amenities and cruise options. A sports lover's paradise, the resort boasts the massive Disney's Wide World of Sports complex, 18-hole and mini golf courses, and activities such as hiking, horseback riding, tennis, watersports, and race car driving. Accommodation options are equally varied, with several resorts and a camping ground.

The Primeval Whirl®, a thrilling ride at Disney's Animal Kingdom®, Walt Disney World® Resort

◁ Cinderella's Castle, a fairy-tale fantasy in full bloom at Magic Kingdom®

Exploring Walt Disney World® Resort

L ET YOUR IMAGINATION take flight at this world-class entertainment center, where there is something for everyone, regardless of their age. Plan to spend at least a day in each of Disney's "big four" – Magic Kingdom, Epcot, Disney-MGM Studios, and Disney's Animal Kingdom. Don't miss a chance to cool off at the two water parks – Blizzard Beach and Typhoon Lagoon. Or you might choose to let off steam at Disney's Wide World of Sports complex; golf courses; hiking and riding trails; and pools and lakes for swimming, boating, waterskiing and much more. With 31 resorts on the premises, you can go back to your hotel to rest before returning to one of the parks for the fireworks finale or checking out a show at Downtown Disney.

Magic Kingdom®
Seven Lands of fantasy and adventure encircle the stunningly beautiful Cinderella's Castle.

SIGHTS AT A GLANCE

Blizzard Beach ❺
Disney-MGM Studios ❸
Disney's Animal Kingdom® ❹
Downtown Disney® ❽
Epcot® ❷
Fort Wilderness Resort & Campground ❼
Magic Kingdom® ❶
Typhoon Lagoon ❻

0 meters   500
0 yards   500

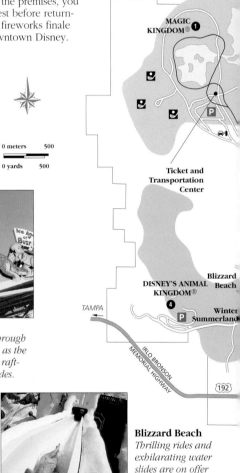

MAGIC KINGDOM® ❶

Ticket and Transportation Center

DISNEY'S ANIMAL KINGDOM® ❹

Blizzard Beach

TAMPA

Winter Summerland

IRLO BRONSON MEMORIAL HIGHWAY

192

Disney's Animal Kingdom®
Experience the thrill of the wild through encounters with animals, as well as the pure fun of African safaris, river rafting, treks, and some enjoyable rides.

KEY

🅿   Parking
⛽   Gas station
⛳   Golf course
—   Monorail
═   Interstate highway
▬   Major highway
═   Secondary route

Blizzard Beach
Thrilling rides and exhilarating water slides are on offer at this cleverly designed and delightful 66-acre (27-ha) water theme park.

Epcot®
Travel across continents, blast into space on a rocket to Mars, embark on an underwater adventure, and take a peek into the future with remarkable discoveries and inventions.

Disney-MGM Studios
There's no business like show business at the Disney-MGM Studios, where guests of all ages are immersed in the glitz, glamor, and magic of Hollywood.

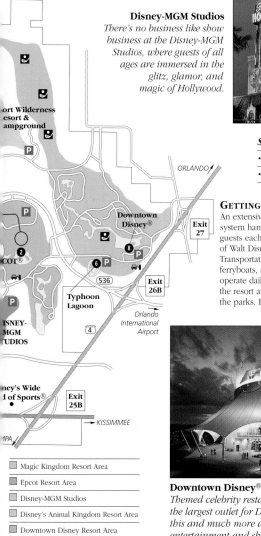

ORLANDO

Downtown Disney®

Exit 27

Exit 26B

Orlando International Airport

Typhoon Lagoon

(536)

ISNEY-MGM UDIOS

ort Wilderness esort & ampground

ey's Wide l of Sports®

Exit 25B

KISSIMMEE

1PA

See Also
• *Where to Stay* pp140–142
• *Where to Eat* pp150–152

GETTING AROUND
An extensive, efficient transportation system handles an average of 200,000 guests each day. The transportation hub of Walt Disney World is the Ticket and Transportation Center (TTC). Monorails, ferryboats, and motorcoach shuttle services operate daily. Additionally, hotels outside the resort area offer free shuttle services to the parks. For further details, see page 76.

☐ Magic Kingdom Resort Area
☐ Epcot Resort Area
☐ Disney-MGM Studios
☐ Disney's Animal Kingdom Resort Area
☐ Downtown Disney Resort Area

Downtown Disney®
Themed celebrity restaurants, nightclubs, and the largest outlet for Disney merchandise – all this and much more are on offer at this exciting entertainment and shopping complex.

Magic Kingdom® ❶

As DISNEY'S QUINTESSENTIAL THEME PARK, Magic Kingdom makes a popular reappearance in similar form in California, Japan, and France. Cartoon characters and nostalgic visions of how the world, and particularly America, once was and how it might be again fill its relentlessly cheerful 107 acres (43 ha). The park is made up of seven Lands evoking a particular theme or era, such as the Wild West, Colonial America, and the future. Symptomatic of the park's effervescence are elaborate parades, entertaining musical street performers, and three-dimensional Disney characters.

TACKLING THE PARK

UNLESS YOU ARE a guest at one of the Disney hotels, plan your visit at midweek or toward the end of the week as the park is busiest on weekends and early in the week. If you are staying at a Disney resort, you are in luck. As their guest, you will have access to early entry privileges on two days a week –

Thursday and Sunday. Take this excellent opportunity and reach the entrance turnstiles an hour and a half before the official opening time. This will allow an extra 90 minutes of precious time to enjoy Fantasyland and Tomorrowland before the rest of the park opens.

Upon arrival at the park, you will receive a leaflet listing the Lands and rides as well as the timings for the shows and parades. A notice board at the top of Main Street also offers this information and, additionally, gives a list of waiting times at various attractions. Getting around the park is relatively easy as the Lands emanate from the central hub, in front of Cinderella's Castle.

The most popular attractions are situated at opposite ends of the park, a considerable distance apart. As a result, you will probably end up walking more than you might expect. However, there are also other, more novel forms of transport. Main Street has a series of vehicles which, in keeping with the Disney storytelling ideal, serve to tell the story of transport from the horse-drawn tram to the motor car. A steam train makes a 20-minute circuit of the park, stopping at Main Street, Frontierland, and Mickey's Toontown Fair.

EATING & DRINKING

THE PARK OFFERS a wide selection of fast foods and an equally vast range of quick service places to choose from. For a reasonable meal, try the Liberty Tree Tavern.

Visitors on Main Street, USA® with Cinderella's Castle in the background

◁ **A dazzling display of fireworks at the Wishes™ Nighttime Spectacular, Magic Kingdom®**

If you would like a quieter dining experience, the Crystal Palace is a good option. Cinderella's Royal Table, located within the castle itself, gives you a taste of royalty with its stately and regal ambience. Their specialty is prime ribs and, overall, the food is agreeable. The frequent appearances by Disney characters keep the kids entertained and makes for a magical meal. However, it is a good idea to make advance reservations in order to ensure a table at this popular eatery.

If you're looking for sandwiches, Aunt Polly's on Tom Sawyer Island is one of the best places to head for. However, this is the only fare on offer here.

WALT DISNEY'S VISION

Walt Disney (1901–66), the father of Mickey Mouse, was a pioneer in the field of animation. Watching his children at play in a squalid amusement park, Disney was struck by his ultimate inspiration – to build a place that was clean and filled with various attractions that parents and kids could enjoy together. He envisioned a theme park revolving around five Lands: Main Street, a setting plucked from late-19th/early 20th-century America; Adventureland, imbued with the mystery of exotic locales; Frontierland, a homage to the pioneers; Fantasyland, a place of whimsy inspired by the song "When You Wish Upon A Star;" and Tomorrowland, with a futuristic theme fit for the emerging Space Age. Disney picked a 160-acre (65-ha) site in Anaheim, California, and oversaw every aspect of the planning and construction of Disneyland. When Magic Kingdom opened its gates in 1955 and 28,000 people stormed in, tears reportedly streamed down Walt Disney's cheeks – his great dream had finally become a reality. Today, the Disney empire stretches across the globe, with theme parks in Paris and Tokyo. Orlando's Walt Disney World® Resort opened on October 21, 1971.

1 DAY ITINERARY

If you really want to cover the Magic Kingdom in one day, be warned, it's a daunting task because of the distances involved. This is specially true in the summer.

1. After leaving the turnstiles, head immediately for the central hub. If the entire park is open, turn right and head for **Space Mountain**. There might be ropes across areas at the hub. If so, wait at the rope entrance to Tomorrowland and head for Space Mountain when the rope drops. This is an exciting ride for those looking for thrills. Alternatively, if you'd prefer a tamer start, you can also make a beeline for **Buzz Lightyear's Space Ranger Spin**.

2. After Space Mountain, choose between the **Tomorrowland Indy Speedway** and the **Tomorrowland Arcade**. If you have preschoolers, you should head for Fantasyland through Tomorrowland (keep the speedway on your right and turn left at the Mad Tea Party) and ride **The Many Adventures of Winnie the Pooh**.

3. After Winnie, turn left and head across Dumbo the Flying Elephant toward **Peter Pan's Flight** and enjoy the ride.

4. Exit left, head to Liberty Square and visit **The Haunted Mansion** on the right.

5. On leaving Haunted Mansion, turn to the right and continue to **Splash Mountain**. If the waiting period is more than half an hour, it might be a good idea at this point to get a Fastpass for this ride. Turn right from here and cross to the **Big Thunder Mountain Railroad**.

6. Take the exit from Big Thunder and cross the bridge bearing right to **Pirates of the Caribbean**. Take the ride.

7. Now you can return to ride the Splash Mountain.

8. After Splash Mountain, backtrack to the **Jungle Cruise**. If the time slot is right, ride, otherwise see the **Enchanted Tiki Room**.

9. Obtain a Fastpass for **Mickey's PhilharMagic** and grab a light lunch.

10. By the time lunch is over, you should be due to see Mickey's PhilharMagic.

11. Afterward, take preschoolers to Mickey's Toontown. If you have older children with you, take them to the rest of Fantasyland: **it's a small world**, **Peter Pan's Flight**, **Snow White's Scary Adventures**, **Dumbo the Flying Elephant**, **Ariel's Grotto**, or the **Mad Tea Party**.

12. Cross the central hub to Tomorrowland and obtain a Fastpass ticket for **Buzz Lightyear**.

13. Visit the **The Timekeeper**, **Astro Orbiter**, and **Walt Disney's Carousel of Progress**.

14. Return to ride Buzz Lightyear.

15. Cross the central hub to Frontierland, and find a comfortable, vantage spot to enjoy the full splendor of the **afternoon parade**.

16. Following the parade, you have a chance to take one last relaxing ride before dinner. Choose between the **Jungle Cruise** in Adventureland or climb aboard the **Liberty Belle Riverboat**.

17. Following dinner, don't miss the **SpectroMagic Parade**. If the park is closing early, view the parade from the Town Square. If it's open late, it's a good idea to see the parade from Main Street on the Tomorrowland side so that, when the parade has passed, you can return to the attractions in Tomorrowland, Mickey's Toontown Fair, and Fantasyland to catch any rides you missed (or ride particular favorites again).

18. Finally, enjoy dinner at the California Grill (see p151) and watch the fireworks in comfort from the restaurant's wall of windows overlooking Magic Kingdom.

TOP 10 ATTRACTIONS

1. **SPLASH MOUNTAIN**®
2. **BIG THUNDER MOUNTAIN RAILROAD**
3. **BUZZ LIGHTYEAR'S SPACE RANGER SPIN**
4. **IT'S A SMALL WORLD**
5. **PIRATES OF THE CARIBBEAN**
6. **SPACE MOUNTAIN**®
7. **THE MAGIC CARPETS OF ALADDIN**
8. **THE HAUNTED MANSION**
9. **PETER PAN'S FLIGHT**
10. **THE MANY ADVENTURES OF WINNIE THE POOH**

MAIN STREET, USA®

O N ENTERING Main Street, take a step into Disney's fantasy of a small-town Victorian America that never was. As you walk down Main Street, you pass beneath the Main Street Station. From here, you can catch the train for a ride around the park. The trains run every ten minutes. Beneath the station are lockers where, for a small fee, you can store valuables and bags.

As you enter the Town Square, **City Hall** lies to your left. This is a good place to visit first if you are looking for information regarding the shows being performed and any special events that might be taking place during your stay. The **Town Square Exposition Hall** lies to the right as you enter the square. You can pick up film rolls and other camera supplies here, but the main shops are, as you would expect, along Main Street.

Main Street itself is a magnificent melange of color, shapes and music, all in astonishing detail. At night, the entire street assumes a magical ambience as thousands of glittering lights bring a resplendent glow to the spotlessly clean sidewalk. It's also an excellent place to see the popular **SpectroMagic Parade** *(see p39)*, a shimmering fantasy of music, live action and illuminated floats.

ADVENTURELAND®

L USH FOLIAGE, evocative drumbeats, and Colonial buildings combine to conjure up vivid images of Africa and the Caribbean. Reached via a wooden bridge from the central hub, Adventureland is an exciting and entertaining fusion of the exotic and the tropical.

One of the first attractions you come across in this Land, the **Swiss Family Treehouse** is a great way to start your tour of this area of the park. The large, man-made replica of the elaborate treehouse described in the beloved 19th-century children's tale is magnificent to behold. Replete with little details and small signs, the tree is reminiscent of the ingenuity and Christian values of the fictional castaways. Climbing the tree provides you with a splendid overhead view of this section of the park. The exhibit also offers a refreshingly shady and breezy educational tour that is certain to capture the interest of pre-teen kids.

Guests enjoying The Magic Carpets of Aladdin ride, Adventureland®

The **Jungle Cruise** boat ride takes its guests around a variety of animatronically designed settings of deepest Africa, India, and South America. A much sought-after ride, it owes a huge part of its popularity to the immense entertainment value of the "boatman" whose often wacky and infectious humor never fails to amuse.

The recently much improved **Enchanted Tiki Room** is an amusing and cleverly animated attraction. It is also a pleasant way to spend 20 minutes or so if you want to get out of the heat. Featuring characters from *Aladdin* and *The Lion King*, it is certainly worth a visit, just to see the walls change shape.

The **Pirates of the Caribbean** is an extremely entertaining and remarkably

The Jungle Cruise, a journey into deep forests with a zany boatsman

detailed voyage. This thrilling journey takes you on a seemingly realistic cruise through crumbling, underground prisons, past fighting galleons of the 16th century, and through scenes of debauchery and mayhem. The colorful characters and loving detail have ensured that it remains one of the best of the original rides. Following the runaway success of the film version, this ride has recently been given a facelift. Although it has been said that it is not as good as the version presented in Disneyland Paris, the Audio-Animatronic® effects are still extremely well done and the ride is certainly a firm favorite with park visitors.

In another popular ride, **The Magic Carpets of Aladdin**, four-passenger carpets circle around a giant replica of a genie's bottle; the carpets move at the "command" of the riders, while whimsical camels "spit" at the airborne guests.

At the exit, you will find one of the most interesting stores in the park. An excellent selection of essential Disney accessories and memorabilia is available for purchase here.

The careening Big Thunder Mountain Railroad ride

TOP TIPS

- *The Swiss Family Treehouse's pinnacle offers some spectacular picture opportunities for the rest of Adventureland.*
- *Most Magic Kingdom parades begin in Frontierland, near Splash Mountain, so this is the best place to watch them.*
- *Try to arrive there about 45 minutes before the parade begins to get a good viewing spot and wait for the Disney characters to arrive.*
- *Daytime parades run from the Splash Mountain area to the Town Square and the nighttime parades usually perform this route in reverse.*
- *To visit Splash Mountain first, board the train at Main Street before the park opens. The train departs at opening time and reaches Frontierland 7 minutes later. This station is next to Big Thunder and Splash Mountain.*

FRONTIERLAND®

SET IN a Hollywood-inspired Wild West, this Land abounds with raised walkways and trading posts. The **Frontierland Shootin' Arcade** is reminiscent of both the Wild West and of country fairs gone by. The **Country Bear Jamboree**, on the other hand, provides a completely animatronic musical animal show, much liked by youngsters, and a welcome respite on a hot summer's day.

A stunningly conceived and superbly executed journey through America's Wild West on an out-of-control mine train, **Big Thunder Mountain Railroad** remains one of the park's enduring attractions. In roller coaster terms, it's a relatively gentle experience, although the rear cars provide a wilder ride than the front. It acquires long lines of people from early in the day, so this is a ride to be enjoyed sooner, rather than later.

Opposite Big Thunder Mountain is the landing stage from where a raft can be taken to **Tom Sawyer Island**. Complete with a fort, swinging bridges, waterfalls, and tunnels, this is a child's dream adventure playground.

An outstanding attraction which threatens to get you a lot wetter than it actually does is **Splash Mountain**®. This is the epitome of what Disney does best, with a seamless integration of music, special effects, and beautifully crafted creatures. This, combined with a multitude of small drops prior to the big one, makes it one of the finest flume rides in the world. Guaranteed to make you want to repeat the adventure, the ride soon develops long queues that remain until closing. Fastpasses for Big Thunder Mountain Railroad and Splash Mountain are highly recommended.

Plunging down on the thrilling Splash Mountain® ride

LIBERTY SQUARE

THE SMALLEST OF all the Lands, Liberty Square is set in post-Colonial America and hosts three attractions: the **Liberty Belle Riverboat**, **The Hall of Presidents**, and **The Haunted Mansion**. The Liberty Belle Riverboat is a relaxing trip back in time to the days of the new frontier, the Louisiana Purchase, and the birth of the Southern culture. The ride is usually not very crowded and is a great way to beat the summer heat.

Another interesting option is a visit to the never-crowded Hall of Presidents. This is an impressive animatronic show that features the recorded voice of the current president joining in on readings by the great presidents from the past. The animatronic portion is preceded by a multimedia film showcasing the trials and tribulations of the early days of the United States. The film takes an unusually honest and candid look at slavery and ends on a stirringly patriotic note.

The first ride constructed at Walt Disney World, The Haunted Mansion still holds its own as one of the best. While the scare factor has ebbed noticeably over the years, the clever introduction, ingenious ghostprojection, and attention to detail throughout the ride still warrant admiration. The

ride's ability to take in large groups of people nearly continuously ensures that even long lines – now rare – move quickly. Very young children may still be frightened by some of the sudden "gotchas," but most others will find this more wonderfully amusing than frightfully scary.

Cinderella's Golden Carrousel, against the backdrop of the Castle

FANTASYLAND®

DOMINATED BY THE soaring spires of Cinderella's Castle, this Land forms the core of the Magic Kingdom. The delightfully designed attractions inspire feelings of amazement and enchantment in even the most cynical.

A relaxing ride on the Liberty Belle Riverboat

TOP TIPS

• *A little known shortcut from Mickey's Toontown Fair to Tomorrowland is just to the right of the train station.*
• *The benches in Mickey's Toontown Fair opposite Mickey's house provide a good vantage point from which to watch the fireworks.*
• *The Tomorrowland Arcade (see p40) can be a useful place to "park" easily bored youngsters while you take toddlers to savor the delights of Mickey's Toontown Fair or take in some of the quieter shows.*

SHOWS & PARADES

Don't miss checking out at least one of these amazing events. The shows – Mickey's PhilharMagic, a wonderful 3-D film experience, and The Enchanted Tiki Room – are superb in their own right but the parades are unique. Floats of towering proportions, surrounded by a multitude of actors and dancers, travel on a set route between Frontierland and Town Square on Main Street. There is always an afternoon parade and, during the peak holiday season, the SpectroMagic Parade takes place twice in the evenings, usually at 8:30pm and 10:30pm. The evening also features the Wishes™ Nighttime Spectacular, a brilliant choreography of fireworks and music.

This Land is usually the first destination for kids as their favorite storybook characters come to life here. **Dumbo the Flying Elephant** proves a compelling draw for young children whilst **Cinderella's Golden Carrousel**, a genuine 1917 restoration, seems to entice both old and young onto its gallopers. **Snow White's Scary Adventures**, which recounts the fairy-tale, is a basic tracked ride and may be slightly frightening for very young children. **Peter Pan's Flight**, however, is deservedly popular, combining the feeling of flying with the delight of perfectly matched music and movement. Opposite this is **it's a small world**, a waterborne journey through a series of animated tableaux. This is accompanied by a rather persistent melody which, if you're not careful, you'll find hard to get out of your head for the rest of the day.

The newest attraction, **The Many Adventures of Winnie the Pooh**, incorporates the latest in ride vehicle technology, lighting, and multi-channel sound effects. A popular attraction, it is justifiably worthy of its Fastpass status.

Inspired by the Mad Hatter and the March Hare's nonsensical "unbirthday" party in *Alice in Wonderland*, the **Mad Tea Party** ride has guests sitting in teacups that go right and left in circular motions. This musical ride is a must for young children.

As the only show here, **Mickey's PhilharMagic** offers a welcome respite from relentless walking and embodies the usual high performance standards associated with Disney. Of all the 3-D films that are shown around the Disney parks, this newest one may be the most perfected. For starters, it features an especially strong plotline – Donald Duck getting into trouble after appropriating Mickey's Sorcerer's Hat during a warm-up for an enchanted symphony. This sends the hapless duck spiraling through several of Disney's most popular animated musicals, trying to undo his mischief. The music at Mickey's PhilharMagic is magnificent, the addition of 3-D to beloved scenes from Disney's stable of hits is incredible, and the sensory enhancement of certain moments is used extremely well and often for comic effect.

Ariel's Grotto hosts the interestingly named "interactive fountain" and greeting area. Here, small children can play in an aquatic environment, meet the Little Mermaid herself, and get totally soaked.

MICKEY'S TOONTOWN FAIR®

THIS LAND APPEALS mainly to younger children. Here, Mickey's and Minnie's houses await, with the opportunity to have your picture taken with Mickey himself. Both the houses are walk-through attractions but Mickey's is actually a queuing area for the Judge's Tent where you can meet Mickey Mouse "in the flesh." An alternative character encounter can be found at the **Toontown Hall of Fame**. This has three entrances, but lines move very slowly and a great deal of time can be spent waiting to see one of the characters.

The Barnstormer at Goofy's Wiseacre Farm is the only "thrill" ride as such, but hardly lives up to its name.

Donald's Boat, a playground and fountain, offers further opportunities for the very young to have a whale of a time getting wet.

Whirling round in teacups on the Mad Tea Party ride

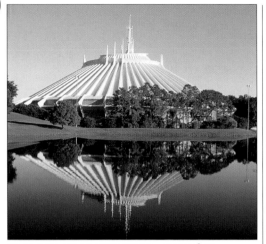

The futuristic building that houses the Space Mountain® ride

TOMORROWLAND®

BASED ON A futuristic theme, Tomorrowland has undergone numerous reformations in Disney's efforts to revitalize the Land. Management continues to routinely close, replace, or add rides in its efforts to find the right mix. The seriously terrifying ExtraTERRORestrial Alien Encounter, for example, was finally judged – after complaints – to be too scary for Disney and is now closed. This has been replaced by **Stitch's Great Escape!**, in the fall of 2004. Inspired by the film *Lilo and Stitch*, the ride showcases the mayhem caused by the mischievous Stitch's adventures in outer space.

There is plenty more to enjoy here. **Space Mountain®** is a fast ride through tight bends and sharp drops in the dark against projections of asteroids and the like. The impression of traveling through space is excellent, but the ride, though wilder than Big Thunder Mountain (*see p37*), may seem somewhat tame for seasoned thrillseekers.

Next door to Space Mountain is the **Tomorrowland Arcade**, an enormous showcase of video games and various high-tech demonstrations.

Handling large crowds with ease, the **Carousel of Progress** is a sit-down attraction where the auditorium rotates around a central stage. It examines the transformations in domestic life through the times and, although rather quaint, is a firm favorite, particularly late in the evening.

A 360-degree Circle-Vision trip through time, **The Timekeeper** has proved to be a very popular show. A standing attraction, it draws large crowds and takes 1,000 people a showing. It is also a wonderful place to escape the afternoon heat.

Visitors can soar high on silvery rockets on the **Astro Orbiter** ride, which affords an excellent view of Tomorrowland. The **Tomorrowland Transit Authority** is a serene, quiet, and interesting 10-minute ride which uses linear induction drives. This journey through the Land affords some of the best views of the park and an opportunity to relax after a great deal of walking. Almost never busy, it travels through Space Mountain and offers glimpses inside several other attractions as well.

One of this Land's recent innovations is **Buzz Lightyear's Space Ranger Spin**. An extremely fast loader, it's one of the park's best rides. This highly addictive journey through comic books sets you in a two-seater car, fitted with laser cannons and electronic scoreboards. A control allows you to rotate the car rapidly for a better aim. Shooting at all the targets with a red laser beam causes bangs, crashes, and rapid increases in your scores. It's one of the few rides that kids have to tear their parents away from.

Guests fly high in the sky during a ride on the Astro Orbiter

The peaceful Tomorrowland
Transit Authority ride

SHOPPING

There are shops everywhere in the Magic Kingdom and they sell just about every type of clothing, confectionery – except chewing gum! – and badged merchandise imaginable. All Lands have their own shops selling items based on the theme of the Land and on the nearest ride. Much piratical memorabilia can be purchased near Pirates of the Caribbean, for instance. Do your shopping on your way out so that you don't have to carry your purchases around with you all day.

Located on the border of Mickey's Toontown Fair is the new **Tomorrowland® Indy Speedway**, a large, safe course where kids and adults 4.3 ft (1.3 m) and taller can drive their own race cars around a twisting track – smaller children must have an adult drive with them. Nowhere near as difficult, or as thrilling as Epcot's Test Track *(see p46)*, the ride is more in line with family-oriented go-kart race courses.

RIDES & SHOWS CHECKLIST

This chart is designed to help you plan what to visit in the Magic Kingdom. The rides and shows are listed alphabetically within each Land.

		WAITING TIME	HEIGHT/AGE RESTRICTION	BUSIEST TIME TO RIDE	FASTPASS	LOADING SPEED	MAY CAUSE MOTION SICKNESS	OVERALL RATING
ADVENTURELAND®								
R	JUNGLE CRUISE	○		11am–5pm	➡	❷		▼
R	THE MAGIC CARPETS OF ALADDIN	○	3 yrs +	9am–7pm		❶	✓	▼
R	PIRATES OF THE CARIBBEAN	○		10am–5pm		❷		◆
S	THE ENCHANTED TIKI ROOM	◗		noon–4pm		❷		▼
FRONTIERLAND®								
R	BIG THUNDER MOUNTAIN RAILROAD	●	3 ft 4 in	9am–7pm	➡	❶	✓	★
R	SPLASH MOUNTAIN®	○	3 ft 4 in	9am–7pm	➡	❶		★
S	COUNTRY BEAR JAMBOREE	○		10am–7pm		❶		▼
LIBERTY SQUARE								
R	THE HAUNTED MANSION	◗		noon–7pm		❶		◆
R	LIBERTY BELLE RIVERBOAT	◗				❶		▼
S	THE HALL OF PRESIDENTS	○				❶		▼
FANTASYLAND®								
R	DUMBO THE FLYING ELEPHANT	○		10am–4pm		❷		▼
R	IT'S A SMALL WORLD	○		9am–7pm		❷		★
R	MAD TEA PARTY	○		10am–6pm		❶	✓	▼
R	THE MANY ADVENTURES OF WINNIE THE POOH	○		10am–5pm	➡	❷		◆
R	PETER PAN'S FLIGHT	○		10am–5pm	➡	❷		★
R	SNOW WHITE'S SCARY ADVENTURES	○		10am–5pm		❷		◆
S	MICKEY'S PHILHARMAGIC	○		10am–6pm	➡	❶		★
MICKEY'S TOONTOWN FAIR®								
R	THE BARNSTORMER AT GOOFY'S WISEACRE FARM	○		10am–6pm		❶	✓	◆
TOMORROWLAND®								
R	ASTRO ORBITER	○				❶		▼
R	BUZZ LIGHTYEAR'S SPACE RANGER SPIN	○		10am–7pm	➡	❶		◆
R	SPACE MOUNTAIN®	○	3 ft 8 in	9am–7pm	➡	❸	✓	◆
R	STICH'S GREAT ESCAPE!	○		10am–6pm	➡	❶		◆
R	TOMORROWLAND® INDY SPEEDWAY	○	4 ft 4 ft	10am–7pm		❸		◆
R	TOMORROWLAND TRANSIT AUTHORITY	○				❷		◆
S	CAROUSEL OF PROGRESS	○				❷		▼
S	THE TIMEKEEPER	○				❷		▼

Key: Ride – R Show – S; Waiting Time Good – ○ Average – ◗ Bad – ●; Loading Speed Fast – ❶
Leisurely – ❷ Slow – ❸; Overall Rating Good – ▼ Excellent – ◆ Outstanding – ★

Epcot® ❷

Epcot, an acronym for the Experimental Prototype Community of Tomorrow, was Walt Disney's dream of a technologically replete, living community. It was intended to represent a utopian vision of the future but, by the time it opened in 1982, several changes had been made to the original dream and Epcot opened as an educational center and permanent world's fair.

The 250-acre (100-ha) park is divided into two distinct halves: Future World with an emphasis on entertainment and education and World Showcase which represents the art, culture, and culinary expertise of different countries around the globe.

Test Track, one of the most popular rides at Epcot

TOP TIPS

• Early entry guests are allowed into the parks immediately to enjoy certain attractions, so it's a good idea to be at the turnstiles at least 15 minutes before they open.

• Most people ride Spaceship Earth as they arrive in Epcot and waiting times are therefore long. In the afternoon, however, you can walk on with virtually no wait.

• To avoid severe congestion at the end of the day, park in the visitor's car park of the Yacht and Beach Club hotels. Walk into World Showcase through the International Gateway and exit the same way after IllumiNations.

West, and emerge to the Imagination Pavilion to see Honey, I Shrunk the Audience (clock face position roughly 1 o'clock). After this, you can return to Spaceship Earth (6 o'clock) if the lines have shortened or make your way back across to the excellent Ellen's Energy Adventure (7 o'clock) and Wonders of Life (8 o'clock) pavilions. Though this seems like a lot of backtracking, you will have covered the main attractions very quickly and should enjoy a little glow of satisfaction when you see the lines snaking out of the entrances later in the day.

World Showcase holds far more interest for adults than children. However, there are Kidcot Fun Spots in several pavilions where kids can draw and have fun, and the diversionary tactic of buying

TACKLING THE PARK

Epcot is two and a half times the size of Magic Kingdom, which means that at least a day and a half are needed to cover most of the attractions here. World Showcase is not normally open until 11am so the early-morning crowds fill Future World and then gradually migrate to the rope between the two parks waiting for World Showcase to open. As with everything Disney, arriving early is the key to a successful visit. If you are entitled to early entry privileges, arrive one hour and 40 minutes before the official opening time.

Although there are really only a small number of rides in Future World, the newest of these – Test Track and Mission: SPACE – are besieged from the outset, so it's best to get to them early. Pick up a Fastpass for one and ride the other. To reach them, bear left through the huge Innoventions East building. It sometimes helps

to think of Future World as a clock face; if the main entrance is at 6 o'clock, then Mission: SPACE is at 9 o'clock and Test Track at 11 o'clock. This is roughly the equivalent of walking from the entrance of Magic Kingdom right through to Splash Mountain/Big Thunder Mountain Railroad.

After leaving the Mission: SPACE/Test Track area, retrace your steps back through Innoventions East, cross immediately through Innoventions

PIN TRADING

This answer to many a parent's prayer was introduced when Disney noticed that the lapel pins it had produced for special events were re-selling at several times the market value. In a flash of inspiration, they created Pin Stations, small booths in every park selling the hundreds of different Disney pins. Epcot's Pin Station Central, near Spaceship Earth, is the largest booth. The pins usually cost $6–$15 each. Following this with a stroke of genius, Disney created Pin Traders – cast members who could be persuaded to swap pins with guests – and surmounted the whole idea with a set of very simple trading rules, which cast members could break in favor of the guest. This has captured the imagination of children who happily spend hours tracking down the pin they don't have and swapping another for it.

Spaceship Earth, the 180-ft (55-m) geosphere at Epcot's entrance

each child a "passport" to have stamped can prove a blessing. There are minor rides – usually boat rides – in some pavilions and several others show films. The dining at some pavilions is excellent and can be booked ahead through your hotel. The transportation system in the park is not very efficient – you'll always get where you want faster by walking, so good, comfortable shoes are essential. There is also not much shade, so be sure to wear a hat.

FUTURE WORLD

As you enter the turnstiles, dominated visually by the giant geodesic dome that is home to the Spaceship Earth ride, you'll notice a new feature: **Leave a Legacy**, which offers guests a chance to have an image of themselves engraved in metal and attached to a series of modern stone structures. Future World itself comprises a series of huge, modernistic buildings around the outside, the access to which is through Innoventions East and West. Some buildings house a single ride attraction while others afford the opportunity to browse various exhibits – usually hands-on – and enjoy smaller rides within the main pavilion. Most attractions here are sponsored by major corporations, which will be evident from the signs.

Spaceship Earth

Housed in a massive, 7,500-ton geodesic sphere, this continuously loading ride conveys you gently past superbly crafted tableaux and animatronic scenes portraying mankind's progress in technology. Almost as interesting as the ride is the dome which cunningly re-circulates rainwater into the World Showcase Lagoon.

Innoventions

Both buildings, East and West, form a hands-on exhibition of products of the near future which, through ties to consumer electronics manufacturers, is constantly updated.

Its structure – small, self-contained demonstration or game bays – make Innoventions an excellent "quick visit" you can return to throughout the day as you wait for your Fastpass time window or for lines to shorten. Though some of the original games have moved to Downtown Disney (see pp74–5), there's still plenty for kids to do, while parents take in the "live infomercials" that show off, and soft-sell, the latest gadgets.

1 DAY ITINERARY

1. Arrive 1 hour 40 minutes before the official opening time on an early entry day or an hour before on a normal day.
2. Head straight toward **Test Track** and pick up a Fastpass for later. Get in line for **Mission: SPACE**.
3. Upon leaving Mission: SPACE, use your Fastpass for Test Track if your appointment time is close, otherwise cross the park to the **Imagination Pavilion** and grab a Fastpass for **Honey, I Shrunk the Audience**. Visit **Innoventions** if you have a bit of time to kill.
4. Upon leaving Test Track, head for **Spaceship Earth**.
5. Visit Honey, I Shrunk the Audience if your Fastpass time window is open, otherwise turn right from Spaceship Earth and head toward **Wonders of Life**. Ride **Body Wars**.
6. Turn right out of Wonders of Life and head to **Ellen's Energy Adventure**.
7. Head toward **World Showcase** and wait for the rope drop on the left.
8. At rope drop, head to **Mexico**. Ride **El Rio del Tempio**.
9. Leave to the right and go to **Norway**. Ride **The Maelstrom**.
10. Now it's time for a late lunch. Pick a pavilion other than the one you have in mind for dinner, and use the time after lunch to select and make dinner reservations. Time your reservation for two hours prior to the start of IllumiNations if possible. Once the reservations are made, visit **China** (movie), **France** (movie), and **Canada** (movie).
11. Return to Future World and visit **The Land** pavilion. Experience all three attractions there.
12. Leave The Land pavilion to the left and head for **The Living Seas**.
13. Exit The Living Seas to the right, pass through both Innoventions East and West, and return to the Wonders of Life pavilion where you can see **Cranium Command** and **The Making of Me**.
14. Finish exploring Innoventions, or pick up a Fastpass for a repeat ride if any are available. Head for dinner, which should allow you a half-hour to find a good spot for **IllumiNations**.

Epcot: Mission: SPACE

THE NEWEST THRILL RIDE at Epcot, Mission: SPACE takes guests on a journey to the heavens that culminates with a crash landing on Mars. This extremely popular attraction is the ultimate in simulator thrill rides, combining high-speed spinning – to simulate g-forces – with a simulator and a 3-D visual interactive storyline. The result is a completely mesmerizing and convincing rocket launch and high-speed trip to Mars, which also involves a ride around the moon. Particularly impressive are the wholly realistic re-creations of a liftoff into space and a problem-fraught landing. The most technologically advanced of Disney's attractions, the ride is a creation of Disney imagination, but is based on scientific fact and theory provided by astronauts, scientists, and engineers.

INTERNATIONAL SPACE TRAINING CENTER

THE STORY IS SET at the International Space Training Center (ISTC) in the year 2036. In this future time of space exploration, many countries have joined together to train a new generation of space explorers. Mission: SPACE participants become astronaut candidates on their first training mission.

The ISTC building is a gleaming, metallic affair, complete with curved walls and a state-of-the-art, Space Age look. The curvy steel exterior surrounds the courtyard, called **Planetary Plaza** – from the moment visitors step into this courtyard, they are taken straight into a futuristic world. Huge replicas of Earth, Jupiter, and the moon fill Planetary Plaza, and its walls feature quotations from historical figures about space

travel and exploration. The moon model displays brass plaques indicating the location of every US and Soviet manned and unmanned touchdown during the 1960s and 70s. The interior of the ISTC is compartmentalized into various areas for different levels of training. There are four ride bays, with ten capsules in each bay; each capsule can hold four guests.

TRAINING

BEFORE EMBARKING on their flight, the explorers must follow a series of procedures in order to prepare for their "mission." These training and briefing sessions also go a long way in making the wait times for the show seem shorter, as they keep the crowds entertained prior to the actual ride portion of the show: the ambience is well-executed and slightly

militaristic – a rare feature at Disney parks. At the **ISTC Astronaut Recruiting Center**, explorers learn about training and view a model of the X-2 Trainer, the futuristic spacecraft they will board for their journey into space.

The second station of the mission is the **Space Simulation Lab**, a slowly spinning 35-ft (10-m) high gravity wheel containing work quarters, exercise rooms, sleeping cubicles, and dining areas for space teams. One of the highlights of the lab is an authentic Apollo-era Lunar Rover display unit on loan from the Smithsonian National Air and Space Museum, which describes mankind's first exploration of the moon.

Participants then enter the **Training Operations Room**, which bustles with the activity of various training sessions in progress. Several large monitors show live video feeds of ongoing ISTC training sessions. In **Team Dispatch**, a dispatch officer meets participants. Here, participants are split into teams of four people and sent to the **Ready Room**. This is the point at which each team member accepts an assignment: commander, pilot, navigator, or engineer. Each member is supposed to carry out the tasks associated with his or her assigned role

Replicas of planets standing out dramatically against the metallic façade of the Mission: SPACE building

during the flight. It is here that the explorers meet Capcom – the capsule communicator – who will act as the astronauts' guide through the flight. In the **Pre-flight Corridor**, explorers receive their final instructions for the mission. A uniformed flight crew member then escorts the team to a capsule – the X-2 Space Shuttle.

FLIGHT & LANDING

THE TEAM members board the X-2 training capsule and are securely strapped in, with individual "windows" just inches away. The countdown begins and then there is a pulse-racing liftoff: the roar of engines, the clouds of exhaust, and the motion of the capsule all combine to generate in the participants sensations similar to those that astronauts feel during actual liftoff.

The cabin's windows are actually state-of-the-art video flat screens that use a combination of LCD glass and electronic video cards to present an ultra-sharp full-motion video based on actual data taken from Mars-orbiting satellites. The spectacular

views of planets Earth and Mars that participants glimpse through the capsule windows, reinforce their illusion of traveling through space.

The members of the space team must work in unison, performing the roles of pilot, commander, navigator, and engineer in order to successfully face challenges and accomplish their mission to Mars. Throughout the flight, crew members receive instructions from Capcom regarding their duties, which consists of pressing buttons; the capsule obeys the commands very convincingly. Unexpected twists and turns keep participants on the edge of their seats, and call for tricky maneuvers with joysticks. Apart from the exhilarating "slingshot" around the moon, other thrills include a brief experience of "weightlessness" and dodging asteroids on the way to Mars.

The four-minute ride comes to a crashing finale with the Mars landing, complemented by superb sound effects that are achieved by the use of a stereo woofer built right into the back of the space capsules. Pioneering astronauts such as Buzz Aldrin and Rhea Seddon have taken their turn on the ride, comparing it favorably to actual space travel.

The g-forces that come into play during Mission: SPACE are, in fact, of lower intensity than in a typical roller coaster but they are of much greater duration.

ADVANCE TRAINING LAB

AFTER THE ride, guests can go around the Advance Training Lab, a colorful interactive play area where they can test their skills in space-related games for people of all ages. You can explore this area even if you choose not to go on the ride itself. There is no minimum height requirement here.

In **Space Race**, two teams are involved in a race to be the first to complete a successful mission from Mars back to Earth. The teams are

composed of up to 60 guests, who are required to work together to overcome numerous challenges and setbacks in their mission. **Expedition: Mars** is another fun endeavor at the Advance Traning Lab. In this sophisticated video game, the player's mission is to locate four astronauts stranded on Mars. **Space Base** is targeted at junior astronauts. It is an excellent interactive play area where kids can climb, slide, crawl, explore, and get rid of excess energy. You can also send **Postcards from Space** at a kiosk in the Advanced Training Lab. Here, guests make a video of themselves in one of several space-related backdrops to create a fine memento of their Mission: SPACE experience, and can email the result to friends and family.

Beyond the Advance Traning Lab is the **Mission: SPACE Cargo Bay**, a shopping area spreading over 1,500 sq ft (139 sq m). A 4-ft (1.2-m) high 3-D figure of Mickey Mouse dressed as an astronaut greets visitors, and the area is dominated by a 12-ft (3.6-m) mural depicting various Disney characters in space gear on the surface of Mars. Here, visitors can purchase a large variety of souvenirs, from inexpensive to costly, as a remembrance of their "space experience."

FUTURE WORLD CONT...

Ellen's Energy Adventure

A passably entertaining film is enlivened by some fascinating technology and hosts Ellen DeGeneres and Billy Nye. The entire theater rotates before breaking into self-powered, moving sections – each seating over a 100 people – which then proceed to take the audience through a prehistoric landscape, inhabited by some fairly convincing antediluvians.

The Living Seas

The technology behind this attraction is quite stunning in its own right, but the reason most come here is to visit Sea Base Alpha, Epcot's most ambitious research project. A pre-show presentation prepares you for your journey to the bottom of the ocean, after which you take the "hydro-lators" to the sea bed. There you board a continuously moving train of small cars, which carry you past astonishing views of sharks, dolphins, giant turtles, and manatees. Disembarkation brings you to the base itself, where you can browse through exhibits, get close up to the manatees, and watch the sealife through transparent walls.

Wonders of Life

This rambling, noisy pavilion deals, as its name suggests, with the functioning of the human body. **The Making of Me** is a pleasant film about the events preceding childbirth while **Cranium Command** is an amusing and often overlooked anima-tronic presentation about the operation of the brain. **Body Wars** – Epcot's first simulator thrill ride – takes you through the human body, having first miniaturized you. This, however, although popular, is a violent and jerky ride which induces motion sickness in quite a few people.

Test Track

One of the most popular rides at Epcot, this has long lines forming quickly at park opening time and increasing rapidly because of frequent malfunctions. Test Track uses the most sophisticated ride vehicle technology available, placing you in a simulator that moves on tracks at high speed. Essentially, you are the passenger in a six-seater prototype sports car being tested prior to going into production. Although the ride puts you through brake tests, hill climbs, sharp turns, near crashes, and paint spraying bays, the climax is the outside lap of the ride where the vehicle exceeds 66 mph (102 km/h) on a raised roadway around the outside of the Test Track building. So advanced is the technology that the ride is kept running 24 hours a day, as the start up procedure is so lengthy. However, the system has frequent stops – usually because the advanced safety systems have cut in and halted the entire run. While this is obviously reassuring in some ways, Test Track is so

TOP TIPS

• *Test Track is exceptionally popular but unreliable. To avoid the long lines, try to ride this first. On leaving, take a Fastpass ticket for another ride later.*

• *If a breakdown occurs during your ride, after disembarking ask the cast member if you can ride again, immediately.*

• *Because Test Track runs continuously – even when the park is closed – you can jump back on it for a repeat ride in the last minutes before park closing.*

• *Ellen's Energy Adventure show is exceptionally long (45 minutes). Take it in for a break from the heat or while you wait for a Fastpass ride window to become available.*

• *Although the lines for Ellen's Energy Adventure are long, it takes 600 guests every 17 minutes, so you won't have long to wait.*

• *The Land is an agriculturist's dream pavilion, but of little interest for teens (though young children will be entertained by the giant produce). For older kids, The Living Seas (recently modified to take advantage of Disney's monster hit Finding Nemo) is a better bet, though both are tame in nature.*

popular that the lines outside continue to grow until, by the evening, you can expect a wait of between 90 minutes and two hours for this 4 minute ride. The ride itself, however, is so good you will want to try it again and again. Be aware that the Fastpass machines outside the entrance have normally exhausted their allocation by lunchtime. After the ride, you can wander at leisure through what appears to be a large General Motors showroom.

The Imagination Pavilion

The Imagination Pavilion houses a show, a ride, and an interactive demo area. The show is the charming and funny 3-D presentation **Honey, I Shrunk the Audience**, the ride is **Journey into Imagination with Figment**, and the interactive showcase is a playground of audio-visual sensory games and demonstrations. Honey, I Shrunk the Audience

Feeding time for the residents of The Living Seas

is another example of the advances in sensory and visual 3-D storytelling. Dr. Nigel Channing, the always funny Eric Idle, hosts the Inventor of the Year Award Show, showing off the inventions that feature in the movie *Honey, I Shrunk the Kids!* – if things could just stop going wrong for a few moments. The clever plotline does indeed shrink the viewer and induces many laughs.

The Journey Into Imagination with Figment ride is an upbeat, light-hearted trip in search of ideas in the arts and sciences. However, it is overcomplicated and overlong. You move past several different animated scenes which present optical illusions and sound effects.

The **ImageWorks Lab** offers visitors a chance to manipulate sound and vision interactively, from making music by waving your arms to experimenting with fast- and slow-motion video to making music by doing aerobics. Highly

The tremendously funny "Honey, I Shrunk the Audience" show

recommended for the kids, it appeals to adults as well.

The Land
Ecology and conservation form the main themes and permeate the attractions housed around the fast food restaurant. As a consequence, these attractions become much busier during lunchtimes. *The Lion King* characters lead **The Circle of Life**, a hymn to conservation

expressed through film and animation. Dangers to the environment as well as potential solutions are presented through this entertaining and inspirational show. **Living with the Land** is a cruise through the past, present, and future of US farming. The Land pavilion also offers a walking tour to accompany the boat ride, which is certainly worth taking for those interested.

RIDES & SHOWS CHECKLIST

This chart is designed to help you plan what to visit at Epcot. The rides and shows in Future World and World Showcase are listed alphabetically.

		Waiting Time	Height/Age Restriction	Busiest Time To Ride/Attend	Fastpass	May Cause Motion Sickness	Overall Rating
FUTURE WORLD							
R	**Body Wars**	◗	3 ft 4 in	10am–2pm		✓	◆
R	**Journey into Imagination with Figment**	◗		11am–2pm			◆
R	**Mission: SPACE**	●	3 ft 8 in	All day	➡	✓	★
R	**Spaceship Earth**	◗		9am–noon			★
R	**Test Track**	●	3 ft 4 in	All day	➡	✓	★
S	**Circle of Life**	○		noon–2pm			▼
S	**Cranium Command**	○					◆
S	**Ellen's Energy Adventure**	◗		10am–1pm			◆
S	**Honey, I Shrunk the Audience**	○		10am–5pm	➡		★
S	**The Living Seas**	○		11am–3pm			◆
S	**Living with the Land**	●		noon–2pm	➡		◆
S	**The Making of Me**	○					▼
WORLD SHOWCASE							
R	**Maelstrom**	●		11am–5pm	➡		◆
R	**The River of Life**	○		noon–3pm			▼
S	**The American Adventure**	○					▼
S	**Impressions de France**	○					◆
S	**O Canada!**	○					◆
S	**Reflections of China**	○					★

Key: Ride – R Show – S; Waiting Times Good – ○ Average – ◗ Bad – ●;
Overall Rating Good – ▼ Excellent – ◆ Outstanding – ★

The gateway of the China pavilion

WORLD SHOWCASE

THE TEMPLES, churches, town halls, and castles of these 11 pavilions or "countries" are sometimes replicas of genuine buildings, sometimes merely in vernacular style. But World Showcase is much more than just a series of architectural set pieces. Every pavilion is staffed by people from the country it represents, selling high-quality local products as well as surprisingly good ethnic cuisine.

At set times, which are given on the guide map, native performers stage live shows in the forecourts of each country: the best are the excellent acrobats at China and the bizarre and comic Living Statues at Italy. Only a couple of pavilions include rides, while a number have stunning giant-screen introductions to their country's history, culture, and landscapes. A few even have art galleries, though these often go unnoticed.

The fastest way to get around the 1.3 mile (2 km) perimeter is to walk, but the easiest way to get from the entrance to the back end, where the American pavilion is located, is to take the ferries that crisscross the lagoon, linking the Canada pavilion to the Morocco pavilion and Mexico to Germany.

Mexico
A Mayan pyramid hides the most remarkable interior at World Showcase. Musicians and stalls selling sombreros, ponchos, and papier-mâché animals (*piñatas*) fill a plaza bathed in a purple twilight. The backdrop to this is a rumbling volcano. Hidden among the splendor of the main area are little art galleries and an arts-and-crafts play space for children.

The tranquil **El Río del Tiempo** ("The River of Time") boat ride passes through Audio-Animatronics and cinematic scenes of Mexico, while the restaurant outside the pavilion offers a great viewing spot for IllumiNations (*see p52*) later in the day.

Norway
The architecture in this pavilion includes replicas of a stave church – a medieval wooden building – and the 14th-century fortress above Oslo harbor called Akershus Castle, arranged attractively around a cobblestone square.

You can buy trolls and sweaters and other native crafts, but the essential element here is **Maelstrom**, a short but exhilarating journey down fjords in a longboat into troll country, and across an oil-rig-flecked North Sea – before docking at a fishing port. The ride is followed by a short film about Norway. The film is not mandatory – you can pass through the theater and exit directly if you choose – but it is a well-done look at the past and present of the country.

China
In this pavilion the *pièce de résistance* is the half-size replica of Beijing's well-known landmark, the Temple of Heaven. The peaceful scene here contrasts with the more rowdy atmosphere in some of the nearby pavilions.

For entertainment, there is **Reflections of China**, a Circle-Vision film shown on nine screens all around the audience simultaneously, which makes the most of the country's fabulous, little-seen ancient sites and scenery. Note that you must stand throughout the film. China, the country, also sends a near-continuous stream of acrobatic and other performing troupes that put on mini-shows throughout the day all year long.

The pavilion's extensive shopping emporium sells everything from Chinese lanterns and painted screens to tea bags. Unfortunately, the restaurants are nothing to write home about.

The striking wooden structure at the entrance to the Norway pavilion

◁ **The unmistakable globe of Spaceship Earth, the focal point of Future World**

Architectural elements of Venice at the Italy pavilion

TOP TIPS

• *The World Showcase opens later than Future World, but also closes significantly later, so save your tour of the World Showcase for the afternoon or evening.*

• *The interactive fountain on the walkway between Future World and World Showcase is a must for young children during hot spells.*

• *Boats cross the World Showcase Lagoon fairly regularly. A bonus is that they're air conditioned, and so offer some respite from the heat in the middle of the day.*

• *As you walk around the World Showcase, take a moment to make note of the menus at the restaurants in each showcase – you can usually make reservations on the spot for later meals.*

Germany
The happiest country in World Showcase is a mixture of gabled and spired buildings gathered around a central square, St. Georgsplatz. They are based on real buildings from all over Germany, including a merchants' hall in Freiburg and a Rhine castle. If you have children, try to time your visit so that it coincides with the hourly chime of the *glockenspiel* in the square.

An accordionist sometimes plays, and the shops are full of quirky or clever gifts such as beautifully crafted wooden dolls. However, you really need to dine here to get the full flavor of Germany.

Italy
The bulk of Italy's relatively small pavilion represents Venice: from gondolas moored alongside candycane poles in the lagoon to the tremendous versions of the towering redbrick campanile and the 14th-century Doge's Palace of St. Mark's Square; even the fake marble looks authentic. The courtyard buildings behind are Veronese and Florentine in style, and the Neptune statue is a copy of a Bernini work.

The architecture is the big attraction, but you should also stop off to eat at one of the restaurants or browse around the shops where you can pick up pasta, amaretti, wine, and so forth.

America
This is the centerpiece of World Showcase, but it lacks the charm found in most of the other countries. However, Americans usually find **The American Adventure** show, which takes place inside the vast Georgian-style building, very moving. For others, it will provide an interesting insight into the American psyche. The show is an openly patriotic yet thought-provoking romp through the history of the United States up to the present day. It incorporates tableaux on screen and some excellent Audio-Animatronics figures, particularly of the author Mark Twain and the great 18th-century statesman, Benjamin Franklin.

WORLD SHOWCASE: BEHIND THE SCENES
If you'd like more than just a superficial view of Walt Disney World, its behind-the-scenes tours may appeal. In World Showcase, two-hour Hidden Treasures tours provide a closer look at the architecture and traditions of the countries featured in the park, while in the Gardens of the World tours the creation of the World Showcase gardens is explained; you are even given tips on how to create a bit of Disney magic back home. These tours cost around $25 per person. If you have $160 and seven hours to spare, you might want to sign up for the Backstage Magic tour, which includes all three theme parks. One of the highlights is the visit to the famous tunnel network beneath Magic Kingdom. Call up for information on all Disney tours (*see p77*).

The lovely architecture and landscaping at the Japan pavilion

ILLUMINATIONS: REFLECTIONS OF EARTH

The one Epcot show that you mustn't miss is the nightly IllumiNations. Presented near closing time around World Showcase Lagoon, it is a rousing *son et lumière* show on an unbelievably extravagant scale with lasers, fire- and waterworks, and a symphonic soundtrack that highlight the 11 featured nations. Best viewing spots are a seat on the veranda at the Cantina de San Angel in Mexico, the outside restaurant balcony in Japan, and the International Gateway bridge near the United Kingdom.

WORLD SHOWCASE CONT...

Japan

This is a restrained, formal place with a traditional Japanese garden, a Samurai castle, and a pagoda modeled on a seventh-century temple in Nara – whose five levels represent earth, water, fire, wind, and sky.

The Mitsukoshi department store, a copy of the ceremonial hall of the Imperial Palace in Kyoto, offers kimonos, wind chimes, bonsai trees, and the chance to pick a pearl from an oyster. Kabuki theater troupes and other performers appear throughout the day. However, Japan really only comes to life in its restaurants, where visitors can sample delicacies such as sushi and tempura. On the second level of the pavilion, chefs work dexterously with flashing knives, demonstrating the Japanese art of tableside cooking.

Morocco

Morocco's appeal lies in its enameled tiles, its keyhole-shaped doors, its ruddy fortress walls, and the twisting alleys of its *medina* (old city), which is reached via a reproduction of a gate into the city of Fez. The use of native artists gives the show a greater sense of authenticity.

Morocco offers some of the best handmade crafts in World Showcase. The alleys of the old city lead you to a bustling market of little stores selling carpets, brassware, leatherware, and shawls.

There are several interesting dining experiences on offer. The Tangerine Café serves a variety of Moroccan sandwiches and specialty pastries. Try the couscous, steamed and served with lamb or chicken, at the Restaurant Marrakesh. It is also the place to see belly dancers perform in a stimulating show.

France

A Gallic flair infuses everything in the France pavilion, from its architecture to its upscale stores. Architectural highlights include a one-tenth scale replica of the Eiffel Tower, Parisian Belle Epoque mansions, and a rustic village main street. Among the authentic products from France sold here are

Detailed replica of the famous prayer tower in Marrakesh at the Morocco pavilion, across a promenade

The Canada pavilion, featuring examples of Canadian architecture

perfumes – such as the famous Guerlain range – wine, and berets. Excellent French food can be sampled in a couple of restaurants in the pavilion and a patisserie selling sinfully rich croissants and cakes.

A film entitled **Impressions de France** is the main entertainment. The film, shown on five adjacent screens and set to the sounds of French classical music, offers a whirlwind tour through the country's most beautiful regions.

United Kingdom

The Rose and Crown Pub is the focal point in this pavilion. It serves traditional English fare such as Cornish pasties, fish and chips, and even draft bitter – chilled to suit American tastes. There's also a "chip shop" takeaway booth next door for those in a hurry or wanting a smaller, less expensive meal. The pub also sports a genuine singalong most evenings. Pleasant gardens surround the pub, as well as a medley of buildings of various historic architectural styles. These include a castle based on Hampton Court, an imitation Regency terrace, and a thatched cottage.

There is not much to do here in this pavilion other than browse around the shops, which sell everything from quality tea and china to sweaters, tartan ties, teddy bears, and toy soldiers. The terrace of the Rose and Crown, however, offers good views of IllumiNations.

Canada

A Native Indian village with a log cabin and 30-ft (9-m) high totem poles, a replica of Ottawa's Victorian-style Château Laurier Hotel, a rocky chasm, and ornamental gardens make up the large but rather staid Canadian pavilion.

The country in all its diversity, and particularly its grand scenery, comes to life much better in the Circle-Vision film **O Canada!** – though China's Circle-Vision film is even better. The audience stands in the middle of the theater and turns around to follow the film as it unfolds on no fewer than nine screens. Shops at Canada sell a wide range of Native Indian and Inuit crafts and various edible specialties, as well as wine. Le Cellier Steakhouse restaurant serves tasty Canadian seafood and steaks along with wines and beer from Canada.

EATING & DRINKING

Dining well is fundamental to visiting Epcot and particularly World Showcase. Some of the latter's pavilions have decent fast-food places, but the best restaurants (including those listed below unless otherwise stated) require reservations. Call Dining reservations *(see p77)* as soon as you know when you'll be at Epcot or book early in the day, using the TV monitors of the WorldKey Information Satellite, which provide up-to-date information on everything at Epcot. Most restaurants serve lunch and dinner; try unpopular hours such as 11am or 4pm if other times are unavailable. Lunch is usually about two-thirds of the price of dinner, and children's menus are available at even the most upscale restaurants.

Recommended in World Showcase are:
Mexico: the San Angel Inn serves interesting but pricey Mexican food. It is the most romantic place to dine at Epcot.
Norway: Restaurant Akershus offers a good-value *koldtbord* (buffet) of Norwegian dishes in a castle setting.
Germany: the Biergarten has a beer hall atmosphere, with a cheap and plentiful buffet and hearty oompah-pah music.
Italy: L'Originale Alfredo di Roma Ristorante is enormously popular and engagingly chaotic, with sophisticated dishes.
Japan: you can eat communally, either in the Teppan Yaki Dining Rooms around a grilling, stir-frying chef, or at the bar of Tempura Kiku for sushi and tempura (no reservations).
France: there are three top-notch restaurants here: the upscale Bistro de Paris (dinner only); Les Chefs de France, the most elegant restaurant in Epcot, with haute cuisine by acclaimed chefs *(see p151)*; and the terraced Chefs de France Steakhouse for steaks, escargots, and crêpes.
United Kingdom: Harry Ramsden's "chippy" booth sells only modest-sized, inexpensive pub fare; it makes for a great "lunch on the go" and the terrace adjoining it is the most relaxing spot in the World Showcase.

Recommended in Future World are:
The Land: the revolving Garden Grill passes a re-created rainforest, prairie, and desert.
The Living Seas: at the expensive Coral Reef you can eat fish and watch them through a transparent, underwater wall.

Disney-MGM Studios ❸

THE SMALLEST THEME park in Walt Disney World Resort, Disney-MGM Studios was launched in 1989 as a full-fledged working film and TV production facility. In January 2004, however, the animation department was shut down, and the "working" side of the equation has been almost completely abandoned, although some film and TV production – mostly for the Disney cable channel – is still undertaken here. Regardless of these changes, the park remains a famed tourist destination, with top-notch shows and rides based on Disney and Metro-Goldwyn-Mayer films and TV shows, which offer a tribute to the world of Hollywood and showbiz. Constantly evolving, the park has introduced new and spectacular shows, such as Fantasmic! and Beauty and the Beast – Live on Stage, which have taken its popularity to new heights. Like its competitor Universal Orlando *(see pp88–99)*, Disney-MGM Studios' educational yet highly entertaining interactive experiences are geared toward adults and teenagers.

TOP TIPS

• The best place to watch the afternoon parade is on the bench nearest the popcorn and drinks stand located opposite Sounds Dangerous. You still, however, have to get there first.
• During the parades, most of the other attractions are quiet, but almost impossible to reach if you're not on the correct side.
• Avoid parking in the Disney-MGM or Animal Kingdom lots if you are visiting multiple parks throughout the day. Trams to these parking lots stop running long before the last show at the Magic Kingdom and it can take a long time for you to get back to your vehicle.

TACKLING THE PARK

THE LAYOUT OF this park differs from that of the other theme parks, although Hollywood Boulevard takes on the role of "Main Street, USA" with the purpose of directing guests toward the numerous attractions.

Over the past few years, Walt Disney World has successfully expanded the scope and magnitude of the park's attractions, building some of the finest in Orlando. With scores of tourists lining up for the rides and shows, arriving early is the key to avoid waiting for long periods in line. It's also worth bearing in mind that some of the attractions might be particularly intense and can frighten young children.

The entertainment schedule changes frequently and streets can be closed off for either celebrity visits or in case of a live filming session. Although events such as these usually take place in winter, it's a good idea to find out about times, locations, and shows as soon as you enter the park from Guest Services, which is located on the left of the main entrance.

At about 3:30pm, the park holds its afternoon parade, usually based on one of Disney's recently animated movies. Be aware that, due to the open plan of the park, the heat can become quite uncomfortable for guests.

Fantasmic! takes place at night – once a night during the slow season and twice during peak periods. Despite seating about 10,000 people at a time, you may need to turn up quite early – up to two hours ahead of time – during peak periods to ensure a seat.

HOLLYWOOD BOULEVARD

DELIGHTFUL ART DECO styled buildings vie with a replica of Mann's Chinese Theater to present an image of Hollywood that never was. It's here that your picture will be taken and you might see

Visitors heading for the Rock 'n' Roller® Coaster starring Aerosmith ride

The famous Hollywood Brown Derby Restaurant, Hollywood Boulevard

TOP 10 ATTRACTIONS

1. **THE TWILIGHT ZONE TOWER OF TERROR™**
2. **FANTASMIC!**
3. **ROCK 'N' ROLLER® COASTER STARRING AEROSMITH**
4. **JIM HENSON'S MUPPET* VISION 3-D**
5. **STAR TOURS**
6. **INDIANA JONES™ EPIC STUNT SPECTACULAR!**
7. **WHO WANTS TO BE A MILLIONAIRE – PLAY IT!**
8. **VOYAGE OF THE LITTLE MERMAID**
9. **THE GREAT MOVIE RIDE**
10. **THE MAGIC OF DISNEY ANIMATION**

some of the cast members, acting as reporters or police, chasing celebrities. Moreover, it is on the boulevard that the cast members will try to direct you to Echo Lake's Indiana Jones Epic Stunt Spectacular! – a live action show featuring stunts from the Indiana Jones films.

Halfway up the boulevard, a street breaks off to the right. This is known as Sunset Boulevard, and is home to two of Disney-MGM Studios' most popular rides: The Twilight Zone Tower of Terror and the Rock 'n' Roller Coaster starring Aerosmith.

At the junction of Sunset and Hollywood boulevards lies an enormous canopy that is shaped like Mickey's hat from *The Sorcerer's Apprentice*.

This is a combination store, shady spot, and pin station (see p42), where budding traders can ambush the cast and swap badges.

At the top of Hollywood Boulevard lies the Central Plaza, which is dominated by the replica of Mann's Chinese Theater. Here you can experience **The Great Movie Ride**, a trip through movie history that features every film genre, ranging from musicals to horror films to gangster movies. Huge ride vehicles carrying 60 guests apiece track silently past the largest movie sets ever built for a Disney ride. As always, Disney's vast experience in the movie industry has led to the creation of some superb sets. Memorable cinematic

moments, such as Gene Kelly singing in the rain and Dorothy going down the Yellow Brick Road on her way to Oz, are re-created with the help of highly realistic Audio-Animatronic figures. Combined with old film clips, special effects, and some fun live action sequences, this is an enjoyable 25-minute ride that ends on a very upbeat and optimistic note. The Great Movie Ride is one of the few attractions where the queuing is almost as good as the ride itself.

1 DAY ITINERARY

1. Upon entering the park, immediately get a Fastpass to **The Twilight Zone Tower of Terror**.
2. Stroll back up Sunset Boulevard and get in line for **The Great Movie Ride**.
3. As you exit, head for Animation Courtyard and take in the various shows (which usually have minimal wait times) – **The Magic of Disney Animation, Voyage of the Little Mermaid**, and **Walt Disney: One Man's Dream**. Try and get a Fastpass for **Who Wants to Be a Millionaire – Play It!**
4. If your time window for the Tower of Terror has arrived, go back down Sunset to ride it. Wait in line for the **Rock 'n' Roller Coaster starring Aerosmith** after you ride the Tower (if the wait time is less than one hour; otherwise come back to it later).
5. Enjoy lunch in the large restaurant area on Sunset, or take in the **Beauty and the Beast – Live on Stage** show.
6. Attend your scheduled Millionaire show, then walk down to the southeast end of the park and get a Fastpass for **Star Tours**. Head to the **Jim Henson's Muppet Vision 3-D** show and walk down New York Street after you're done there.
7. Just before heading into Star Tours, get a Fastpass for the **Indiana Jones Epic Stunt Spectacular!**
8. Dine at your pre-reserved restaurant.
9. Head for your scheduled Indiana Jones show, then walk across the park for your last chance to re-ride either Tower of Terror or Rock 'n' Roller Coaster if the wait times have fallen to under one hour. Time this so that you emerge from the ride about 90 minutes to one hour prior to the start of **Fantasmic!**
10. As darkness descends on the park, head for the Amphitheater to catch Fantasmic! and end the day on a perfect note.

SUNSET BOULEVARD

LIKE HOLLYWOOD Boulevard, Sunset Boulevard is a rose-tinted evocation of the famous Hollywood street in the 1940s. Theaters and storefronts – some real, some fake – have been re-created with characteristic attention to detail. The Hollywood Tower Hotel lies at one end of the boulevard. This decrepit, lightning-ravaged hotel is home to one of Orlando's scariest rides – **The Twilight Zone Tower of Terror**™. The ride straps you into a runaway service elevator for a voyage inspired by the 1950s TV show *The Twilight Zone*. The pre-show area is a library into which you are ushered by a melancholic bellhop. From here you enter what appears to be the boiler room of the hotel and you walk through to board the freight elevators fitted with plank seats. The elevator doors sometimes open to allow glimpses of ghostly corridors. As you reach the 13th floor, the elevator actually trundles horizontally across the hotel. But it's hard to concentrate on anything other than the ghastly 13-story plunge that everyone knows will come – but not exactly when. The original single drop has now been increased to seven and, during the first drop, enormously powerful engines actually pull you down faster than free fall. Terrifyingly brilliant, this ride is a technological masterpiece. You can also enjoy a brief, fleeting view of the whole park, and indeed outside the park – a break with Disney tradition – before you begin the scary descent. The Tower of Terror ride is not to everyone's taste, but diehard enthusiasts and novices alike pack this ride from the outset.

An indoor extravaganza, the **Rock 'n' Roller® Coaster starring Aerosmith** ride accelerates from 0 to 60 mph (96 km/h) in just 2.8 seconds. Strapped into "stretch limos," guests experience 5G pulls as they hurl through the twists and turns. Replete with loops, steep drops, and corkscrew spins, the Rock 'n' Roller Coaster employs a fully synchronized and very loud soundtrack as it hurls you toward the neon-lit equivalent of oblivion. Those who enjoy sitting in the front can get to the seats via the lower ramp. The pre-show is a rather tame affair and presents a recording session of the popular American band, Aerosmith.

The boulevard also features two outdoor arenas for shows. The **Theater of the Stars** is a huge, covered amphitheater with 1,500 seats. The **Beauty and the Beast – Live on Stage** show is performed several times throughout the day here. The production is about 30 minutes long and has beautifully choreographed scenes adapted from the movie of the same title. The exquisitely detailed sets, and costumes are works of art. Since the show is extremely popular, go early to get a good seat. The gigantic **Hollywood Hills Amphitheater** is home to the spectacular and dazzling show, **Fantasmic!**

TOP TIPS

• *Fastpasses to the top rides – the Tower of Terror and the Rock 'n' Roller Coaster – are usually gone by early afternoon. If you do not arrive early at the park, your only chance to ride these rides will be to either wait in the "standby" line for up to two hours each, or stay in the park until it's nearly closing time, when the line wait times drop to around 45 minutes.*
• *In the boiler room of the Tower of Terror, take any open gateway to the lifts – don't worry if the other guests do not do the same. You'll get a better seat and a better view.*
• *Many people leave the park during bad weather or as night approaches, but this is in fact the best time to head for the Tower of Terror ride.*

Sunset Boulevard also offers a large seating area, where guests can choose from a wide range of food stands and restaurants. Visitors can opt for a quick snack, a light meal, or a full lunch. There is something to suit every budget.

FANTASMIC!

Each of the Disney parks aim to bring down the curtain with a spectacular show, but Disney-MGM's Fantasmic! extravaganza outdoes them all. It is, quite simply, the finest event of its kind in Florida. Combining lasers, fan fountain projection, animation, and a cast of more than a 100 actors and dancers, Fantasmic! manages to choreograph the entire event with split second accuracy to music, fireworks, and lighting. Set on an island in a lagoon meant to represent Mickey Mouse's imagination, the "story," such as it is, cleverly weaves elements of all the classic Disney films into a single battle between good and evil.

Illuminated boats, flying floats, and a lake that bursts into flames are but some of the remarkable features of this enchanting event. Playing to audiences of 10,000 per showing, Fantasmic! completely mesmerizes adults as well as children with incredible special effects and their interaction with live performers. The wide array of famous characters represented will bring squeals of recognition and delight from all ages.

As expected, the show is exceptionally popular with most visitors as a finale for the evening, which means that arriving early is a must if you want to sit near the front – be aware that you may get wet in the first few rows. Seating opens approximately two hours before showtime, and the earlier show tends to fill up faster than the final performance. Even in the quietest time of the off-peak season, all 10,000 places are taken up to 30 minutes before the show starts. However, this truly is one event you would never forgive yourself for missing.

◁ **The sinister exterior of The Twilight Zone Tower of Terror**™**, Disney-MGM Studios**

Bear and his friends at Playhouse Disney – Live on Stage!

ANIMATION COURTYARD

THE ORIGINAL idea behind Animation Courtyard was not just to give visitors an inside look into the history and process of animation, but also a glimpse at all forthcoming Disney animated films as they were being made. With the shutting down of Disney's animation unit in January 2004, this area of the park is now less popular, but still has features worth visiting.

The **Magic of Disney Animation**, which used to be a tour of the working spaces in the Animation Department, is now a guided visit with a sole Disney artist and some films exploring Disney's rich history in animated films. The artist does live sketches on the spot and answers questions about how films are made. The "tour" concludes with the audience – mostly children – sitting at tables and working with the artist to create their own Disney character. For adults, the most interesting aspect of this attraction are the sketches from Disney classics, along with copies of the Academy awards the unit has won over the years.

The **Voyage of the Little Mermaid** show is enacted by cartoon, live, and Audio-Animatronic characters. Special effects use lasers and water to create the feel of an underwater grotto. It is one of the most popular shows in the park, though young children sometimes find the lightning storm scary.

Playhouse Disney – Live on Stage! is also geared toward youngsters and features singing and dancing Disney Channel characters. There's the lovable Bear in the Big Blue House and the cute and cuddly Winnie the Pooh. This 20-minute production encourages audience participation. Don't miss it.

MICKEY AVENUE

THIS CONNECTS Animation Courtyard to the **Disney-MGM Studios Backlot Tour**. Sound stages line the avenue and currently are the premises for **Who Wants to be a Millionaire – Play It!**, a re-creation of the ABC game-show phenomenon. Also, look out for Mickey, who may be signing autographs here.

Next door is the new attraction: **Walt Disney: One Man's Dream**. This could be dismissed as simple propaganda, but it is difficult not to admire Walt's great vision and risk-taking ability. A fascinating "museum" features collections of early Disney memorabilia, multimedia appearances of the man himself, and plenty of scale models and historical props from the parks. Wind your way to the cinema to see a film on Walt Disney. Despite the title, the film and photos make it pretty clear that Walt

---

SHOPPING

Most of the best shops are on Hollywood Boulevard, which stays open half an hour after the rest of the theme park has closed. Mickey's of Hollywood is the big emporium for general Disney merchandise. Celebrity 5 & 10 has a range of affordable movie souvenirs, such as clapper boards and Oscars®, as well as books and posters. More expensive is Sid Cahuenga's One-Of-A-Kind, where you can buy rare film and TV memorabilia such as genuine autographed photographs – of Boris Karloff and Greta Garbo, for example – or famous actors' clothes. Limited-edition "cels" in Animation Gallery in Animation Courtyard are also very expensive and will make an even bigger dent in your wallet; the same shop sells Disney posters and books too.

◁ **The electrifying Rock 'n' Roller® Coaster starring Aerosmith ride, Disney-MGM Studios**

TOP TIPS

Disney received extensive help from his family – particularly brother Roy, who worked arduously to complete and expand Walt Disney World after his brother's death in 1966. Especially admirable is Walt's enthusiasm for the expansion of his dream – the plans for Disney World and his dream project, Epcot. However, Walt would probably be fairly shocked at the size, scope and appeal of the company these days, having humbly said: "Never forget, it started because of a mouse."

Although it never fails to be entertaining, the half-hour Disney-MGM Studios Backlot Tour best comes to life when a film is actually being shot. The tour begins with a show explaining how the effects of controlling the weather and the forces of nature – such as the sea – are accomplished on film. Members of the audience are roped in for some of the demonstrations. A tram then takes you through various departments – props, makeup, costume, and so on – and finally down Residential Street, where different exteriors illustrate how the mood of a film is set. You also get to look in on three sound stages, where, if you're lucky, a TV show, commercial, or movie might be being filmed. If any actual television or film production happens to be taking place, the audience is usually allowed to walk onto the sound stage and observe the work in progress.

The most memorable part of the tour is a visit to the **Castastrophe Canyon**, a highly realistic and terrifying journey through floods, explosions, earthquakes, and various other disasters. The newest addition to the tour, **Lights, Motors, Action! Extreme Stunt Show**, features special cars, motorcycles, and jet skis.

NEW YORK STREET

THE BRICKS and stone in this version of New York are in fact just painted on plastic and fiberglass, the buildings' façades simply propped up with girders. Washing on the line outside a brownstone, a Chinese laundry, and the Empire State Building – painted in forced perspective to make it appear tall – add authenticity to the Big Apple. The streets were once closed to the public, but visitors can now wander around freely – even though the set is still used for filming.

Toy Story Pizza Planet is a trumped up arcade made to resemble Andy's favorite hangout. It is packed full of video games.

Jim Henson's Muppet™ Vision 3-D is a highly enjoyable, slapstick 3-D movie, starring the Muppets. The 25-minute show is a favorite with kids. Trombones, cars, and rocks launch themselves at you out of the screen; they are so realistic that children often grasp the air expecting to touch something. A full Muppet orchestra plays music in a pit. Audio-Animatronic characters and the excellent special effects, such as a cannon blowing holes in the walls of the theater, enhance the show's impact.

Visitors on an exhilarating ride through the Catastrophe Canyon, Disney-MGM Studios Backlot Tour

A giant ant at the Honey, I Shrunk the Kids Movie Set Adventure

The 12-minute pre-show is pure Muppet mischief. Here you will see Kermit and Miss Piggy at their best. In addition, the actual 3-D movie – hosted by Audio-Animatronic Statler and Waldorf – is full of playful comedy for all ages.

If you've got young children, don't miss the imaginative **Honey, I Shrunk the Kids Movie Set Adventure**. Everything is larger than life in this playground that is specifically designed for the younger set

to burn off their excess energy. As you enter, you are surrounded by 30-ft (9-m) high blades of grass, a slide made from a roll of film, and an ant the size of a pony. The huge tunnels, slides, giant spiders, and other props keep children amused for hours. Since the area is not very large, the playground can get very crowded, and it's a good idea to head for it early. Due to its popularity, parents find it difficult to get kids to leave.

ECHO LAKE

THE INTEREST here is focused on three shows and one thrill ride. Children also enjoy the sight of Gertie, the great green dinosaur, which houses an ice cream stand. The shows reveal the tricks of the film and TV trade.

In a nice change of pace, the audio portion of Hollywood's "magic" is given its due with the whimsical film **Sounds Dangerous – Starring Drew Carey**. Popular comedian/actor Drew Carey is a police detective who goes undercover with a hidden camera that keeps losing its picture, but never its sound. In an innovative twist, part of the film – about seven continuous minutes – takes place in complete darkness, leaving the audience with only the headphones to help them imagine what is going on.

Nearby, the **Academy of Television Arts and Sciences Hall of Fame** features the likenesses of many television legends, who have been honored for their outstanding achievements either in front of or behind the camera.

The storyline of the sensational ride **Star Tours** is based on the *Star Wars* films. Your spaceship, a flight simulator similar to those used to train astronauts, takes

An explosive scene from the Lights, Motors, Action! Extreme Stunt Show, Mickey Avenue

a wrong turn and then has to evade meteors and fight in an inter-galactic battle. The craft's movements synchronize perfectly with the action on screen, adding to the illusion.

The large-scale show **Indiana Jones™ Epic Stunt Spectacular!** re-creates well-known scenes from the *Indiana Jones* movies to deliver lots of big bangs as well as daredevil feats to thrill the audience. Death-defying stuntmen leap between buildings as they avoid sniper fire, sudden explosions, and dangerous traps. As an educational side-line, the stunt director and real stunt doubles demon-strate how some of the action sequences are realized. Try to arrive early if you want to take part as an extra in the show.

Surrounding Echo Lake are many eating spots that have been designed to look like sets from films.

EATING & DRINKING

It is definitely worth going through the trouble of making a reservation at one of the full-service restaurants at Disney-MGM Studios, though more for their atmosphere than their food. You can reserve a table by calling *(see p77)*, or by going directly to the Dining Reservation Booth, at the crossroads of Hollywood and Sunset boulevards, or to the restaurants themselves.

The exclusive and costly Hollywood Brown Derby repli-cates the Original Brown Derby in Hollywood, where the stars met in the 1930s – right down to the celebrities' caricatures on the walls and the house specialties of Cobb Salad and grapefruit cake. Kids usually prefer the Sci-Fi Dine-In Theater Restaurant, a 1950s drive-in where customers sit in mini-Cadillacs to watch old science-fiction movies, while munching on popcorn, burgers, and sandwiches. In the 50's Prime Time Café, you are served by maternal waitresses in 1950s kitchens with the TV tuned to period sitcoms; the food – which includes items such as meatloaf, pot roast, fried chicken, and milk shakes – is homey. Adults in search of beverages can visit the Tune-In Lounge next door.

The best place to eat without a reservation is the self-service Art Deco-themed cafeteria Hollywood & Vine, where you can choose from a varied buffet that includes pasta, salads, seafood, ribs, and steaks. It also has an excellent selection of desserts. The recently opened Mama Melrose's Ristorante Italiano serves pizza, pasta, seafood, and other favorites in a typical Italian diner environment.

RIDES, SHOWS & TOURS CHECKLIST

This chart is designed to help you plan what to visit at Disney-MGM Studios. The rides, shows, and tours are listed alphabetically within each area.

		WAITING TIME	HEIGHT/AGE RESTRICTION	BEST TIME TO RIDE /ATTEND	FASTPASS	MAY CAUSE MOTION SICKNESS	OVERALL RATING
HOLLYWOOD BOULEVARD							
R	THE GREAT MOVIE RIDE	○		Any			◆
SUNSET BOULEVARD							
R	ROCK 'N' ROLLER® COASTER STARRING AEROSMITH	●	4 ft	►11	➡	✓	◆
R	THE TWILIGHT ZONE TOWER OF TERROR™	●	3 ft 4 in	►11	➡	✓	★
S	BEAUTY AND THE BEAST – LIVE ON STAGE	◗					◆
S	FANTASMIC!	●					◆
ANIMATION COURTYARD							
S	PLAYHOUSE DISNEY – LIVE ON STAGE!	◗		Any			▼
S	VOYAGE OF THE LITTLE MERMAID	●		Any	➡		◆
T	MAGIC OF DISNEY ANIMATION	◗		Any			◆
MICKEY AVENUE							
S	WALT DISNEY: ONE MAN'S DREAM	◗					▼
S	WHO WANTS TO BE A MILLIONAIRE – PLAY IT!	◗		Any	➡		▼
T	DISNEY-MGM STUDIOS BACKLOT TOUR	○		Any			★
NEW YORK STREET							
S	JIM HENSON'S MUPPET™ VISION 3-D	●		Any			★
ECHO LAKE							
R	STAR TOURS	◗	3 ft 4 in	►11	➡		★
S	INDIANA JONES™ EPIC STUNT SPECTACULAR!	●		Any		✓	◆
S	SOUNDS DANGEROUS – STARRING DREW CAREY	◗		Any			▼

Key: Ride – R Show – S Tour – T; Waiting Times Good – ○ Average – ◗ Bad – ●; Overall Rating
Good – ▼ Excellent – ◆ Outstanding – ★; Time to Ride: Anytime – Any Before 11am – ►11

Disney's Animal Kingdom® ❹

WHILE THE OTHER DISNEY theme parks host a healthy collection of fish, birds, and other examples of nature, Disney's Animal Kingdom practically overflows with life and nature in all its forms. Quixotically, it is both the largest of the theme parks – five times the size of Magic Kingdom – and yet the easiest to cover, since a large portion of that extra space is accessible only by safari tour. Children and adults will find great delight in the never-ending array of animals and exotic landscapes and architecture, both real and mythical – but teens and other thrill seekers may find the rides too few and far-between for their tastes. This may change in 2006, when an exciting new attraction, Expedition Everest, is scheduled to open in the Asia section of the park. Construction is in progress for this high-speed train adventure, set in a reproduction of the Himalayas, which promises thrills galore.

Carvings on the bark of The Tree of Life in Discovery Island®

TACKLING THE PARK

THE PARK IS divided into seven Lands: The Oasis, Discovery Island, Dinoland USA, Camp Minnie-Mickey, Africa, Asia, and Rafiki's Planet Watch. Navigation within the park is quite different from other parks. When you first pass through the turnstiles, you enter **The Oasis** – a foliage-festooned area offering several routes to the park's central hub, Safari Village. The Oasis contains many little surprises, most of which are missed by visitors who race through to reach the attractions. Time spent waiting quietly at the various habitats will be well-rewarded. The park has a strong emphasis on leisurely walks – with dozens of semi-hidden nature paths and byways filled with scenic views – and shows rather than rides, but

the rides Animal Kingdom does have are all outstanding and get very crowded.

There's plenty for young children to enjoy as well, with three areas of the park more or less dedicated to the little ones. If you love animals or are interested in conservation issues, this park is a heaven on earth, but time is needed to really absorb the experience – this is not a place for hurried tourists seeking quick excitement. Keep your camera charged and loaded – you'll want to take lots of stunning pictures.

DISCOVERY ISLAND®

AS YOU EMERGE into the open space of the village, **The Tree of Life** looms – this is a massive, 14-story structure that is the signature landmark of the park. It holds sway over a pageant of brightly colored shop fronts and a multitude of pools and gardens, each holding a variety of wildlife. The main shops, baby care, and first aid post all face The Tree of Life. Embedded in the tree and of endless fascination and

The It's Tough to be a Bug® show in Discovery Island®

The popular DINOSAUR ride, which brings dinosaurs back to life

Top 10 Attractions
1. **Kilimanjaro Safaris®**
2. **Festival of the Lion King**
3. **It's Tough to be a Bug®**
4. **Kali River Rapids®**
5. **DINOSAUR**
6. **Tarzan™ Rocks!**
7. **Flights of Wonder**
8. **Primeval Whirl®**
9. **TriceraTop Spin**
10. **Mickey's Jammin' Jungle Parade**

delight to visitors are over 325 carvings or other images of various animals. While waiting in line for the shows or character greetings, children in particular spend time trying to identify them all. Under its branches lie the bridges that cross to the other Lands and within the trunk itself is the **It's Tough to be a Bug®** show. Held in a stunningly detailed "underground" theater, this 3-D film and sensory experience is one of the finest in the whole of Walt Disney World and not to be missed. Hosted by Flik and featuring many of the characters from Disney and Pixar's hit film *A Bug's Life*, the show combines animatronics and sensory enhancement to heighten the realism of the computer-animated 3-D. The show cleverly plays on our natural fear of insects and the audience is generally kept alternating between laughter and repulsion; the delightfully creepy finale keeps the crowd laughing right out the door.

Dinoland USA®

This land is a mixed bag of children's play areas, rides, and serious exhibits of dinosaur artifacts. Fans of dinosaur lore will enjoy the actual dinosaur skeletons that lead you to the popular ride **DINOSAUR**, in which guests board a mobile motion simulator that travels back in time and bucks and weaves violently, trying to avoid carnivorous dinosaurs. Very young children may find the ride, which is mostly in the dark, quite scary. The pre-show is an excellent opportunity to educate yourself on Earth's past. The recreated layers of sedimentary soil and rock provide an insight into the history of the planet, and is accompanied by occasional narration from science entertainer Bill Nye.

Younger children will get a lot more fun, and dizziness, out of the carnival atmosphere of the outdoor rides, including the **Primeval Whirl®** and the **TriceraTop Spin**, a roller coaster with spinning cars. There's also **The Boneyard**, a playground where children can dig for dinosaur bones. For all-round family entertainment, the featured show in Dinoland USA is the **Tarzan™ Rocks!** extravaganza. This show is loud, rockin', and filled with stunts and songs that will impress. It has absolutely nothing to do with dinosaurs; however, children will be so taken with the in-line skaters, the gymnastic and aerialist stunts, and the high-energy performances of the singers, dancers, and musicians that it is very likely they won't care.

The thrilling Primeval Whirl® ride at Dinoland USA®

CAMP MINNIE-MICKEY

DESIGNED primarily for guests to meet Disney characters, this Land also has the park's two live stage productions. Lines for the **Camp Minnie-Mickey Greeting Trails** – at the end of which the youngsters get to meet with the characters – can, predictably, become very long and sometimes become entwined with the lines for the stage shows.

A very popular show, and hands-down the finest live-action show in the whole of Walt Disney World, the **Festival of the Lion King** encourages cheering and singing like no other. Exceptionally well-choreographed and costumed, this colorful spectacle is one of the most elaborate shows seen outside Broadway and, now that the theater is fully enclosed and air conditioned, it's a

must-not-miss attraction that is best seen at the beginning or the end of the day, though wait times can be exceptionally long.

Pocohontas and Her Forest Friends At Grandmother Willow's Grove lacks the punch of the Festival of the Lion King but is a favorite with little girls. The music is pleasant enough but the general feel is somewhat sugary. The theater is small and lines frequently long.

A daily parade that winds through the park, **Mickey's Jammin' Jungle Parade** brings a menagerie of abstract animal images to life in the form of towering animated puppets in fun costumes. Elaborate rickshaw taxis put selected guests in the middle of the parade, while party patrols of "animals" interact with guests and invite them to sing along with the music.

AFRICA

ENTERED THROUGH the village of Harambe, Africa is the largest of the Lands. The architecture is closely modelled on a Kenyan village and conceals Disney cleanliness behind a façade of simple, run-down buildings and wobbly telegraph poles.

The **Kilimanjaro Safaris®** is the park's busiest attraction, though it gets quieter in the afternoon. Guests board open sided trucks driven into an astonishing replica of the East

Lions and rhinos, to be glimpsed on Kilimanjaro Safaris®

African landscape. During this 20-minute drive over mud holes and creaking bridges you have the opportunity to see many African animals including hippos, rhinos, lions, and elephants, all roaming apparently free and undisturbed. It isn't unusual for a white rhino to get close enough to sniff the truck.

Affording an excellent opportunity to see gorillas close up, the **Pangani Forest Exploration Trail®** leads visitors into a world of streams and splashing waterfalls. It can get rather congested with guests exiting the safaris. The trail gets less busy in the late afternoon and you can actually spend some time watching the animals. The pleasant Wildlife Express, a re-creation of the African train system, takes you to **Rafiki's Planet**

Visitors savoring the sights of a re-created East African landscape on Kilimanjaro Safaris®

EATING & DRINKING

Disney's Animal Kingdom has only one full-service restaurant, the Rainforest Café near the entrance of the park, so reservations are a must. Character dining takes place at the amusing Restaurantosaurus, an all-you-can-eat buffet. Restaurantosaurus also features a full McDonald's. On opposite sides of Discovery Island are Pizzafari and the Flame Tree Barbecue lunch restaurants, while Africa boasts the Tusker House Restaurant. Asia offers only snack stands, which are also located throughout the other areas of the park. Feeding the animals or throwing coins in the water supplies is strongly discouraged.

The swirling water adventure ride, Kali River Rapids®

Watch, which features two educational programs, Conservation Station and Habitat Habit, and Affection Section, a shaded petting yard.

ASIA

THIS LAND FEATURES gibbons, exotic birds, and tigers set in a re-creation of post-Colonial Indian ruins. **Kali River Rapids®** offers you a chance to get completely drenched. This short ride presents some of the most striking and detailed surroundings in the park, which you may miss as yet another wave saturates the parts still merely damp. Tapirs, Komodo dragons, and giant fruit bats can be found on the **Maharaja Jungle Trek**, the climax of which is undoubtedly the magnificent Bengal tiger roaming the palace ruins. Through glazed walled sections of the palace, you can get within arm's length of the tigers.

A campy, funny show with an unexpected amount of thrills, the **Flights of Wonder at the Caravan Stage** showcases exceedingly beautiful birds demonstrating natural behavior with polished trainers and a clever "story."

Be aware that the birds fly extremely low and graze the tops of the audience's heads, but ducking down just makes the birds fly lower.

Slated to open in 2006, **Expedition Everest** will involve a high-speed train bound for Mount Everest, which takes passengers on a daring ride on rugged terrain and along icy slopes. The ride will incorporate roller coaster thrills and yeti mystique.

RIDES, SHOWS & TOURS CHECKLIST

This chart is designed to help you plan what to visit at Animal Kingdom. The major rides, shows, and tours are listed alphabetically within each area.

		WAITING TIME	HEIGHT /AGE RESTRICTION	BEST TIME TO RIDE /ATTEND	FASTPASS	MAY CAUSE MOTION SICKNESS	OVERALL RATING
DISCOVERY ISLAND®							
S	IT'S TOUGH TO BE A BUG®	○		Any	➡		◆
DINOLAND USA®							
R	DINOSAUR	◗	3 ft 4 in	Any	➡	✓	▼
R	PRIMEVAL WHIRL®	●	4 ft	➤11	➡	✓	◆
R	TRICERATOP SPIN	●		➤11		✓	★
S	TARZAN™ ROCKS!	◗		Any			◆
AFRICA							
R	KILIMANJARO SAFARIS®	●		Any	➡	✓	★
T	PANGANI FOREST EXPLORATION TRAIL®	●		Any			◆
ASIA							
R	KALI RIVER RAPIDS®	◗	3 ft 2 in	Any	➡	✓	★
S	FLIGHTS OF WONDER AT THE CARAVAN STAGE	◗		Any			★
T	MAHARAJA JUNGLE TREK®	●		Any			◆
CAMP MINNIE-MICKEY							
S	CAMP MINNIE-MICKEY GREETING TRAILS	●		Any			◆
S	FESTIVAL OF THE LION KING	◗		Any			★
S	POCAHONTAS AND HER FOREST FRIENDS	◗		➤11			▼

Key: Ride – R Show – S Tour – T; Waiting Time Good – ○ Average – ◗ Bad – ●; Time to Ride: Anytime – Any Before 11am – ➤11; Overall Rating Good – ▼ Excellent – ◆ Outstanding – ★

Water Parks

WALT DISNEY WORLD FEATURES two of the best water parks in the world, including the second-largest on record. A third water park, River Country – the first to be built in Walt Disney World – is now closed. While playing second fiddle to the major theme parks of the resort, the water parks manage to attract huge numbers of visitors, particularly during the hot summer months.

Typhoon Lagoon bears only a pretense of a theme, a whimsical pirate/nautical motif that features everything from thrilling slides to winding rapids to gentle rivers. Apart from the chance to snorkel with real sharks and other fish, it's a normal water park, only Disney-fied. On the other hand, Disney's Blizzard Beach is a wonderful working "flooded ski resort" that throws visitors into a "failed" winter wonderland and substitutes flumes and slides for skis and toboggans. This truly clever idea keeps the area covered in "snow" but with nice warm water almost all year round.

Sliding down Mount Gushmore at Blizzard Beach

A watery game of hide-and-seek in progress at Blizzard Beach

Blizzard Beach ❺

DURING A "freak" winter storm – or so the legend goes – an entire section of the Disney property was buried under a pile of powdery snow. Disney Imagineers quickly set to work, building Florida's first ski resort, complete with ski lifts, toboggan runs, and a breathtaking ski slope. However, the snow started to melt quickly, and the Disney people thought all was lost until they spotted an alligator snowboarding himself down the mountainside. In a flash, they reinvented the ski resort as a water/ski park, Blizzard Beach; they turned luge runs into slides and the mountain into the world's longest and highest flume, and created creeks for inner-tube enthusiasts to paddle around in.

The centerpiece of Blizzard Beach is the 120-ft (36-m) high **Summit Plummet**, which rockets particularly brave visitors at speeds of over 60 mph (96 km/h). Incredibly popular with teens, it's too intense for children – you must be at least 4 ft (1.2 m) tall to ride it.

The Slusher Gusher and Toboggan Racer are similar, but less frightening, water slides. There's also the Snow Stormers flumes and Downhill Double Dipper racing slides, a favorite with families.

The thrills continue with the **Teamboat Springs** whitewater raft ride, a rollicking race through choppy waters that lasts far longer than you'd expect but leaves you wanting more anyway. The Runoff Rapids is another speedy trip through harrowing waterways, this time in an inner tube.

For those with a more relaxed agenda, there is the lovely chair lift to carry you up the side of **Mount Gushmore**, where you can go rock-climbing or hiking. Or you may choose to lazily float around the entire park by tubing down Cross Country Creek, enjoy the pool area called Melt-Away Bay, or take a slide down the mild Cool Runners.

Kids' areas include the Blizzard Beach Ski Patrol Training Camp, aimed at older children, and Tike's Peak for the little ones.

TOP TIP

• *Blizzard Beach and Typhoon Lagoon have their own, free, parking lots; Winter Summerland shares the Blizzard Beach lot. You don't need to wait for Disney transportation if you've got a vehicle – you can drive to the water parks and park right there.*

Swimmers head almost straight down Summit Plummet

◁ **Snorkeling amid colorful fish at Shark Reef, Typhoon Lagoon**

Typhoon Lagoon ❻

THIS WATER PARK offers less in the way of man-made thrills and more natural excitement, though it features some traditional water park favorites as well. Where Blizzard Beach trades on its novelty, Typhoon Lagoon revels in natural beauty and sealife encounters, and boasts a surf pool that is the world's largest, at 650,000 cu ft (18,406 cu m). The motif of this park is that of a shipwreck – the "Miss Tilly" which got caught in a storm so severe it landed on the peak of **Mount Mayday** – in a tropical paradise.

At the top of Mount Mayday, visitors will find three whitewater raft rides of varying intensity – the thrilling Gang Plank Falls, the incredibly high and wild Mayday Falls, or the relatively tame Keelhaul Falls.

Also on Mount Mayday are the body-slide rides known collectively as Humunga-Kowabunga. Great fun but highly intimidating, these rides involve falls of roughly 50 ft (15 m) at speeds of 30 mph (48 km/h) almost straight down. The Storm Slides offer three flumes that go twisting and turning inside the mountain itself; these rides are less intense but still delightful.

More relaxing is the powerful **Wave Pool** which

The Wave Pool, with "Miss Tilly" in the backgound

offers 6-ft (1.8-m) high waves alternating with gentler periods. The other peaceful attraction in Blizzard Beach is the highlight of the park for adults – the meandering, relaxing, and stunningly beautiful **Castaway Creek**, where you can inner-tube your troubles away for what seems like forever. Children can spend many happy hours at the aquatic playground,

Ketchakiddee Creek, and the smaller wave pools. Of special note is the **Shark Reef**, which offers visitors the chance to either observe tropical fish and live, small sharks from the safety of a "overturned freighter" or to grab a snorkel and mask and go one-on-one with them. It's perfectly safe and offers lovely views of incredibly colorful sealife.

Getting up close and personal with sealife at Shark Reef

WINTER SUMMERLAND

Although Fantasia Gardens, on Buena Vista Drive, was the first themed mini-golf park on Disney property, Winter Summerland is unique in that it continues the motifs of the neighboring water parks, Blizzard Beach and Typhoon Lagoon, but adds a Christmas twist, with two elaborately-designed 18-hole courses – the Winter and Summer courses. The two courses were supposedly built by St. Nick's elves, who were divided into two camps – those who missed the North Pole and those who preferred the Florida heat.

Both courses feature plenty of interactive elements and are surprisingly challenging. Generally the most popular, the Winter Course is widely perceived as being slightly easier, with "snow" and holiday elements abounding. A few of the holes on each course are identical except for the substitution of sand for snow on the Summer holes. The Summer Course features surfboards, water sprays, and other tropical obstacles, including a sand-buried snoozing Santa. The two courses converge for the final two holes in a log cabin-style lodge.

Disney Cruise Line®

WITH A CRUISE LINE that offers two gorgeous, larger-than-average ships, private destinations, and an all-inclusive fare, Disney World, in 1998, extended its reach to the high seas of the Caribbean. In addition to the popular three- and four-night trips, there are now extended itineraries available to passengers, which offer more island ports and longer duration cruises. Disney's Cruise Line has a pair of powerful incentives no other cruise line can match: apart from its outstanding reputation for quality and comfort, it offers vacations that include stays at Walt Disney World as part of the total package.

A Disney Cruise Line® ship docked at a pier

A Disney Cruise Line® ship at Castaway Cay

THE SHIPS & THE DESTINATION

THE TWO DISNEY cruise ships, the **Disney Magic** and the **Disney Wonder**, have staterooms that are around 25 percent larger than those of most other cruise ships. The usual out-of-fashion stylings of most other ships are replaced with the stately elegance of European vessels of old, with an Art Deco theme for the Magic and Art Nouveau for the Wonder.

Dining in style at Palo restaurant aboard a Disney ship

Both ships offer theater, restaurants, spas, and fitness centers among several other amenities. **Castaway Cay**, Disney's own private island, is the end point of every Disney cruise, and is very much a tropical extension of Walt Disney World's hotels and resorts. There are uncrowded beaches, snorkeling, bicycling, glass-bottom boat tours, watersports, and much more on offer. In addition, there is always plenty to do for children on board and off – so much so that you may see very little of them during your trip.

THE SHORT (THREE–FOUR NIGHT) CRUISES

THE ITINERARY ON the shorter cruises for both ships is the same – after arriving at Port Canaveral by charter bus and checking in, you cast off and arrive in Nassau in the Bahamas the next day. The following day you arrive at Castaway Cay, and leave there in the evening to return to Canaveral at 9am the following morning. The four-night cruise adds a day at sea with the occasional stop in Freeport before returning to Port Canaveral.

THE LONG (SEVEN–TEN NIGHT) CRUISES

DISNEY OFFERS both an Eastern Caribbean and a Western Caribbean tour for their longer cruises, which include stops in St. Maarten and St. Thomas in addition to Castaway Cay for the eastern cruise, or Grand Cayman and Cozumel along with Castaway Cay for the western cruise. Plans are afoot for additional seven-night tours as well as a 10-night cruise that includes stops in Antigua, San Juan, St. Lucia, and Key West.

TOP TIPS

• Keep in mind that the all-inclusive fare does not include things such as tips for servers, stateroom hostess, assistant server, and head server. Other additional charges are for soft drinks at the pool, and alcoholic beverages. There is a $10 per person charge for eating in the adults-only specialty restaurant. Shore excursions are also extra significant charges – port charges as well as government taxes are added to the fee.

• It is a good idea to plan ahead for shore excursions to avoid waiting in a line to sign up for them once on the ship and taking a chance. You can log on to the website (see p77) to sign up for shore excursions.

Fort Wilderness Resort & Campground ❼

A CAMPGROUND WOULD SEEM to be at odds with the provide-every-luxury mentality of most Disney World accommodations, but Fort Wilderness, which opened in 1971, still represents one of Walt Disney's aims – to foster an appreciation of nature and the outdoors. Located on Bay Lake in the Magic Kingdom resort area, it has more than 750 shaded campsites and over 400 cabins to provide various levels of "roughing it." While wildlife is fairly sparse in this area, amenities and even entertainment are plentiful. The center of Fort Wilderness is Pioneer Hall, home to several restaurants and the hugely popular dinner show, Hoop-De-Do Musical Revue *(see p75)*. There is convenient boat transportation to Magic Kingdom and motorcoach conveyance to all theme parks.

Riders enjoying a canter at Fort Wilderness Resort & Campground

A cabin at Disney's Fort Wilderness Resort & Campground

ACCOMMODATIONS & COMMUNITY AREAS

THE CAMPSITES at Fort Wilderness are small but reasonably secluded, with electric and water "hookups" at all locations. All the cabins offer house-like comfort in confined quarters *(see p138)*.

There are 15 air-conditioned "comfort stations" all around the campground, with facilities such as laundries, showers, telephones, and even ice machines, open 24 hours a day. Two "trading posts" offer groceries and rent out recreational equipment.

RECREATION

THERE IS PLENTY to keep visitors happily occupied at Fort Wilderness Resort. The **Tri-Circle D Ranch** has two heated pools, guided horseback tours, and pony rides. Other recreational facilities include tennis, volleyball, and basketball courts, bike and boat rentals, fishing, an exercise trail, nightly wagon rides, horseshoes and shuffleboard, carriage rides, a petting zoo, and video arcades. You can also opt for skiing, parasailing, and wakeboarding. Equipment is usually available for rental. Reservations are required for the guided tours on horseback or for fishing.

In addition, Fort Wilderness offers a **Campfire** program with singalongs and outdoor movies. Available to all Disney guests – and not just Fort Wilderness residents – the program features an hour of singalongs complete with toasted marshmallows and the American delicacy "smores" – melted marshmallow and chocolate on graham crackers. Hosted in part by the Disney chipmunks Chip 'n' Dale, the singalong leads into the screening of a Disney animated feature. An additional attraction is the nighttime **Electrical Water Pageant** *(see p75)*, which goes by Fort Wilderness Resort at 9:45pm. There is a nice all-you-can-eat breakfast buffet at Pioneer Hall.

SPORTS AT WALT DISNEY WORLD

Besides Fort Wilderness, all Disney resorts have sports and fitness facilities, though available only for residents. In 1997, **Disney's Wide World of Sports**® complex was opened, primarily as a training camp and athletic haven for exhibition games, Olympic training, and other recreational activities *(see p178)*. While the DWWS experience is largely passive, the same cannot be said for what is Disney's most "hands-on" experience to date: **The Richard Petty Driving Experience** *(see p177)*, where visitors can train and become NASCAR-style race car drivers, actually driving real race cars at speeds in excess of 100 mph (161 km/h) around a race track. Unlike most Disney experiences, you are in full control of the vehicle. These cars boast over 600 horsepower engines so the thrill is most decidedly real. As might be expected, safety instruction takes top billing for this sport.

Downtown Disney® 8

SHOPPING, FINE DINING, exciting shows, and concerts and dancing 'til the last club closes at 2am, are on offer at Downtown Disney, giving visitors plenty to do at Walt Disney World Resort after the theme parks have closed. Three distinct areas collectively make up Downtown Disney – the Marketplace, a lovely outdoor mall; West Side, featuring stores, eateries, and concert venues; and the centerpiece of late-night Disney, Pleasure Island, a floating non-stop party complete with clubs, shows, and fireworks. Downtown Disney offers free parking, and the West Side and Marketplace areas have no charge for admission. Pleasure Island, which doesn't open until 7pm, requires separate admission unless you have the Ultimate Park Hopper or Park Hopper Plus passes *(see p76)*; you must be at least 18 – or 21 for some venues – to enter. DisneyQuest, a five-story "indoor interactive theme park," also charges separate admission, except for Ultimate Park Hopper and Premium Annual pass holders. Buses run almost continually to the on-property resort hotels.

Fireworks at Pleasure Island in Downtown Disney®

PLEASURE ISLAND

THIS ULTIMATE party zone consists mainly of eight nightclubs, each with a different theme. By far the most relaxing and surprising one is the **Adventurers Club**, which is more like a performance-art piece than a nightclub. Visitors walk into the year 1937 and a stately, exquisitely decorated British gentlemen's club where they are recruited as "new members." Club activities may involve a "radio broadcast" or a "balderdash" storytelling competition. There are odd surprises at every turn, from talking exotic masks to bar stools that raise and lower themselves.

Another all-time favorite is the **Comedy Warehouse**, which hosts hourly improvised comedy shows. The innovative decor of the club consists of "retired" Disney signage.

The most popular of the music clubs is **Mannequins Dance Palace**, which offers up-to-date music and DJs spinning the mostly electronica/techno rhythms alongside a stunningly elaborate light show. **Motion** is squarely aimed at the younger crowd and goes for the most popular sounds straight from the Top 40, played deafeningly loud. Older visitors can relive the rock era by visiting the **Rock 'n' Roll Beach Club**, which offers live bands re-creating the reliable crowd-pleasing hits of yesterday and today. The disco era is the

theme of **8 Trax**, an accurate representation of 1970s styles and music. The **BET Soundstage Club** and the **Pleasure Island Jazz Company** require patrons to be 21 and up, with the former playing the latest hip-hop, reggae, and R&B music, while the latter focuses on more sophisticated genres like jazz, blues, and swing music performed live. There is a handful of shops on the island as well as a bevy of live street performers and outdoor stages, plus a daily New Year's Street Party, with a concert, countdown, and fireworks display at midnight.

WEST SIDE

EACH STORE, restaurant, or business on Downtown Disney's West Side has a unique feel to it, making for a splendid evening's exploring. Among the do-not-miss shops are the gigantic **Virgin Megastore**, selling music, books, and paraphernalia; the **Magnatron** shop, with magnets and similar kitschy items; the **Magic Masters** trick shop, which features continuous live magic demonstrations; and the **Candy Cauldron** where sweets are made on the spot. There's also the state-of-the-art stadium-seating **AMC Cinema**.

Full-service restaurants here include the popular Cuban and Latin fare of **Bongo's Café**, the gourmet entrées of the upstairs **Wolfgang Puck's Café**, the Southern US cuisine of the **House of Blues** restaurant, and the American food

Downtown Disney® West Side glittering in the evening

Pirates of the Caribbean: Battle for Buccaneer Gold at DisneyQuest®

of movie-memorabilia-studded **Planet Hollywood**. Quick bites can be obtained from **Wetzel's Pretzels**, featuring hot pretzels and cold Häagen-Dazs ice cream, and the lower level of Wolfgang Puck's Café, which serves brick-oven pizzas and salads. The West Side has three special attractions that require separate admissions: the House of Blues concert hall – part of the national chain, which attracts major music acts – the **Cirque du Soleil®** show La Nouba™, and the electronic funhouse called **DisneyQuest®**.

In addition to regular shows by national artists – with a side stage for smaller acts – the House of Blues offers a Sunday Gospel Brunch that features live

La Nouba™ show at Cirque du Soleil®

gospel performers showing off their uniquely American religious singing. The Cirque du Soleil show, which is a theatrical production based on a circus, is so popular that it is always sold out. This fabulous show has 64 performers on stage at the same time, performing a variety of gymnastic feats. Reservations are a must. DisneyQuest is extremely popular with teens and younger kids and features state-of-the-art video arcades, virtual reality experiences, and other computer-driven and 3-D "interactivities" along with an assortment of traditional arcade games such as Skee-ball. Among the best of the various "zone" offerings are the virtual

reality "rides" – you wear a special helmet with glasses – such as **Aladdin's Magic Carpet Ride**, **Ride the Comix**, and **Invasion!**, along with the two-man shooter rides such as **Pirates of the Caribbean: Battle for Buccaneer Gold**.

MARKETPLACE

An OPEN-AIR MALL with some excellent shops and a good variety of restaurants, the Marketplace makes for a relaxing walk when you're not pressed for time. Among the highlights, especially for children, is the **LEGO Imagination Center**, which features photo-op displays of wonderful LEGO constructions, from a spaceship to a dragon in the pond next to the store. Also of interest to kids will be the **Once Upon a Toy** and **Disney's Days of Christmas** stores. Kids and adults alike will be awed by the sheer size of the **World of Disney** emporium, the largest Disney memorabilia store in the world and the "mother lode" for all Disney souvenirs. Restaurants include the colorful **Rainforest Café, Fulton's Crab House** with its superb seafood and riverboat ambience, and **Ghirardelli's Soda Fountain & Chocolate Shop** with its malt-shop atmosphere. Quick bites can be found at **Cap'n Jack's** floating restaurant and the **McDonald's, Wolfgang Puck Express**, and **Earl of Sandwich** chain stores.

The superbly constructed LEGO dinosaur at the Marketplace

AFTER DARK EVENTS

Apart from the Downtown Disney attractions, other prime after-dark entertainment includes **dinner shows** and the **Electrical Water Pageant**. A floating parade that wanders around park resorts such as Polynesian and Contemporary, the Electrical Water Pageant is best viewed from the unobstructed beach in Fort Wilderness. This kids' favorite showcases 20 minutes of dazzling electrical animation – dolphins jumping out of the water, whales swimming by, even a fire-breathing dragon. Around since 1971, it often serves as an opening act or postscript for the Magic Kingdom and Epcot fireworks. Disney's two long-running dinner shows, Hoop-Dee-Doo Musical Revue and Disney's Spirit of Aloha, should not tempt visitors to leave the theme parks early but they are still enjoyable. The first is a popular Western comedy show at Fort Wilderness' Pioneer Hall; the second features authentic Polynesian music, dance, and food. Another show, Mickey's Backyard BBQ, provides country 'n' western fun.

Essential Information

SPREAD OVER A LARGE AREA of 47 sq miles (121 sq km) and brimming with attractions, Walt Disney World® Resort can provide entertainment for the whole family for at least a week. Guests who do not have much holiday time need to plan carefully to make the most of their visit to this dream vacationland. The information here is geared toward aiding them in this task.

WHEN TO VISIT

THE BUSIEST TIMES of the year are Christmas, the last week of February until Easter, and June to August. At these times, the parks begin to approach capacity – some 90,000 people a day in Magic Kingdom alone. All the rides will be operating and the parks are open for longer periods. During off-season, 10,000 guests a day might visit the Magic Kingdom, only one water park may be operating, and certain attractions may be closed for maintenance. The weather is also a factor – in July and August, hot and humid afternoons are regularly punctuated by torrential thunderstorms. Between October and March, however, the temperatures and humidity are both more comfortable and permit a more energetic touring schedule.

BUSIEST DAYS

EACH OF THE theme parks is packed on certain days. The busiest days are as follows: Magic Kingdom: Monday, Thursday, and Saturday. Epcot: Tuesday, Friday, and Saturday. Disney-MGM Studios: Wednesday and Sunday. Note, however, that after a thunderstorm, the water parks are often almost empty – even at the peak times of the year.

OPENING HOURS

WHEN THE theme parks are busiest, opening hours are the longest, typically 9am to 10–11pm or midnight. In less busy periods, hours are usually 9am to 6–8pm. Call to check. The parks open at least 30 minutes early for pass holders and guests at any of the WDW hotels and resorts.

LENGTH OF VISIT

TO ENJOY Walt Disney World to the full, you may want to give Magic Kingdom and Epcot two full days – or one and half days, with half a day at a water park – each, leaving a day for Disney-MGM Studios and Animal Kingdom. Set aside three nights to see Fantasmic!, IllumiNations, and Wishes firework displays.

THE IDEAL SCHEDULE

TO AVOID THE worst of the crowds and the heat:
• Arrive as early as possible and visit the most popular attractions first.
• Take a break in the early afternoon, when it's hottest and the parks are full.
• Return to the parks in the cool of the evening to see parades and fireworks.

TICKETS & TYPES OF PASSES

THERE ARE SEVERAL types of passes available for visitors. You can buy one-day, one-park tickets, but if you're staying for more than three days consider the **Park Hopper Pass**. This offers you one-day admission to each theme park on any four or five days. For most, one of these multi-day park hopper passes will suffice.

The **Park Hopper Plus** offers unlimited access to theme parks, water parks, and Pleasure Island on any five, six, or seven days.

However, one of the best passes is the **Ultimate Park Hopper Pass**, exclusively available to Disney hotel guests. It offers unlimited admission to theme parks, Pleasure Island, water parks, and the sports complex. Prices are determined by the length of your stay. Non-Disney guests visiting for more than ten days should consider the **Annual Pass** or the **Premium Annual Pass**, which costs little more than a seven-day Park Hopper. Separate Annual Passes are offered by the water parks, DisneyQuest, and Pleasure Island. Child ticket pricing applies to ages three through nine.

Passes are available at Disney stores, the airport, the Tourist Information Center on I-Drive, and the official Disney website. In addition, passes are sometimes included in package deals.

GETTING AROUND

AN EXTENSIVE, efficient transportation system handles an average of 200,000 guests each day. Even if you stay outside Walt Disney World Resort, many nearby hotels offer free shuttle services to and from the theme parks, but you can check this when you make your reservation.

The transportation hub of Walt Disney World is the **Ticket and Transportation Center (TTC)**. Connecting it to the Magic Kingdom are two monorail services. A third monorail links the TTC to Epcot. Ferries run from the TTC to the Magic Kingdom across the Seven Seas Lagoon.

Ferries connect the Magic Kingdom and Epcot with the resorts in their respective areas, while buses link everything in Walt Disney World, including direct links to the Magic Kingdom. All ticket holders can use the entire transportation system for free.

Although Disney transportation is efficient, you may wish to rent a car if you want to enjoy the entire area without inconvenience. The theme parks are spread out and, especially for visits to swimming attractions such as Blizzard Beach and Typhoon Lagoon, Disney transportation is not always the best option for children. Young children who are wet and tired from swimming will not welcome waiting for the Disney bus.

COPING WITH LINES

LINES TEND TO BE shortest at the beginning and end of the day, and during parade and meal times. Lines for the rides move slowly, but the wait for a show is rarely longer than the show itself. The Fastpass *(see p34)* allows visitors to reserve time at 25 of the most popular attractions rather than wait in long lines. Disney parks fill rapidly after the first hour of opening. Until then, you can usually just walk onto rides for which you'll have to line up later.

DISABLED TRAVELERS

WHEELCHAIRS can be borrowed at the park entrance and special bypass entrances allow disabled guests and carers to board rides without waiting in line. Staff, however, are not allowed to lift guests or assist with lifting for safety reasons.

VERY YOUNG CHILDREN

AS WALT DISNEY WORLD can be physically and emotionally tiring for children, try to adapt your schedule accordingly. If you've come with preschool-age kids, focus on Magic Kingdom.

The waiting and walking involved in a theme park visit can exhaust young children quickly so it's a good idea to rent a stroller, available at every park entrance. Each stroller is personalized when you rent it, but if it should go missing when you leave a ride, you can get a replacement with your rental receipt. Baby Care Centers for changing and feeding are located all around the parks.

In a system called "switching off," parents can enjoy a ride one at a time while the other parent stays with the child – without having to line up twice.

MEETING MICKEY

FOR MANY YOUNGSTERS, the most exciting moment at WDW Resort is meeting the Disney characters. You will spot them in all the theme parks, but you can have more relaxed encounters in a number of restaurants, usually at breakfast. Each theme park and many of the resorts also offer "character dining," though you must call well ahead of time to make a reservation.

SAFETY

THE RESORT'S excellent safety record and first rate security force mean problems are rare and dealt with promptly. Cast members watch out for young unaccompanied children and escort them to lost children centers. Bags of all visitors are checked.

STAYING & DINING

LODGING IN THE Disney-run hotels and villa complexes is of a very high standard. However, even the lowest-priced places are more expensive than many hotels outside Walt Disney World. But do keep in mind that, apart from Disney quality, your money also buys:
• Early entry into the theme parks (up to 60 minutes).
• Guaranteed admission to the theme parks even when the parks are otherwise full.
• The delivery of shopping purchases made anywhere in Walt Disney World Resort.

For dining at any full-service restaurant in Walt Disney World, especially in Epcot, book a Priority Seating – the table booking equivalent of the Fastpass.

For more information, see pages 140–47 and 150–57.

PARKING

VISITORS TO Magic Kingdom must park at the TTC and make their way by tram or foot; Epcot, Disney-MGM Studios, and Animal Kingdom have their own parking lots. Parking is free for Disney resort residents – others must pay, but only once a day no matter how many times they move their vehicle. The lots are very large, so it's important to remember the character name and row of the section where you are parked.

DIRECTORY

GENERAL

General Information
℡ (407) 939-6244.
W http://disneyworld. disney.go.com/wdw/

Accommodation Information/ Reservation
℡ (407) 939-6244.

Dining Reservations (including Dinner Shows)
℡ (407) 939-3463.
Operational 7am–11pm Sat–Sun.

Disney Tours
℡ (407) 938-8687.

Golf Reservations
℡ (407) 939-4653.

THEME PARKS & ATTRACTIONS

Blizzard Beach
℡ (407) 560-3400.

Disney Cruise Line®
℡ (888) 325-2500.
W www.disneytravelagents.com

Disney-MGM Studios
℡ (407) 824-4321.

Disney's Animal Kingdom®
℡ (407) 824-4231.

Disney's Wide World of Sports®
℡ (407) 828-3267.

Downtown Disney®
℡ (407) 828-3058.

Epcot®
℡ (407) 934-7639.

Fort Wilderness Resort & Campground
℡ (407) 824-2900.

Magic Kingdom®
℡ (407) 934-7639.

The Richard Petty Driving Experience
℡ (407) 939-0130.

Typhoon Lagoon
℡ (407) 560-4141.

ORLANDO'S OTHER THEME PARKS

WITH EVERYTHING FROM *roller coasters to performing killer whales, filmy fantasy to amazing shopping and dining experiences, the theme parks at Orlando provide endless entertainment options, and have catapulted the city into the ranks of the world's top vacation destinations. The pioneering effort was, of course, Walt Disney World in 1971; other parks quickly followed.*

SeaWorld, the marine-based park, opened in 1973. With its range of educational and entertaining programs, the park brings visitors in close touch with whales, sea lions, manatees, and many other marine creatures. It also features sea-themed rides such as Kraken, one of the world's tallest and fastest floorless roller coasters. Located across from SeaWorld, Discovery Cove, which opened in 2001, is a tropical paradise where guests can swim with dolphins, snorkel with fish, and hand-feed exotic birds.

Universal Orlando, which came onto the scene in 1990 with the opening of its park, Universal Studios Florida, is going great guns. A lively entertainment venue, Universal CityWalk, followed in 1998; then came a second Universal theme park, Islands of Adventure. With its wildly exciting, high-tech rides and shows, based on blockbuster movies, Universal Orlando has emerged as serious competition to Disney. Another popular attraction is Wet 'n' Wild, the world's first water park in 1977, which now boasts a variety of thrill rides.

The theme parks are constantly evolving, with exciting areas and new, jazzy rides being added at regular intervals. For instance, SeaWorld recently opened The Waterfront, a 5-acre (2-ha) village suffused with the flavor and festivity of the most vibrant cities by the sea, while Universal Orlando's new Revenge of the Mummy ride showcases cutting-edge technology.

A mother-child pair of dolphins gamboling at Discovery Cove

◁ **The 150-ft (46-m) high monster roller coaster, Kraken®, at SeaWorld® Orlando**

Exploring Orlando's Other Theme Parks

CONVENIENTLY LOCATED in the area around International Drive *(see pp112–13)*, Universal Orlando, SeaWorld, Discovery Cove, and Wet 'n' Wild do not lag far behind Walt Disney World in the entertainment stakes. SeaWorld and Discovery Cove focus on the natural world with their beautifully re-created habitats that hold various creatures of the deep. SeaWorld's shows, such as Odyssea and Shamu Adventure, and its world-class rides provide plenty of excitement. The other two major theme venues are geared more toward older childen and adults. The water park Wet 'n' Wild is an out-and-out big-thrill rides experience, while Universal Orlando entices with two theme parks full of movie magic and amazing rides laden with special effects, as well as an exuberant entertainment district.

SIGHTS AT A GLANCE

Discovery Cove ❷
SeaWorld® Orlando ❶
Universal Orlando ❸
Wet 'n' Wild® ❹

Key West Dolphin Fest at SeaWorld® Orlando

Universal Orlando's new Revenge of the Mummy – The Ride

SEE ALSO

- **Where to Stay** p143
- **Where to Eat** pp152–3

GETTING AROUND

To the northeast of Walt Disney World, Orlando's other major theme parks are connected to each other and to Disney by I-4, the crucial artery of the Orlando region. Universal Orlando is at one end, situated off exits 29 and 30B from I-4. At the other end is Discovery Cove, across the road from SeaWorld, which is located at the intersection of I-4 and the Bee Line Expressway. Wet 'n Wild is situated off I-4, exit 75A.

Apart from the connections offered by the public bus service LYNX, there are private charters as well as free shuttle services provided by some hotels to the various theme parks. If you wish to cover a lot of ground in less time, the best option is to rent a car. However, keep in mind that I-4 is a high traffic zone. For more details, see pages 193–7.

KEY

	Interstate highway
	Major highway
	Secondary route
	Tourist Information

0 km   1

0 miles   1

A couple having fun at The Blast, a ride at Wet 'n' Wild®

SeaWorld® Orlando ❶

IN TERMS OF SCALE AND CREATIVITY, the world's most popular marine life adventure park is a match for any of Orlando's other theme parks. Opened in 1973, the park is home to thrilling rides as well as beautifully choreographed and flawlessly executed shows, including the highly popular Shamu Adventure show that stars Shamu, SeaWorld's mascot killer whale, and his many friends. Some attractions even allow you to touch or feed the marine life – an experience of a lifetime. The park also provides a platform for the promotion of educational, research, and conservation programs. Each presentation at the park illustrates ways and means by which people can protect and safeguard the environment and the wildlife that occupies it.

TACKLING THE PARK

SEAWORLD is usually less crowded than Orlando's other theme parks. Its gentler pace means that a visit after 3pm affords a cooler and less crowded experience. Try to set aside at least an entire day to cover all the attractions the park has to offer. Pick up a map from Guest Services, and plan your day. You can use the 400-ft (122-m) high Sky Tower as a point of reference while navigating the park.

Most of the presentations are walk-through exhibits or sit-down stadium shows. The stadiums seat so many that finding a good spot is seldom a problem. Bear in mind that if you sit near the front you may get wet. It is also worth noting that the shows are timed so that it's all but impossible to leave one show just in time for another. This is done to reduce crowding, but it is possible to get a seat in the Clyde and Seamore (Sea Lion and Otter) show if you leave the Shamu stadium about four minutes early – while all the performers are taking their bows at the end of the show.

During peak season, head for the Wild Arctic, Journey to Atlantis, Shark Encounter, and Kraken attractions early in the day as they get very crowded later on and form long lines. Young children enjoy meeting the actors in furry suits who play the parts of Shamu and the crew – a killer whale, a penguin, a pelican, a dolphin, and an otter. They are usually found near the park's exit around closing time. SeaWorld also has several restaurants to choose from if you are hungry.

Tourists touching and feeding the friendly dolphins in a lagoon at Dolphin Cove®, Key West at SeaWorld®

Sea lions basking on the rocks at Pacific Point Preserve®

ANIMAL ATTRACTIONS

THE METICULOUSLY designed habitats at SeaWorld offer a rare look at marine creatures, such as dolphins, penguins, and sharks, as they would be in their natural settings.

Key West at SeaWorld®
One of the park's most visited animal attractions, Key West at SeaWorld is a tropical paradise featuring animals of the Florida Keys. Spread over 5 acres (2 ha), the attraction's Dolphin Cove® and Stingray Lagoon® are home to several bottlenose dolphins and more than 200 stingrays. Guests can also experience the thrill of feeding and touching these animals. At Turtle Point®, various species of endangered and threatened sea turtles can be seen, and an underwater viewing area offers a peek at a beautiful coral reef.

Sunset Celebration, which takes place every night at Key West, is a colorful and festive affair abuzz with live music and entertainers.

Pacific Point Preserve®
Designed as a replica of the Northern Pacific coast, this 2.5 acre (1 ha) area has many beaches and rocky outcroppings. Visitors enjoy the antics of sea lions, harbor seals, and fur seals as they play, jump, and have a great time at this attraction. Don't miss the highly entertaining feeding sessions as the sea lions and other mammals dive around for food and swallow an entire fish in one gulp. Check at the information desk for timings.

Manatees: The Last Generation?®
Named the country's best zoological exhibit by the American Zoological Association, the attraction offers an up close and personal look at these doleful and appealing herbivores. This highly educational exhibit includes a film show. Injured manatees are brought to the park by an animal rescue team, and are released back into their habitat once they have recovered.

Penguin Encounter®
A re-creation of the polar regions, this glacial terrain is covered with snow and has a sub-zero temperature. Four

Rockhopper penguins on icy ledges at Penguin Encounter®

VISITORS' CHECKLIST

Orange Co. 7007 SeaWorld Dr, intersection of I-4 & Bee Line Expressway. (407) 351-3600. 8, 42 from Orlando. 9am–7pm daily; until 11pm in summer. www.seaworldorlando.com/seaworld/fla

species of penguins – gentoo, rockhopper, chinstrap, and king – waddle along the rocky cliffs and swim gracefully in the icy waters, while puffins play close at hand. A 120-ft (35-m) long moving walkway passes through the habitat and gives guests a close view of the birds.

Shamu: Close Up!®
This research and breeding center facilitates the study of killer whales as part of SeaWorld's ongoing efforts to create awareness and educate people about these powerful creatures. The Shamu Underwater Viewing area presents a massive 7 million gallon (26 million liter) habitat, which offers a close look at these giant mammals.

Shamu, the park's official mascot

Shark Encounter
Walk through an underwater tunnel surrounded by hair-raising creatures such as poisonous fish, scary barracudas, creepy eels, and predatory sharks. The 60-ft (18-m) long tunnel is made up of acrylic panels – each weighing almost 5000 lbs (2268 kg) – and offers a close but safe look at these dangerous animals.

Those looking for a more thrilling experience can try the interactive Sharks Deep Dive program, which is a part of the Shark Encounter. Here, visitors wear special wetsuits and snorkel or scuba dive in a shark cage while more than 50 sharks swim around them. This two-hour program is expensive and permits only two guests at a time. Note that children below the age of ten are not allowed.

MISTIFY®

Held each night at The Waterfront *(see p85),* SeaWorld's fireworks show Mistify is an absolutely stunning finale to a day at the park. The show uses laser projection techniques and highly advanced special effects to create 100-ft (30-m) tall fountains, giant displays of marine life, dancing flames, and a brilliant sky and underwater light show – all accompanied by dazzling fireworks. The best place to watch this spectacular event is from the shores of The Waterfront's seaport village.

RIDES & SHOWS

SPECTACULAR STUNTS, hilarious animal antics, and exhilarating thrills characterize SeaWorld's rides and shows.

Wild Arctic®
Journey to the North Pole in a highly realistic simulated helicopter flight through blizzards and avalanches. At the end of this perilous "flight," visitors embark on an exploration of the frozen landscape. They also meet the region's animal inhabitants, such as giant walruses, frisky harbor seals, beautiful beluga whales, and two playful polar bears called Snow and Klondike.

Journey to Atlantis®
Unpredictable drops, twists, and turns are what riders can expect from this high-speed part water and part roller coaster adventure ride – the most thrilling being a terrifying drop, almost straight down, from a height of 60 ft (18 m). Eight riders, aboard an old Greek fishing boat, are pitchforked into a battle for the

lost city of Atlantis and face lugelike plunges and curves interlaced with amazing special effects as they fight their way through to safety.

Kraken®
Named after a giant mythical sea monster, the floorless roller coaster Kraken is one of the fastest coasters in Orlando.

SEAWORLD'S SERIOUS SIDE

The buzzwords at the nonprofit Hubbs-SeaWorld Research Institute are Research, Rescue, and Rehabilitation – the "three Rs." SeaWorld's animal rescue teams are on call 24 hours a day and have helped

thousands of ill and injured whales, dolphins, manatees, and turtles. In fact, the park's manatee rescue program is the largest in the world. The animals are nursed and, if necessary, operated on in the park's rehabilitation center. Those that recover sufficiently are released back into the wild. SeaWorld also runs several educational tours, such as the Saving a Species tour, which offer a glimpse into their conservation programs.

SeaWorld's animal rescue team providing aid to a manatee calf

Riders are taken to a height of 149 ft (45.5 m) and then dropped 144 ft (44 m), while taking seven hair-raising loops that turn them upside down – all at an incredible speed of 65 mph (104 km/h). Adding to the thrill are the open-sided seats, offering only shouder restraints as support and leaving nothing for riders to hold on to as they are hurled through the air.

The Shamu Adventure®
The excitement of seeing a killer whale erupt out of the water carrying one of the SeaWorld trainers on its nose is hard to overstate. In Shamu Adventure, stunts such as this are supplemented by a giant video screen, ShamuVision, which provides close-ups of the action and footage of the huge mammals in the wild. The show is hosted by the famous animal expert, Jack Hanna, and features the killer whales performing remarkable acrobatic flips and jumps. There are five orcas, which take turns to perform, as well as a baby killer whale.

Key West Dolphin Fest
Atlantic bottlenose dolphins and false killer whales perform with speed and amazing agility in this well-choreographed and enjoyable show. The mammals leap, do back flips, and play with their trainers, as well as interacting with members of the audience. The show's highlight, however,

Riders plummet down a sharp drop at the Journey to Atlantis® ride

A trainer performing tricks with a killer whale, Shamu Adventure® show

is the dolphins' synchronized leaps over a rope.

Clyde & Seamore Take Pirate Island®
Held at the Sea Lion and Otter Stadium, this hilarious show features two sea lions – Clyde and Seamore – otters, and a walrus, who, along with their trainer, embark on a swashbuckling adventure filled with lost treasure, pirate ships, and comical mix-ups at sea.

Odyssea
SeaWorld's Nautilus Theater hosts this mystical show, which takes viewers deep into the ocean with the help of stunning visual effects. Following a non-traditional circus theme, the show features spellbinding acrobatic feats, dramatic music, and imaginative costumes. This is one of the most sought-after attractions at SeaWorld.

Pets Ahoy!
This amusing show has an all-star cast of animals such as cats, birds, dogs, pigs, skunks, and many others performing amazing tricks and funny skits. Almost all of the animals featured here have been rescued from animal shelters. Toward the end of the show, the trainers also provide guests with tips on training pets at home.

Shamu Rocks America®
Blaring music greets visitors as they enter this nighttime rock 'n' roll show, held at the

Shamu Stadium. SeaWorld trainers and killer whales perform astounding acrobatics to the beat of the music, complete with huge splashes of saltwater waves and excellent theatrical effects.

Tours & Other Attractions
Smaller exhibits at SeaWorld include Shamu's Happy Harbor®, a 3-acre (1.2-ha) play area for younger kids; Dolphin Nursery for new dolphin moms and their calves; and Caribbean Tidepool, which encourages close examination of tropical

fish, starfish, sea anemones, and other marine life. The Polar Expedition Tour takes guests on a 60-minute educational exploration of the polar regions and a look at the park's Penguin Research Facility, while Adventure Express Tour offers reserved seats, guided tours of SeaWorld, animal feeding opportunities, and backdoor access to rides.

EATING, DRINKING & SHOPPING

A recent addition, The Waterfront at SeaWorld™ is a world-class dining, entertainment, and shopping area spread over 5 acres (2 ha), which offers merchandise and foods from all over the world. Guests may choose from nine restaurants, ranging from full-service to cafeteria-style. They include Voyagers Wood Fired Pizzas; The Seafire Inn, which offers stir fried dishes and hosts the Makahiki Luau show; the Sandbar pub, which serves sushi and martinis; and The Spice Mill, which features international cuisine. The Dine with Shamu restaurant, located at Shamu Stadium, allows guests to eat alongside killer whales, while at Sharks Underwater Grill (see p152), guests are served "Floribbean" fare as they eat just inches away from menacing sharks. The shops at The Waterfront include Allura's Treasure Trove, where kids can design their own porcelain dolls, and Under The Sun, which offers knick-knacks and several collectibles. Souvenirs are mainly soft toys and Shamu memorabilia; Shamu's Emporium has the largest selection.

Stuffed turtle and dolphin toys from SeaWorld shops

Discovery Cove ❷

LOCATED JUST ACROSS the road from its big sister, SeaWorld, Discovery Cove is an enticing tropical paradise with beaches, reefs, and lagoons. Although the entry price is high enough to make all but lottery winners blink, the park's relaxing and tranquil setting offers some exceptional and unforgettable experiences, the highlight of which is a 30-minute opportunity to swim with Atlantic bottlenose dolphins. Forgoing the dolphin experience, however, can reduce the cost of a visit by half. In contrast to Florida's other theme parks, Discovery Cove has a capacity of only 1,000 guests a day – the car park is limited to only 500 cars – and it is advisable to make reservations well in advance.

VISITORS' CHECKLIST

Orange Co. 6000 Discovery Cove Way. ☎ *(407) 370-1280* 🚌 *8, 42 from Orlando* 🕐 *9am–5:30pm daily.* ♿ 🛍 🍴 [W] www.discoverycove.com

Aquamarine lagoons surrounded by lush foliage at Discovery Cove

TACKLING THE PARK

WHITE SANDY beaches, lush green surroundings, and picturesque waterfalls create a serene atmosphere and allow guests to explore the park at a leisurely pace. Make sure you set aside an entire day to cover the park's animal attractions and enjoy the beaches.

The price is steep at $229 plus taxes per person – with no reductions for children – and include the Dolphin Swim experience, swimming and snorkeling gear, the use of beach amenities such as towels, umbrellas, and lockers, one main meal, and unlimited admission to SeaWorld or the Busch Gardens Tampa Bay for seven consecutive days. Note that children below the age of six are not permitted to swim with the dolphins.

Since admission is limited, the lack of crowds ensure attentive service as visitors are greeted by a personal guide, given a photo ID card, and taken on a familiarization tour through the park.

Cameras are allowed at most of the attractions except at Dolphin Lagoon, but avoid wearing jewelry as it might be distracting for the animals. Guests with disabilities are welcome and special outdoor wheelchairs, with oversized tires for easy maneuvering on the beach, are available.

There is only one restaurant at Discovery Cove, Laguna Grill, which is self-service. However, the quality of food is good and the staff delivers food to the beaches as well.

ATTRACTIONS

DISCOVERY COVE is divided into five main areas – Coral Reef, the Aviary, Ray Lagoon, the Tropical River, and Dolphin Lagoon. These beautifully designed habitats are home to several exotic birds as well as marine life such as stingrays, tropical fish, and dolphins. The attractions provide a memorable interactive experience as guests are allowed to feed, touch, and even play with the animals.

Coral Reef

Explore an underwater world filled with hundreds of tropical fish as they swim through grottos, reefs, and the remains of an artificial shipwreck. Here, visitors have the unique opportunity to swim and snorkel alongside exotic fish and encounter giant stingrays. A transparent plexiglas partition that separates you from large sharks and barracudas, nevertheless creates the thrilling illusion of swimming with these predatory creatures.

Another striking feature of this artificially created habitat are the eye-catching colors of the coral reefs.

The Aviary

Trickling streams, stone tombs, bridges, and fountains create a beautiful setting for this bird sanctuary. Towering high above the rest of Discovery Cove, this recently expanded free-flight aviary is now home to more than 300 tropical birds. The new small bird sanctuary is filled with several types of finch, hummingbirds, and honeycreepers, which you

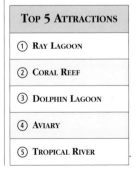

TOP 5 ATTRACTIONS

① RAY LAGOON

② CORAL REEF

③ DOLPHIN LAGOON

④ AVIARY

⑤ TROPICAL RIVER

Having fun with colorful, friendly birds at the Aviary

can feed by hand, while the large bird sanctuary features emus, toucans, and the red-legged seriema – some of the large birds are almost 4 ft (1.2 m) tall. The park's guides provide you with food for the birds, and introduce you to the various species, their habits, and the ongoing conservation programs.

The Aviary is accessible from the Discovery Cove beaches as well as from the waterfalls of the Tropical River.

Ray Lagoon
This large, secluded tropical pool is filled with several southern and cownose rays. Some of these rays are fairly large and can grow to almost 5 ft (1.5 m) in length and about 4 ft (1.2 m) in diameter. However, they are harmless and gentle creatures, and allow guests to swim and snorkel along with them. Those feeling more adventurous can even reach out and touch the surprisingly velvety skin of the rays as they softly glide past.

Tropical River
Following a serpentine route through most of Discovery Cove, the warm waters of this tropical river are inviting to say the least. Swimmers and snorkelers can float lazily past blue lagoons or take in the scenery around them as they wade through a thick rainforest. One of the most popular stopovers on the river are the cascading waterfalls, where guests can cool off from the heat of the Florida sun. Those

interested can also stop and take a look at various species of birds at the colorful Aviary. The river also features a specially designed underwater cave, which families can explore, as well as an underwater viewing window for a peek into Coral Reef.

Dolphin Lagoon
Discovery Cove's most famous attraction offers the amazing opportunity to swim and play with several bottlenose dolphins in Dolphin Lagoon. The experience begins with a 15-minute orientation program, held in beach cabanas, where trainers show a brief film on the habits and characteristics of the dolphins, and teach guests ways to communicate with the mammals by using special hand signals. Following this, groups of seven to eight guests are led into the shallow waters of the lagoon, which are home to around 30 of these friendly animals. The next 30 minutes, spent under the watchful eyes of the trainers, are simply unforgetable as you get the chance to talk to, hug, and even kiss the gentle dolphins.

Trainer for a Day
A new addition to the park's repertoire of offerings, this program allows up to 12 participants to work alongside

animal trainers, interact with the birds, tropical fish, sharks, dolphins, and other sealife, and take part in the behind-the-scenes animal training sessions at Discovery Cove for a day. Guests who wish to participate in the Trainer for a Day program must be physically fit and children below the age of six are not allowed. Note that the package is costly at $399 plus taxes.

> **TOP TIPS**
>
> • *Don't put any sunscreen on before you visit as the price includes Discovery Cove's own "fish friendly" screen, the only sunscreen allowed.*
> • *You don't need to be an expert swimmer for the Dolphin Swim experience – just comfortable in the water. You will be given a flotation jacket, which you must wear at all times while you are in the pool.*
> • *The Dolphin Lagoon is cooler than the rest so a wet suit will be provided if you feel too cold.*
> • *Make sure at least one person in your group is wearing a watch at all times as it is otherwise easy to forget your Dolphin Swim time slot.*
> • *It's a good idea to split your group into two and take turns in clicking photographs. This will help you avoid the high charges of the resident photographers.*

A family and a dolphin sharing a special moment at Dolphin Lagoon

Universal Orlando ❸

Once a single movie park, competing with the other local attractions, Universal Orlando has transformed into an expansive resort destination, which includes two theme parks, Universal Studios Florida and the Islands of Adventure; a 30-acre (12-ha) entertainment complex, Universal CityWalk; and three resorts (see p143). Together, these diverse options present a formidable reason to spend time away from Disney. Located off exits 29 and 30B from I-4, Universal's car parking brings guests through CityWalk on a series of moving walkways to a fork where they choose between the two parks.

VISITORS' CHECKLIST

Orange Co. 1000 Universal Studios Plaza, exits 29 or 30B on I-4. ⓘ (407) 363-8000. 🚌 21, 37, 40 from Orlando. ⏰ minimum opening hours 9am–6pm daily; extended evening opening in summer & on public hols. CityWalk: 11am–2am daily. 🏪♿🍴🛍 ⓦ www.universalorlando.com; www.citywalkorlando.com

TACKLING THE PARKS

The busiest times of the year at Universal Orlando are the same as at Walt Disney World (see p76); the weekends are normally busier than the weekdays.

During peak season, the parks are open until late, and two full days are just about long enough to see everything at both of them. However, during off-season, they shut early, and you will need three to four days to cover all the attractions in the area.

Those staying for a longer duration can opt for any one of Universal's multi-day packages – such as 2-Day, 2-Park, 3rd Day Free Pass, the Bonus Pass, or the Annual Pass – which offer cost-effective admissions to the parks and CityWalk, as well as special discounts on hotel stays, food, and merchandise.

Universal Orlando Resort logo

Lines at Universal can sometimes be even longer than those at Walt Disney World, and you might have to wait a considerable time for the best rides. One way of combating the lines is by purchasing the Universal Express pass, which operates in a similar manner to Disney's Fastpass (see p34). Visitors can use this pass to make a reservation at an attraction – only one at a time – and skip the line on returning at the designated time. Moreover, guests staying at any of the Universal Orlando properties can use their room keys as Universal Express passes on all rides – with no limit – and also as a credit card throughout the park, charging food, gift shop items, and other expenditures to their room. On a busy day, visitors might like to consider indulging in the five-hour guided VIP Tour. Accommodating up to 12 people at a time, the tour provides priority admission to at least eight attractions, access to production facilities and sound stages, discounts, and a walk around backstage areas.

Most rides are likely to be too intense for very young children and of course some have minimum height restrictions; the exception to this is ET Adventure. The attractions designed to appeal to youngsters can be found at Woody Woodpecker's Kid Zone, and include A Day in the Park with Barney, and Animal Planet Live!.

Universal Orlando has made special provisions for families traveling with children, and for people with disabilities. Wheelchairs and strollers are available on rent near the entrance of both the parks. All the shopping and dining venues, and most of the attractions, are wheelchair friendly. The Family Service center also offers first aid and several restrooms with nursing and diaper-changing facilities.

The brightly illuminated world of Universal's Islands of Adventure

Exploring Universal Studios Florida®

Everything in this motion picture theme park is designed to take visitors into the magical world of movie-making. Built with the help of Steven Spielberg as a creative consultant, the park opened in 1990 and is home to several state-of-the-art rides, shows, and attractions – all based on popular films and television shows. Even the streets, shops, and restaurants are reminiscent of Hollywood sets, and the life-size reconstructions of New York and San Francisco are unbelievably realistic. The park is divided into six main sections – Production Central, New York, Hollywood, Woody Woodpecker's Kid Zone, World Expo, and San Francisco/Amity.

A scene from the animated Jimmy Neutron's Nicktoon Blast™ ride

Front Lot

The entrance to Universal Studios Park is known as Front Lot because it has been created to resemble the front lot of a working Hollywood film studio from the 1940s. However, the shooting schedule notice board near the turnstiles, with the details of shows being filmed, is real enough.

Logo of the fun ride Shrek 4-D

Just inside the park, the palm-lined Plaza of the Stars has several shops *(see p93)*, but do not linger here on arrival. Instead, you should immediately head off to the main attractions before the lines reach their peak.

Production Central

Although this is the least aesthetic section of the park, two of Universal's most popular rides are located here. **Jimmy Neutron's Nicktoon Blast**™ is a simulated adventure ride, which hurls you through space with the help of special effects, computer animations, and programmable motion-based seats. Evil egg-shaped aliens have stolen Jimmy's new invention, the Mark IV rocket, and are planning to take over the world. Now Jimmy needs your help to get it back. Blast off on a wild chase along with other favorite Nicktoons, including Fairly Odd Parents, Rugrats, Hey Arnold!, Goddard, Wild Thornberrys, and Jimmy's arch rival and nemesis, Cindy Vortex.

Live Filming

While there is no guarantee that you will be able to see live filming on the day you visit Universal Studios Florida, there is a slim possibility that cameras may be rolling on the backlot of the theme park itself. However, there is a good chance, especially from September to December, that you could be in the audience for the taping of a TV show. Those interested can also call ahead and check to find out which shows are being filmed during their visit. Tickets for the shows are issued on a first-come-first-served basis – on the day of filming – and are available at the Studio Audience Center located near Guest Services. Go there as soon as you enter the park to pick some up.

Shrek 4-D™, one of the newer attractions, is a fun-packed ride that features a 13-minute 3-D movie, in which Shrek and his friends set out to rescue Princess Fiona who has been kidnapped. The motion-simulated effects and special "OgreVision" glasses enable you to see, hear, and almost feel the action right in your seat. Starring the voices of Eddie Murphy, Mike Myers, John Lithgow, and Cameron Diaz, the ride is both a sequel to the original film *Shrek* and a bridge to the new instalment in the series, *Shrek 2*.

Amazing special effects enthrall the audience at Shrek 4-D™

Guests experiencing the forces of a tornado at Twister...Ride It Out®

NEW YORK

UNIVERSAL'S reproduction of the Big Apple is uncannily realistic and captures the minutest of details very effectively. The area is home to more than 60 life-size façades, some of which replicate actual buildings in the city of New York, and others which reproduce those that have appeared only on screen. Macy's, the well-known department store, can be found here, as can Louie's Italian Restaurant, which was the location for a shootout in the original *Godfather* movie. Cutouts of structures such as the New York Public Library and the famous Guggenheim Museum cleverly create an illusion of depth and distance.

The washed out storefronts, warehouses, and even the stained and somewhat cracked cobblestone streets have been specially treated by a process called "distressing" to make them appear old.

New York is also host to the newest virtual reality ride at Universal Studios, **Revenge of the Mummy – The Ride**. Based on the phenomenally successful film, *The Mummy* and its equally popular sequel, *The Mummy Returns*, the ride combines extremely advanced special effects, such as space age robotics and high-speed roller coaster engineering, to take guests on a terrifying journey into the dark world of ancient Egypt. As they are swept through Egyptian tombs, passageways, and crumbling columns, riders have to face skeletal warriors and a giant animated figure of the menacing Mummy that jumps aboard the coaster. Fires, swarming bugs, and vengeful creatures add to the scare factor of this three-minute ride.

The other ride at New York is **Twister...Ride It Out®**, based on the movie *Twister*. Located inside a huge compound, the attraction pits visitors against Mother Nature at her most ferocious, as they stand just 20-ft (6-m) away from a graphically simulated tornado. Experience the overwhelming strength of the elements as cars, trucks, and even a cow are swirled up in the air by the ear-splitting, five story-high funnel of winds.

Away from the rides, guests can also head down Delancey Street to take in **The Blues Brothers**, a 20-minute live music stage show, where Jake and Elwood perform a medley of their biggest hits. Relive moments from the original cult movie – starring John Belushi, Dan Aykroyd, Carrie Fisher, and Cab Calloway – as the brothers put on a show in an attempt to save their former school. There's plenty of audience participation, sing-alongs, dancing, and some outrageous humor.

The huge, scary skeletal warriors at Revenge of the Mummy – The Ride

Hollywood Boulevard, a fine example of the park's superbly created sets

HOLLYWOOD

Two of the most attractive sets at Universal Studios are the streets of Hollywood Boulevard and Rodeo Drive. While ignoring actual geography, these sets pay tribute to Hollywood's golden age from the 1920s to the 50s. The famous Mocambo nightclub, the luxurious Beverly Wilshire Hotel, the top beauty salon, Max Factor, and the movie palace, Pantages Theater, are just some notable examples of the wonderful re-creations lining these streets.

Shaped like a hat, the Brown Derby restaurant was once a fashionable eatery where the film glitterati used to congregate; Universal's own version is a fun hat shop. Schwab's Pharmacy, where hopefuls hung out sipping sodas and waiting to be discovered, is brought back to life as an old-fashioned ice cream parlor. The widely recognized Hollywood Walk of Fame, with the names of stars embedded in the sidewalk, just as in the real Hollywood Boulevard, has also been faithfully reproduced.

The top attraction in Hollywood is **Terminator 2: 3D**. Designed with the help of James Cameron, the director of the *Terminator* movies, this exciting ride uses the latest in 3-D film technology and robotics, along with explosive live stunts and giant screens, to catapult the audience into a battle with futuristic cyborgs. The fast-paced 3-D action features the star of the original films, Arnold Schwarzenegger, and other cast members.

A typical sequence, combining film and live action, has a Harley-Davidson "Fat Boy" dramatically bursting off the screen and onto the stage. Note that young children may find this ride a bit scary.

Lucy – A Tribute acknowledges the talent of Lucille Ball, the queen of comedy and one of the world's favorite stage and television stars. The museum showcases clips, scripts, costumes, props, and other memorabilia from the comedian's hit TV show, *I Love Lucy*. The den of Lucy's Beverly Hills home and the set of her show have been meticulously replicated. The tribute also features an interactive game for trivia buffs to test their Lucy knowledge, as well as a gift shop where guests can pick up mementos. The museum is an ideal place to escape from the heat of the afternoon sun as well.

Top 10 Attractions

1. **Revenge of the Mummy – The Ride**
2. **Men in Black™ – Alien Attack™**
3. **Twister...Ride It Out®**
4. **Jimmy Neutron's Nicktoon Blast™**
5. **Back to the Future...The Ride®**
6. **Shrek 4-D™**
7. **Terminator 2: 3D**
8. **Earthquake® – The Big One**
9. **Jaws®**
10. **ET Adventure®**

Another fascinating exhibit at Hollywood is the **Universal Horror Make-Up Show**. The attraction offers a behind-the-scenes look at how movies use makeup to create scary monsters and creepy effects. Props from films, such as the wax head from *The Exorcist*, the chambers where a man was merged with a fly in *The Fly*, and several masks, are on display. In addition, trained workers demonstrate the substitutes that can be used to resemble blood and slime. This partly gory and partly entertaining show takes place in a theater-like setting.

The audience under attack by a giant robot, Terminator 2: 3-D

ET and his alien friends on their colorful home planet, ET Adventure®

WOODY WOODPECKER'S KID ZONE

As the name suggests, this area caters specifically to preschoolers and younger children. Rides, shows, and attractions here have been designed to provide loads of fun with a minimum amount of scare factor.

Based on Steven Spielberg's 1982 movie, **ET Adventure**® is an enchanting, if rather tame, ride. Riders board flying bicycles and embark on a mission to save ET's home planet. Soaring high above a twinkling cityscape and through space, they fly past policemen and FBI agents before arriving at a strange world inhabited by aliens.

A must-see for animal lovers, the **Animal Planet Live!**™ show features a talented troupe of dogs, cats, chimpanzees, birds, and other animals performing tricks and comical skits – some based on popular TV shows and movies. Animals playing the parts of canine superstars Beethoven and Lassie demonstrate how they are trained for film work. Audience participation and the antics of the animals make this an entertaining show.

A Day in the Park with Barney™ appeals only to very young children. A musical show set in a magical park, it features the lovable T-Rex Barney, who plays the lead in *Barney & Friends* – a top preschool-age TV show.

The big purple dinosaur and his fun-loving friends, Baby Bop and BJ, sing, dance, and play with the children.

Inspired by the animated films *An American Tail* and *An American Tail: Fievel Goes West*, **Fievel's Playland**® features a playground as seen through the eyes of a mouse. Larger-than-life props, such as a cowboy hat, boots, glasses, cans, and a teacup have been used to construct tunnel slides, a 30-ft (9-m) spider web climbing area, and a 200-ft (61-m) twisting water slide.

Other attractions at Kid Zone are **Woody Woodpecker's Nuthouse Coaster**® – a gentle and child-friendly introduction to the world of roller coasters – and **Curious George Goes to Town** – a colorful playground with lots of water for kids to splash around in, as well as a ball area where they can play with hundreds of foam balls.

WORLD EXPO

Architecturally inspired by the Los Angeles 1984 Olympics Games and Expo '86 in Vancouver, World Expo has two major attractions. **Men in Black**™ **– Alien Attack**™, based on the *Men in Black* films, is an addictive ride in which visitors join Agent J (as played by Will

Guests fending off an attack by bug-eyed monsters at the Men in Black™ – Alien Attack™ ride

Visitors on a catastrophic train journey in Earthquake® – The Big One

Smith) in a simulator, battling aliens who have escaped after their shuttle crashed on Earth. This ride-through interactive video game is filled with 360-degree spins and lots of gun-fire and infrared bullets, as well as plenty of noise. Each person has their own laser weapons and smoke bombs, and can earn bonus points by hitting certain aliens. Watch out for the giant roach with its huge fangs, because he is most likely to explode. The scores reflect the team's ability to destroy aliens; at the end of the ride, Agent J rates the passengers on their scores.

Located nearby, **Back to the Future...The Ride®** is one of Orlando's most intense rides. No knowledge of the epony-mous films is needed to enjoy this journey in a time-traveling sports car. The car's move-ments are synchronized to the action on a gigantic wraparound screen, making it seem as though you really are plunging over a flow of molten lava, skimming ice fields, and flying right into the mouth of a giant dinosaur. Although you don't leave the room, you will think that you have traveled around the world in this high-tech adventure ride.

SAN FRANCISCO/ AMITY

MOST OF THIS area is based on San Francisco, notably the city's Fisherman's Wharf district. For instance, the Chez Alcatraz snack bar is modeled to resemble the ticket booths for tours to Alcatraz Island. San Francisco's main draw is the amazing special effects

ride, **Earthquake® – The Big One**. The ride has a slow start with an educational show where the audience sees how earthquakes can be simulated using detailed models, and how actors are superimposed onto dramatic scenes. Things start picking up as you board a subway train for a short ride. Suddenly, an earthquake, measuring 8.3 on the Richter scale, hits the train station, and you are trapped amid collapsing ceilings, underground floods, colliding trains, and a burning oil tanker. When it's all over, you can watch the entire set put itself back together. Amity, the other half of this corner of Universal Studios, is named after the fictional village in New England that was the setting for *Jaws*. The **JAWS®** ride begins as a serene cruise around the bay, but soon the deadly dorsal fin appears, and then a 32-ft (9.7-m) long mechanical great white shark is tearing through the water at a terrifying speed and lunging at your boat.

Beetlejuice show's sign

Of more limited appeal is **Beetlejuice's Graveyard Revue™**, a live rock 'n' roll dance concert featuring Beetlejuice, Dracula, and the Frankenstein monster, literally pounding out hit songs.

EATING, DRINKING & SHOPPING

The food at the restaurants in Universal Orlando's theme parks is generally good, and there are plenty of options. Advance reservations are advisable for Lombard's Seafood Grille, specializing in fish dishes, and the Universal Studios Classic Monster Café, which offers Italian and Californian cuisine and has a good value buffet. Mel's Drive-In is definitely the place to go for fast food and shakes; the wonderful 1950s diner is straight out of the 1973 movie American Graffiti.

Most of the shops at the parks stay open after official closing times, and offer a wide range of themed souvenirs. The Universal Studios Store in the Front Lot sells everything from fake Oscars to oven mitts bear-ing the Universal logo, and you can buy auto-graphed, but extremely expensive, photographs of your favourite movie star at the On Location store. Most of Universal Orlando's attractions have their own store.

MEETING THE STARS

Actors in wonderful costumes can be seen all along the streets of Universal Studios, playing the likes of Jake and Elwood from *The Blues Brothers*, Ghostbusters, Franken-stein, the Flintstones, as well as legends of the silver screen such as Marilyn Monroe and the Marx Brothers. They usually tend to congregate at the Front Lot.

Daily during the high season, and twice a week in off-season, guests can eat with the stars at a Character Breakfast in the park an hour prior to the scheduled opening time.

Exploring Islands of Adventure

Logo of Islands of Adventure

One of the world's most technologically advanced theme parks, Islands of Adventure is home to some of the most thrilling roller coaster and water rides in Florida. Spread over an area almost as vast as Universal Studios Florida, the park consists of five themed zones – Marvel Super Hero Island, Toon Lagoon, Jurassic Park, The Lost Continent, and Seuss Landing – all positioned around a central lagoon. Each Island has a creative and imaginative layout, which serves as an introduction to famous comic book, cartoon, and movie characters. Visitors will need to set aside an entire day to cover all the attractions on offer at Islands of Adventure.

Incredible Hulk Coaster®

Marvel Super Hero Island®

Super heros and villains from the Marvel Comics' stable of characters are the inspiration behind this Island's four main attractions.

Arguably the best coaster in Florida, the **Incredible Hulk Coaster®** is a green leviathan that accelerates from zero to 40 mph (64 km/h) in just two seconds. Riders are taken 110 ft (33.5 m) in the air, turned upside down, and sent plummeting down a terrifying 105-ft (32-m) drop. With seven inversions and two drops into deep watery trenches, this stimulating ride is guaranteed to leave you breathless.

Highly advanced 3-D film technology, spectacular special effects, and motion simulated action makes the **Amazing Adventures of Spider-Man®** one of the most sought-after rides at the park. Guests are cast into a battle between Spider-man and villains, as the super hero leaps from tall buildings, saving damsels in distress and others. A scary 400-ft (122-m) simulated free fall is the highlight of this exciting, edge-of-your-seat ride. **Doctor Doom's Fearfall®** catapults its riders high into the air before plunging them down a 150-ft (46-m) fall. The ride also offers a great view of the entire park. **Storm Force Accelatron®** is a more intense version of the Mad Tea Party ride *(see p39)* at Disney.

Toon Lagoon®

Favorite cartoon characters come to life against this Island's colorful backdrop. The Comic Strip Lane, at the entrance, is lined with life-size images of toons such as Betty Boop, Olive Oyl, and Beetle Bailey; the island also hosts scheduled performances of the fun-filled Toon Lagoon Beach Bash.

Based on the Rocky and Bullwinkle cartoons, **Dudley Do-Right's Ripsaw Falls®** is a thoroughly drenching and enjoyable flume ride. Be prepared for the 15-ft (4.5-m) dive into a deep lagoon.

Popeye & Bluto's Bilge-Rat Barges® is a whitewater raft ride where visitors are squirted and splashed by water guns fired from the nearby shores and playgrounds.

Children love exploring **Me Ship, The Olive**, a play area with bells, organs, ladders, tunnels, and whistles. The ship also overlooks the raft ride and offers water cannons to soak riders below.

Jurassic Park®

Step into a lush, tropical, and jungle-like setting as you enter this Island, where all the attractions are based on the *Jurassic Park* films. The **Jurassic Park River**

Top 5 Rides

1. Amazing Adventures of Spider-Man®
2. Incredible Hulk Coaster®
3. Dueling Dragons®
4. Popeye & Bluto's Bilge-Rat Barges®
5. Jurassic Park River Adventure

Fantastic special effects at the Amazing Adventures of Spider-Man®

◁ Tourists flocking to the entrance of Universal Studios Florida

Visitors under attack at the Jurassic Park River Adventure®

Adventure® starts out as a peaceful cruise along a river, where you encounter friendly dinosaurs before an accidental raptor breakout. Suddenly you are faced with a menacing T-Rex and the only escape route is a 85-ft (26-m) drop into a lagoon.

Jurassic Park Discovery Center® is an interactive exhibit, with realistic replicas of dinosaurs, a Beasaurus area, which allows visitors to see and hear things as dinosaurs did, and several games and quizzes. It also offers a virtual demonstration of a raptor egg hatching in the lab.

The remaining three draws at the island are **Pteranodon Flyers®**, a slow sky ride over Jurassic Park, **Camp Jurassic®**, a playground with caves and buried fossils for kids, and the **Triceratops Discovery Trail**, where youngsters can tickle a 24-ft (8-m) Triceratops robot that moves when patted.

THE LOST CONTINENT®

ENTER A MAGICAL world that is inspired by mythical and supernatural creatures, and has mysterious fortune tellers as well as a talking fountain. A favorite with coaster addicts,

Dueling Dragons® has two coasters – Fire and Ice – racing toward each other in a battle to see who will arrive back first. Riders come within inches of each other as the dragons go through several inversions and sharp corners. There is a separate, and longer, line for those who want to sit in the first car of the coasters.

A less thrilling ride, designed primarily for young children, is the **Flying Unicorn®** – a pleasant and non-frightening introduction to roller coasters.

An exciting stage show, **The Eighth Voyage of Sinbad®** is filled with stunts, giant flames, and explosions, as Sinbad embarks on a journey to find treasure.

The best show, however, is **Poseidon's Fury®**, which features a battle between the King of the Seas and the King of the Gods. Visitors walk through a tunnel surrounded by a giant swirling whirlpool, while massive waves crash around them and the gods throw flaming fireballs at each other.

SEUSS LANDING®

BASED ON THE popular Seuss children's books, this Island appeals mainly to the young and fans of the books.

Those with no experience of Seuss might find **The Cat in the Hat™** a somewhat bewildering and chaotic ride. A spinning and whirling couch takes you on a trip with the mischievous cat and characters such as Thing 1 and Thing 2. Some children may find the cat's sudden pounces at the corners scary.

Younger kids enjoy riding **One Fish, Two Fish, Red Fish, Blue Fish™** as they spin around on a remote controlled fish that moves up and down, and try to avoid being squirted by water jets.

Caro-Seuss-El is a merry-go-round with lovable Dr. Seuss characters, such as Dog-alopes, Aqua-MopTops, cow-fish, and elephant-birds among others, as the horses.

If I Ran The Zoo is another playground and the ideal place for kids to burn off energy.

Riders miss each other by inches at the Dueling Dragons® ride

Exploring Universal CityWalk®

Logo of Universal's CityWalk

THE GATEWAY TO Universal Orlando's offerings, CityWalk is a 30-acre (12-ha) entertainment, dining, and shopping complex that offers visitors the opportunity to continue their Universal experience long after the parks have closed – most of the places remain open from 11am to 2am. Restaurants, shops, concerts, nightclubs, and a movie theater present a range of options for an exciting night out. The banks of a sparkling lagoon running through CityWalk are perfect for an after-dinner stroll. While admission to the complex itself is free, most clubs have a cover charge. However, guests can visit all the clubs for the price of one with Universal's Party Pass.

RESTAURANTS

CITYWALK OFFERS a delectable selection of international cuisines to choose from.

Award-winning chef Emeril Lagasse's **Emeril's® Restaurant Orlando** *(see p153)*, serves delicious, but expensive, New Orleans Creole-based cuisine. Those looking for excellent Caribbean, Cajun, and fresh Florida fare should visit **Jimmy Buffett's®**; **Margaritaville®** *(see p153)*, which also offers live entertainment every night.

Munch on tasty Hispanic food from 21 nations at **Latin Quarter**™, while a dance troupe performs the salsa. At the family-style **Pastamoré Ristoranté**, you can dine on superb Italian cuisine, with dishes such as grilled eggplant and chicken parmigiana as well as panini.

More than 1,000 pieces of rock memorabilia can be seen at the famous **Hard Rock Café® Orlando** *(see p153)*. The café serves up great American food at reasonable prices. At **Motown® Café**, get a taste of steaks and barbecue food while listening to old favorites. Unique Motown merchandise is also available for purchase.

The **NASCAR Café®**, an officially sanctioned NASCAR eatery, features authentic racing memorabilia along with a menu of steaks, BBQ, shrimp, chili, and salads. Voted Orlando's best theme restaurant, **NBA City** offers a large viewing area with screens, where basketball fans can watch games while enjoying burgers, steaks, pastas, and sandwiches.

ENTERTAINMENT

LIVE MUSIC, CONCERTS, and hot dance floors fill the many clubs at CityWalk's with energy and a sense of festivity.

Bob Marley – A Tribute to Freedom is a replica of the famous musician's Jamaican home. Nightly performances by local and national reggae bands are the highlight here and can be enjoyed along with Jamaican and Caribbean food.

Another outstanding nightclub, **CityJazz®** features rare instruments belonging to the legends of jazz music, and hosts live concerts every night.

Some of the biggest bands in the music world perform at the **Hard Rock Live!® Orlando** coliseum-shaped concert hall. Guests can call ahead to find out which group will be playing during their visit.

One of CityWalk's most popular dance clubs is **the groove**. The lively atmosphere offers a mixture of hip-hop, rock, and dance music that is played live through the night on the club's impressive sound system.

Duplicating the famed New Orleans watering hole, **Pat O'Brien's®** is a much-celebrated bar, known for its specialty drinks, such as the Hurricane, and the "dueling piano" bar.

Catch a movie at any of the 20 theaters in the state-of-the-art **Universal Cineplex**. In addition, the outdoor stages and areas are settings for street performances and art festivals.

The world's largest Hard Rock Café® and music venue, at CityWalk®

A live music concert in progress at Hard Rock Live!® Orlando

SHOPS

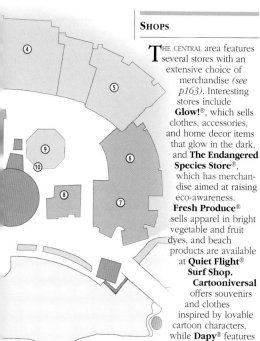

THE CENTRAL area features several stores with an extensive choice of merchandise (see p163). Interesting stores include **Glow!**®, which sells clothes, accessories, and home decor items that glow in the dark, and **The Endangered Species Store**®, which has merchandise aimed at raising eco-awareness. **Fresh Produce**® sells apparel in bright vegetable and fruit dyes, and beach products are available at **Quiet Flight**® **Surf Shop. Cartooniversal** offers souvenirs and clothes inspired by lovable cartoon characters, while **Dapy**® features lava lamps and novelty gifts. Souvenir hunters will also enjoy shopping at **Universal Studios Store**®, which offers a vast collection of products from the park. Sports fans can choose from an impressive selection of sports memorabilia and gifts at **All Star Collectibles**, while watches, leather items, and sunglasses can be purchased at the **Fossil**® store. A superior range of cigars and accessories are available at **Cigarz at CityWalk**. If you want a diamond ring or necklace, but don't want to pay megabucks for it, check out **Elegant Illusions**, which sells affordable copies of designer jewelry.

The well-stocked sports store at NBA City

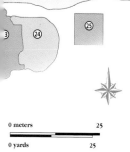

Wet 'n' Wild® ❹

Wet 'n' Wild logo

Oₙₑ of Central Florida's top attractions, Wet 'n' Wild opened in 1977. It focuses on rides of the hair-raising variety, boasting an awesome collection of high-velocity rides – multi-passenger as well as solo, on toboggans, rafts, or inner tubes, down slides and chutes or through tubes. There are activities for smaller kids as well, with miniature versions of the park's popular adult attractions on offer at Kids' Park. A range of family activities and a beach party atmosphere add to Wet 'n' Wild's appeal. Several outlets offer fast food; visitors can also bring in their own picnic hamper.

Knee Ski
Ride a surfboard on your knees in this cable-operated, half-mile (0.8-km) course on the park's lake. You can also wakeboard at the lake.

Black Hole®
Hang on for dear life in a two-person raft propelled by a blast of water through 500 ft (150 m) of twisting tubes in total darkness.

Surge Landing Picnic Area
Beach Club
Lakeside Terrace
Beachside Terrace
The Sands Picnic Area
Birthday Land
Mach 5 Pavilion
The Blast Pavilion
The Blast
Kids Park

Surf Lagoon, a 17,000-sq ft (1,580-sq m) wave pool, features 4-ft (1.2-m) high waves and a waterfall.

The Flyer
Four-seater toboggans descend from a height of 40 ft (12 m), plowing through 450 ft (137 m) of banked curves and racing straight runs in this exhilarating watery ride.

Mach 5
Riders navigate this solo flume ride on a foam mat. On tight turns, ride the flowing water as far up the wall as possible. You can choose from three different twisting-and-turning flumes.

Top Tips

- Steps to the rides and asphalt walkways can get very hot. Wear non-slip footwear as protection.
- High-speed rides can leave you uncovered. Ladies should avoid wearing bikinis or consider adding a T-shirt.
- Rides have a 36-inch (91-cm) minimum height requirement for kids riding solo.
- Be sure to carry sunscreen.

Hydra Fighter

Strapped back-to-back in a swing, armed with water cannons, and in control of the swing's movement, two riders are supposed to create their own ride. A zestful water fight between riders in all eight swings provides loads of fun.

VISITORS' CHECKLIST

6200 International Dr, Universal Blvd, off I-4 at Exit 74A, less than 2 miles (3 km) from Universal Orlando & SeaWorld. **☎** *(800) 992-9453, (407) 351-1800.* **🚌** *21, 38 from Downtown Orlando.* **◯** *10am–5pm daily. Best to call as hours change due to weather conditions.* **💷** *(free for children under 3; afternoon discounts available).* **W** www.wetnwild.com

Blue Niagara®, a six-story drop through 300-ft (92-m) long twisting, interwoven tubes, ends in a bracing fall into a splash-landing tank.

Bomb Bay

A six-story plunge down a nearly vertical slide from a bomb-like capsule, this is one of Wet 'n' Wild's most sensational rides. Der Stuka is a slightly less scary version.

Knee Ski Dock

Bubba Tub Pavilion

Lazy River ● Picnic Pavilion

Bubble Up

Topped by a fountain that squirts water over the surface, this huge, colorful, slippery balloon makes a fun area for kids to climb, jump, and slide on.

International Pavilion

Lazy River®, a mile-long (1.6-km) circular waterway, lets you swim or float gently past swaying palms, orange groves, and waterfalls – a lovely re-creation of Old Florida.

Bubba Tube®

A raft large enough to hold five is the just the thing for watery splashes and fun for the family as it hurtles down a six-story slide with three big drops.

The Storm

Plummet down a chute with mist, thunder, and – at night – lightning effects, then drop into a huge open bowl, to swirl out with a splash into a lower pool in this exciting ride.

ORLANDO & CENTRAL FLORIDA

*T*HE THRILLS AVAILABLE AT THE *numerous theme parks attract the majority of visitors to Orlando but the city and its surrounding region have much more to offer the discerning tourist, from beautiful beaches – quiet, unspoilt havens as well as bustling spots – to lush forests and serene lakes, to the space-related attractions at Cape Canaveral and a plethora of cultural activities.*

As late as the first half of the 20th century, Orlando and neighboring towns such as Kissimmee were small, sleepy places dependent on cattle and the citrus crop. Everything changed with the arrival of Disney World. Its booming entertainment industry, which has spawned several new and exciting entertainment venues, has made Orlando one of the country's fastest growing areas. But quieter pleasures are still available within Orlando, in its numerous museums and leafy suburbs. Outside Orlando, the landscape becomes more bucolic, with huge agricultural fields interspersed between the highways. The charming towns of Sanford and Mount Dora to the north provide a glimpse of Central Florida of a few decades ago. West of the St. Johns River lies the wooded expanse of the Ocala National Forest and,

farther west, the world's largest artesian spring, Silver Springs. Along the Atlantic Coast, broad white sandy beaches flank the popular resort of Daytona Beach, which has been synonymous with car racing ever since the likes of Henry Ford and Louis Chevrolet raced automobiles on the beach during their winter vacations. Farther down, Cocoa Beach is another lively beach, famous for surfing. In between, along the Space Coast, the barrier islands across the broad Indian River boast 72 miles (116 km) of stunning sandy beaches, and there are two enormous nature preserves rich in bird life. Amid all this, set in a preserved marshy vastness beneath giant skies and in surprising harmony with nature, is the Kennedy Space Center, from where rockets are launched dramatically out of the earth's atmosphere.

The busy beach north of Main Street Pier, Daytona Beach

◁ **Silver Glen Springs, Ocala National Forest**

Exploring Orlando & Central Florida

THE PRIMARY REASON THOUSANDS of vacationers come to Central Florida is its theme parks, but the region has many other options for enjoyment. Smaller entertainment venues abound, and Orlando itself has 35 museums which house a diverse range of art. A wealth of retail stores and boutiques will satisfy the most discriminating shopper. Beaches in Central Florida range from empty, wild sands to the action-packed Daytona Beach and the buzzing surfing mecca of Cocoa Beach. Inland, the Ocala National Forest offers dozens of hiking trails, boating, and fishing; snorkeling and diving are also popular pursuits in crystal-clear springs. Kennedy Space Center, on the Space Coast, competes sharply with Orlando's attractions for excitement.

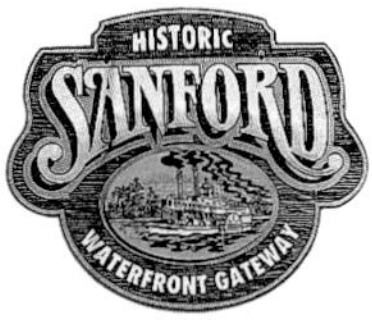

Sign for the town of Sanford

KEY

- Interstate highway
- Major highway
- Secondary route

SIGHTS AT A GLANCE

Blue Spring State Park 4
Bok Tower Gardens 17
Canaveral National Seashore 23
Cocoa 20
Cocoa Beach 19
Cypress Gardens 16
Daytona Beach 7
DeLeon Springs State Park 6
Dinosaur World 15
Fantasy of Flight 13
Florida Southern College 14
Gatorland 10
Kennedy Space Center 25
Kissimmee 11
Merritt Island National Wildlife Refuge 24
Mount. Dora 3
Ocala National Forest 8
Orlando 1
Sanford 2
Silver Springs 9
Southern Cassadaga Spiritualist Camp 5
US Astronaut Hall of Fame 22
Valiant Air Command Warbird Museum 21
Yeehaw Junction 18
A World of Orchids 12

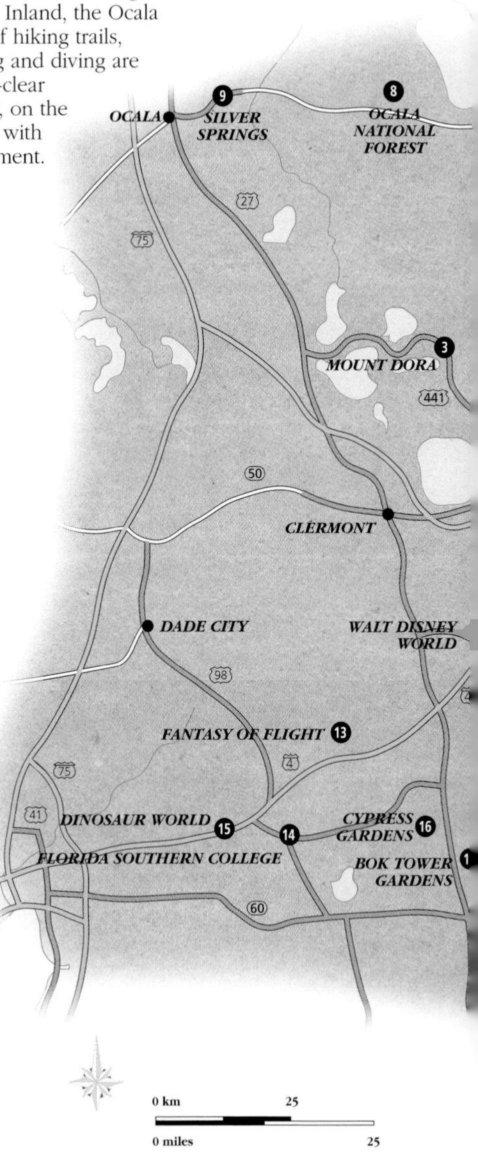

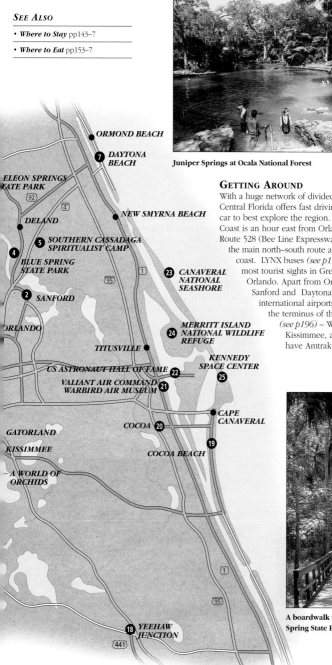

Juniper Springs at Ocala National Forest

GETTING AROUND

With a huge network of divided highways, Central Florida offers fast driving – rent a car to best explore the region. The Space Coast is an hour east from Orlando on Route 528 (Bee Line Expressway). I-95 is the main north–south route along the coast. LYNX buses *(see p196)* serve most tourist sights in Greater Orlando. Apart from Orlando, only Sanford and Daytona Beach have international airports. Sanford – the terminus of the Auto Train *(see p196)* – Winter Park, Kissimmee, and Orlando have Amtrak stations.

A boardwalk trail at Blue Spring State Park

Orlando ❶

VISITORS' CHECKLIST

Orange Co. 👥 180,000. ✈
Orlando International Airport,
1 Airport Blvd, 9 miles (14 km)
SE of Downtown. 🚆 Amtrak
Station, 1400 Sligh Blvd.
🚌 Greyhound Lines, 555 N
John Parkway. ℹ 8723
International Dr, Suite 101,
(800) 551-0181.

N OT MUCH MORE THAN a sleepy provincial town until
the 1950s, Orlando's fortunes were transformed by
its proximity to Cape Canaveral and the theme parks.
Downtown Orlando's glass-sided high-rises mark a
busy business district; it also has a burgeoning arts
and culture scene. In the evening, Orange Avenue,
Orlando's main street, pulsates with an exciting nightclub
scene. Another bustling street is International Drive,
with its many attractions, plenty of shopping opportunities, and excellent restaurants. Winter Park, one of
Orlando's most elegant neighborhoods, boasts a bevy
of cultural attractions from art museums to scenic boat
tours; the nearby suburbs of Eatonville and Maitland
feature quiet attractions, which make a pleasant change
from the thrills and spills of the theme parks.

**Charles Hosmer Morse
Museum of American Art**
in Winter Park features a
lovely collection of glass
by famed designer Louis
Comfort Tiffany (see p114).

**Zora Neale Hurston National
Museum of Fine Arts** in Eatonville
exhibits the works of contemporary
African-American artists. It is named
after African-American writer Zora
Neale Hurston, who grew up in
Eatonville (see p115).

**WINTER PARK,
EATONVILLE
& MAITLAND**
(see pp114–15)

0 km   30

0 miles   20

**DOWNTOWN
ORLANDO**
(see pp107–109)

**Ripley's Believe It Or
Not! Orlando Odddito-
rium**, with its fantastic
collection of the world's
strangest odddities collec-
ted by Robert Ripley dur-
ing his travels around
the globe, is a major
attraction on Interna-
tional Drive (see p113).

I-DRIVE
(see pp112–
13)

Lake Eola Park, a quiet
haven in Downtown Orlando,
has an ornate fountain set
in the center of a picturesque
lake (see p108).

Exploring Downtown Orlando

THE CITY'S FIRST DESIGNATED historic district, Downtown Orlando encompasses eight square blocks and more than 80 buildings constructed between 1880 and 1940, which offer visitors a window into the city's past. Today, these buildings house offices, restaurants, and trendy galleries and boutiques. The crown jewel of Downtown Orlando, Lake Eola Park, separates the historic downtown district from Thornton Park, Orlando's center of new urbanism, with its collection of eclectic shops. The broader downtown area, especially the natural and cultural retreat Loch Haven Park to the north, features several unique and top-quality visual and performing arts centers and museums.

Sculpture at the Mennello Museum of American Folk Art

🏛 Orlando Science Center
777 E Princeton St, Loch Haven Park.
📞 (407) 514-2000. ⏱ 9am–5pm Tue–Thu; 9am–9pm Fri & Sat, noon–5pm Sun. 🎬 🚻 🅿 🛗 ♿
🌐 www.osc.org

Originally called the Central Florida Museum when it was opened in 1960, the museum acquired its current name in 1984. Covering 207,000 sq ft (19,200 sq m) of floor space, the present building was opened in February 1997.

The aim of the center is to provide a stimulating environment for experiential science learning, which it achieves by presenting a huge array of exciting, state-of-the-art interactive exhibits, designed to introduce kids of all ages to the wonders of science. The center's four floors are divided into ten themed zones dealing with subjects that range from mechanics to math, health and fitness to lasers. The Body Zone, for instance, allows guests to explore the intimate workings of the human body. Other fascinating attractions include the DinoDigs exhibit with its collection of dinosaur fossils, which is very popular with children, as is the ShowBiz Science exhibit, which reveals some of the effects and tricks used in the movie business.

The gigantic Dr. Phillips CineDome surrounds visitors with amazing images and films on a range of topics such as Egyptian treasures and ocean life; it is also a planetarium.

🏛 Orlando Museum of Art
2416 N Mills Ave, Loch Haven Park.
📞 (407) 896-4231. ⏱ 10am–4pm Tue–Fri, noon–4pm Sat & Sun.
⏱ public hols. 🎬 🚻 ♿
🌐 www.omart.org

One of Southeastern USA's finest arts museums, the Orlando Museum of Art has a superb permanent collection that includes pre-Columbian artifacts, with figurines from Nazca in Peru; African art; and American paintings of the 19th and 20th centuries. These are supplemented by traveling exhibitions from major metropolitan museums, and smaller shows of regional or local significance. Music, food, and the works of local artists are on offer at a lively get-together on the first Thursday evening of every month.

🎭 John & Rita Lowndes Shakespeare Center
812 E Rollins St, Loch Haven Park.
📞 (407) 447-1700. **Orlando-UCF Shakespeare Festival**
🌐 www.shakespearefest.org

Spread over 50,000 sq ft (4,645 sq m), the elegant Shakespeare Center features the 350-seat Margeson Theater and the smaller Goldman Theater. Since February 2002, this state-of-the-art venue has been host to the nationally recognized **Orlando-UCF Shakespeare Festival**, which has been performing since 1989. It mounts high-quality performances throughout the year – its annual spring festival at Lake Eola Park (*see p108*) is very popular.

🏛 Mennello Museum of American Folk Art
900 E Princeton St, Loch Haven Park.
📞 (407) 246-4278. ⏱ 10:30am–4:30pm Tue–Sat, noon–4:30pm Sun.
⏱ major hols. 🎬 ♿
🌐 www.mennellomuseum.com

This small, lakeside museum houses an unusual collection of paintings by curio-shop owner and Floridian folk artist, Earl Cunningham (1893–1977), and traveling exhibitions of the works of other folk artists. Quirky sculptures are scattered throughout the grounds.

The sparkling exterior of the Orlando Science Center

A bridge across a rocky stream at Harry P. Leu Gardens

♣ Harry P. Leu Gardens

1920 N Forest Ave. ☎ (407) 246-2620. ○ 9am–5pm daily. ● Dec 25. ✎ ♿ 🅿 &. ⓦ www.leugardens.org

The Harry P. Leu Gardens offer 50 acres (20 ha) of serene, beautiful greenery to stroll in. Features such as Florida's largest rose garden are formal while, elsewhere in the park, there are mature woods of spectacular live oaks, maples, and bald cypresses, festooned with Spanish moss; in winter, seek out the mass of blooming camellias. Other attractions are a herb garden and one filled with plants that attract butterflies. Visitors can also tour the early 20th-century Leu House and its gardens, which local businessman Harry P. Leu donated to the city of Orlando in 1961.

⚏ Ivanhoe Row

N Orange Ave.
Shops 10am–5pm Mon–Sat.

Stretching from Colonial Drive to Lake Ivanhoe, this row of antiques shops features an interesting mix of the old and the unconventional. Vintage linens, clothing, jewelry, and various collectibles are on offer here, as is also period furniture ranging from Victorian to Art Deco. The Wildlife Gallery sells original paintings and sculptures of animals, while Art's Premium Cigars offers a range of cigars and smoking paraphernalia. The prices are on the high side, but you might find some unusual treasures here.

Sign for Ivanhoe Row

♣ Thornton Park

E of Lake Eola.

Close to the city's business center, hip and artsy Thornton Park offers a blend of trendy cafés, unique boutiques, stylish eateries such as HUE Restaurant, which serves world-class cuisine, and pretty B&Bs. Most active after 6pm, it is a popular neighborhood for locals to unwind in after work. One of the area's most happening hangouts is Dexter's of Thornton Park (see p153), with its chrome vinyl stools, terrazzo floors, contemporary art, and gourmet food. Other attractions include Urban Think!, a bookshop that features author readings, art shows, and a bar, and Marie-France, a chic jewelry boutique.

♣ Lake Eola Park

N Rosalind Ave & E Washington St. ☎ (407) 246-2827. ○ 5am–sunset daily. **Boat rentals** ☎ (407) 658-4226. &.

Orlando's most visited park, Lake Eola Park is spread over 43 acres (17 ha) and is encircled by a 0.9-mile (1.4-km) pedestrian-only path. This charming park in the heart of the city offers a lovely view of the downtown skyline. Cruise the lake on two-person swan-shaped paddle boats, or feed the swans, drifting along in the lake's shallow water.

The park hosts several annual and seasonal events, including the Fourth of July fireworks show and the superb UCF-Shakespeare Festival. The plays and concerts are performed against the stunning backdrop of the Walt Disney Amphitheater, a band shell with excellent acoustics. The Terrace in the Park restaurant serves fine cuisine, not the usual park fare.

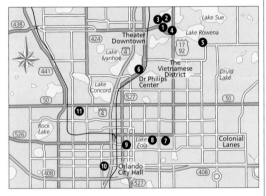

Sights at a Glance

Key

═══ Interstate highway

▬▬▬ Major highway

══ Highway

── Railroad

0 km   1

0 miles   1

A scene in progress from Les Liaisons Dangereuses, Mad Cow Theatre

Mad Cow Theatre
105 S Magnolia Ave. **(407) 297-8788.** **W** www.madcowtheatre.com
Started in late 1997 as a simple project between a band of actors and some directors in a former blueprint studio in Maitland, this theatrical group has developed a reputation for outstanding productions performed at different settings for several years. In 2004, it acquired a permanent home in the heart of Downtown Orlando, at a venue that seats an audience of around 160.

The Mad Cow Theatre presents a quality range of classics, musicals, and original works, and produces an annual Orlando Cabaret in July. Past productions have ranged from Chekhov and T.S. Eliot to Neil Simon. The group also offers educational shows and workshops.

Orange County Regional History Center
65 E Central Blvd. **(407) 836-8500, (800) 965-2030.** 10am–5pm Mon–Sat, noon–5pm Sun. **W** www.thehistorycenter.org
Housed in the former Orange County Courthouse, the Orange County Regional History Center sits on nearly 2 acres (0.8 ha) of land in Heritage Square, the old town center. It has four floors of exhibits and interactive areas for visitors of all ages, offering a glimpse into the history and environment of Central Florida. Everything, from wildlife, and the first

Native Americans in the area, to Walt Disney and the space program, is covered here. Highlights include replicas of a Seminole settlement and an early Florida Pioneer Cracker home. Visitors can also wander though a re-created Timucuan village. The museum has an interesting exhibition on the training of aviators, from World War II pilots to NASA astronauts. The center also offers several educational programs and school field trips for children, and organizes get-togethers such as concerts on a regular basis.

Wells' Built Museum of African American History & Culture
511 W South St. **(407) 245-7535.** 9am–5pm Mon–Fri, Sat by appointment.
The Wells' Built Hotel was constructed in 1912 by Orlando's first African-American physician, Dr. William Monroe Wells, as a lodging for performers on the Chitlin' Circuit, a network of locations throughout southern United States where African Americans stayed and performed music. Many of the day's top black entertainers, including Billie Holiday, Ray Charles, Benny Carter, and Duke Ellington, have stayed here at different times. The building was converted into a museum in 1999.

The museum contains artifacts, photographs, and exhibits relating to Orlando's African-American communities, focusing on locals who were the first African Americans to attain positions of prominence in their professions and the community. There is a photo display of the Chitlin' Circuit.

SAK Comedy Lab
380 W Amelia St. **(407) 648-0001.** **W** www.sak.com
One of the best places for live comedy in Orlando, SAK Comedy Lab stages two hilarious shows per night. The later show is slightly racier, but obscene material is strictly avoided, and the high-energy improvization comedy is a great option for families looking for laughs. Especially popular are the series shows, such as *Duel of Fools*. The 215 seats of the theater are wrapped around the stage, giving all members of the audience a good view. Comedians who have performed here include Wayne Brady – one of the stars on the *Whose Line is it Anyway?* TV show.

Wells' Built Museum of African American History & Culture

Exploring International Drive

GARISH AND GLITTERING International Drive, generally known as I-Drive, is a 3-mile (5-km) ribbon of innumerable attractions, including five major theme parks *(see pp78–101)*. Several of the entertainment venues are open day and night, making the area a zone of frenetic activity 'til late at night. I-Drive brims with hotels and restaurants catering to all budgets, and shopping malls and stores where tourists can pick up souvenirs as well as go in for serious discount shopping. Also located here is Orlando's excellent Official Visitor Information Center, which has coupons for many of the city's attractions, hotels, and restaurants. The most convenient way to take in I-Drive's sights is to hop onto the I-Ride Trolley *(see p197)*.

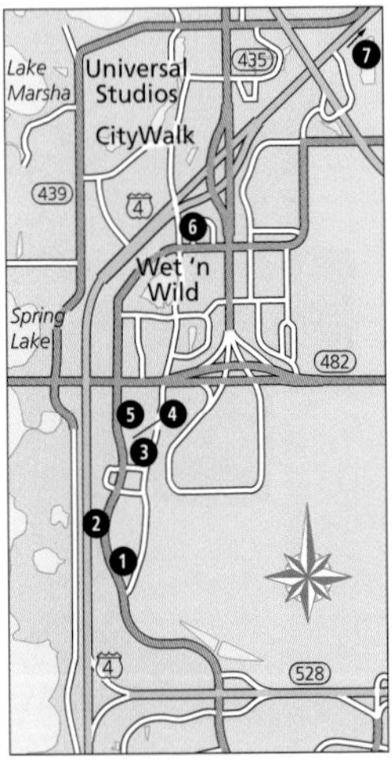

SIGHTS AT A GLANCE

Hard Rock Vault ④
Holy Land Experience ⑦
International Train & Trolley Museum ②
Ripley's Believe It Or Not®! Orlando Odditorium ⑤
Skull Kingdom ⑥
Titanic – The Exhibition ③
WonderWorks ①

KEY

- Interstate highway
- Major highway
- Highway

0 km — 2

0 miles — 2

WonderWorks

Pointe Orlando, 9067 International Dr. ☎ *(407) 351-8800.* 🕒 *9am–midnight daily.* 🎟 [W] www.wonderworksonline.com

One of the most striking buildings on International Drive, WonderWorks looks as though a three-story tall, Neo-Classical building has landed upside down atop a 1930s brick warehouse. This interactive entertainment center boasts numerous hands-on exhibits – some incorporating virtual reality – and demonstrations that the whole family can enjoy. Visitors can experience hurricane-force winds and an earthquake, or even play basketball with a very tall simulated opponent.

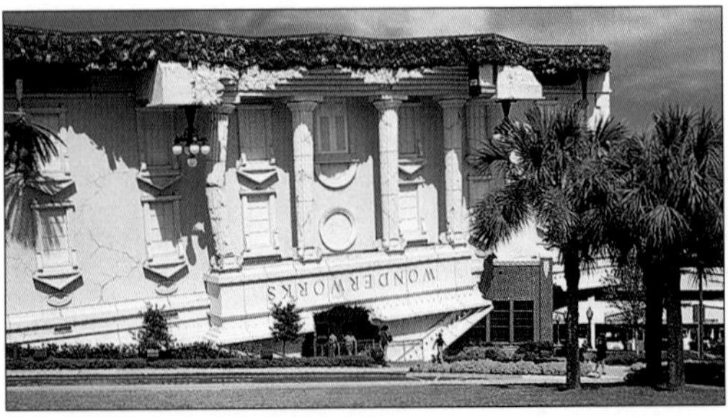

The upside down façade of WonderWorks

Other favorites include the WonderCoaster, where guests can design and ride their own roller coaster in a simulator, and the laser tag video arcade.

International Train & Trolley Museum

8990 International Dr. ☎ *(407) 363-9002.* 🕒 *10am–9pm Mon–Sat, 10am–8pm Sun.* ● *public hols.* 🎟

The importance of the rail industry in the development of the country is underlined by the elaborate displays at this museum, which features one of the world's largest G-gauge layouts occupying 4,800 sq ft (446 sq m) of floor space. The track is beautifully laid out through mountain passes, small towns, and industrial areas, all created with great attention to detail. Visitors can ride a genuine Mason Bogey with two passenger cars and a custom-built California trolley. The highly knowledgeable staff can regale train enthusiasts with related stories and a multitude of modeling tips.

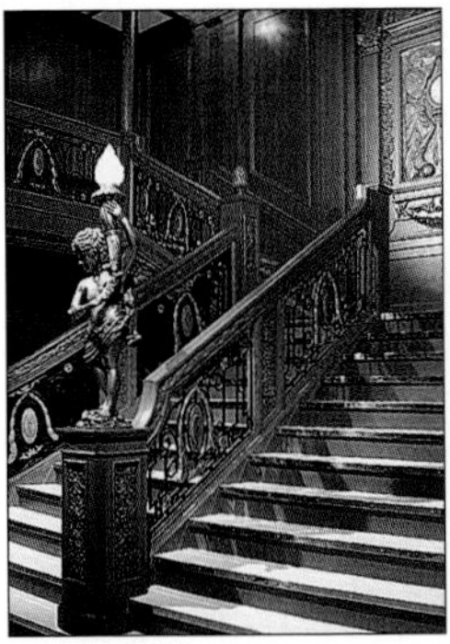

The Grand Staircase at Titanic – The Exhibition

Titanic – The Exhibition

The Mercado, 8445 International Dr. ☎ *(407) 248-1166.* 🕒 *10am–10pm daily. Ticket office: 10am–8pm daily.* ● *public hols.* 🎟 ♿ [W] www.titanicshipofdreams.com

This exhibition allows visitors to re-live the *Titanic*'s mesmerizing drama as it unfolded, share in the inspirational personal stories of those aboard, and marvel at the splendor of one of the finest ships ever built. The doomed ship is impressively re-created here with the help of modern

◁ **The Sun Trust building towering over Church Street, Downtown Orlando**

technology, reproductions of the ship's rooms – including the Grand Staircase – historic artifacts, and interactive interpretations by storytellers in period costume. The exhibit also contains memorabilia from three major Titanic movies, including an outfit worn by Leonardo Di Caprio in the 2001 version.

Holy Land Experience, a reconstruction of biblical Jerusalem

🏛 Hard Rock Vault

The Mercado, 8437 International Dr.
📞 (407) 599-7625. ◯ *9am–midnight daily.* 🖼 🚻 🚹
🌐 www.hardrock.com/vault/vault.asp

Get close to music legends at the Hard Rock Vault, a fascinating interactive rock 'n' roll museum that is part of the worldwide restaurant chain. More than 17,000 sq ft (1,580 sq m) are dedicated to memorabilia and interactive displays, with tour guides and self-guided tours giving fans a glimpse at the evolution of this music genre. The star feature is the guided Total Immersion Tour through five galleries of rock history. The listening room, the Sound Asylum, features its own show. Priceless possessions from music greats such as Elvis Presley, the Beatles, the Rolling Stones, Eric Clapton, and Madonna make this museum a dream come true for rock aficionados.

Logo of Hard Rock Vault

🏛 Ripley's Believe It Or Not!® Orlando Odditorium

8201 International Drive. 📞 (407) 363-4418. ◯ *9am–1am daily.*
🖼 🚹 ♿

Showcasing the bizarre and the extraordinary, Ripley's worldwide chain of attractions displays the fantastic odditities discovered by Robert Ripley (1893–1949) in the course of his travels. Housed in a building that appears to be sinking, the Orlando branch is one of the best of the 27 Ripley's, with 16 galleries of the unusual. Highlights include a 1907 Silver Ghost Rolls Royce – with moving engine parts – that was made from 63 pints of glue and 1,016,711 ordinary matchsticks, a version of the *Mona Lisa* made out of toast, and a holographic 1,069-lb (485-kg) man. The replicas of human and animal odditites on display may make some cringe. There is also a gift shop with collectibles for visitors who wish to take some unusual souvenirs home.

🏛 Skull Kingdom

5933 American Way. 📞 (407) 354-1564. ◯ *10am–11pm daily.*
🚼 *for kids.* 🖼 ♿ *(limited).*
🌐 www.skullkingdom.com

A two-story haunted castle, fronted by a gigantic skull, Skull Kingdom is a fantastic combination of old-fashioned sideshow scares and cutting-edge special effects. Robotics,

detailed light and sound effects, and superb, wonderfully made-up actors keep your spine tingling at every turn as you make your way through caverns, mazes, and haunted hallways. Families are led through the castle by a staff guide to ensure everyone makes it safely to the end of the tour. There are day and night horror shows, with the latter being more intense. The Chamber of Magic Show and Dinner features a magic entertainment show and all-you-can-eat pizza, beer, and soda for a set price.

🏛 Holy Land Experience

4655 Vineland Rd. 📞 (407) 367-2065. ◯ *10am–5pm Mon–Fri, 9am–6pm Sat, noon–6 pm Sun.*
● *Thanksgiving, Dec 25.* 🖼 🚹 ♿
🌐 www.holylandorlando.net

Opened in 2001, this biblical history museum spread over 15 acres (6 ha) re-creates in elaborate and authentic detail the city of Jerusalem and its religious importance between the years 1450 BC and AD 66. Guides in period costume, dramatic enactments of stories from the Old and New Testaments, and high-tech presentations bring Jerusalem to life in this religious theme park. Among the highlights of Holy Land Experience are reconstructions of Jesus's tomb and the limestone caves where the Dead Sea Scrolls were discovered, and displays of rare Bibles and biblical manuscripts. While the museum makes no bones about being a Christ-centric institution, visitors of all faiths can enjoy its evocative journey back in time. A Middle-Eastern-style café serves "Goliath burgers."

The dramatic sinking home of Ripley's Believe It Or Not! Odditorium

Exploring Winter Park, Eatonville & Maitland

Greater Orlando's most refined neighborhood, Winter Park took off in the 1880s, when wealthy northerners came south and began to build lavish winter retreats here, along the area's waterways. Excellent stores and classy cafés afford ample opportunities for strolling and window-shopping, and there are several intriguing museums. Nearby Eatonville, the first incorporated African-American municipality in the USA, has an interesting museum on African-American culture, while Maitland, to the north, has beautiful homes and gardens and boasts an excellent art center.

Sights at a Glance

Albin Polasek Museum & Sculpture Gardens ④
Audubon Center for Birds of Prey ⑦
Central Park ②
Charles Hosmer Morse Museum of American Art ①
Cornell Fine Arts Museum ③
Holocaust Memorial Resource & Education Center of Central Florida ⑨
Maitland Art Center ⑧
Winter Park Scenic Boat Tour ⑤
Zora Neale Hurston National Museum of Arts ⑥

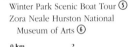

0 km 2

0 miles 2

Key

Interstate highway

Major highway

Highway

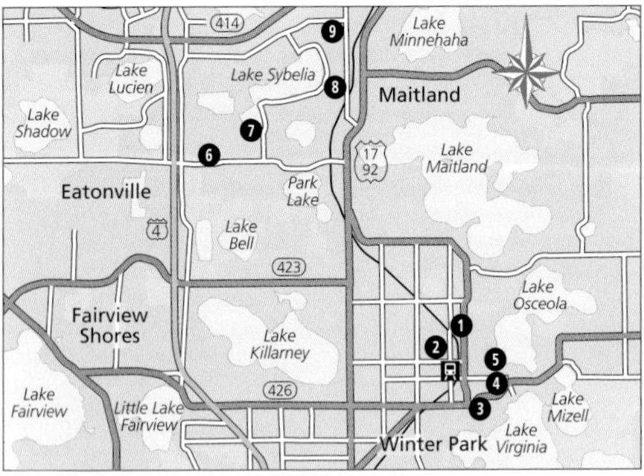

Charles Hosmer Morse Museum of American Art

445 N Park Ave. ☎ *(407) 645-5311.* 🕓 *9:30am–4pm Tue–Sat, 1–4pm Sun.* ● *public hols.* 💲 *(Sep–May: 4–8pm Fri free)* ♿
[W] www.morsemuseum.org

The imposing, windowless walls of this museum rather ironically contain an outstanding collection of beautiful stained-glass windows and objects by the American designer, Louis Comfort Tiffany (1848–1933). Other highlights include American ceramics and representative collections of the late 19th- and early 20th-century American and European paintings, graphics, decorative arts, furniture, and jewelry.

Central Park

Downtown Winter Park. ☎ *(407) 599-3334.* 🕓 *daily.* ♿

Located alongside Winter Park's main street, Park Avenue, Central Park is a lovely shaded area that hosts numerous events throughout the year. Tall oaks, pretty fountains, and a splendid rose garden provide a scenic backdrop to monthly concerts on Sunday evenings by the Orlando Philharmonic. Other events include monthly jazz concerts, the Winter Park Sidewalk Art Festival in March, screening of film classics, month-long Christmas festivities, and school activities. Many carry their own blankets and even chairs to enjoy the various musical events. Sculptor Albin Polasek designed the beautiful fountain called "Emily." Benches are scattered throughout and parking is free at the two lots adjacent to the park.

Cornell Fine Arts Museum

100 Holt Ave. 🕓 *Currently closed for renovation. Expected to reopen in fall of 2005.* ☎ *(407) 646-2526.*
[W] www.rollins.edu/cfam

Located on the scenic Rollins College campus, this small but elegant museum houses Florida's oldest art collection. The diverse and distinguished collection features European and American paintings, sculptures, and decorative arts from the Renaissance to the 20th century, including the works of artists such as Cosimo Roselli, Henry Moore, William Merritt Chase, and Louis Sonntag.

Albin Polasek Museum & Sculpture Gardens

633 Osceola Ave, Winter Park. ☎ *(407) 647-6294.* 🕓 *10am–4pm Tue–Sat, 1–4pm Sun.* ● *public hols, July & Aug.* 💲 ♿
[W] www.polasek.org

Listed on the National Register of Historic Places, the home of Czech-American sculptor Albin Polasek (1879–1965) is a beautifully maintained, serene spot spread over

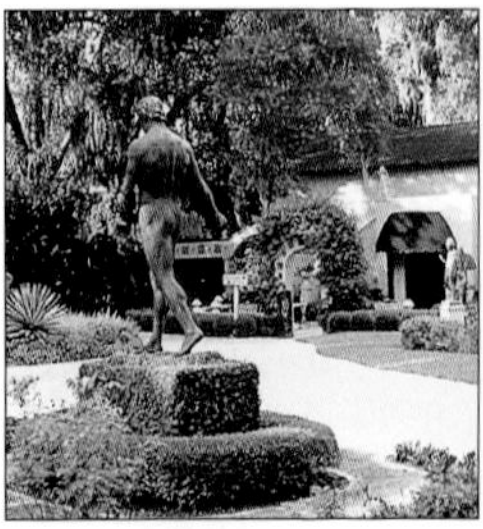

Albin Polasek Museum & Sculpture Gardens

Winter Park Scenic Boat Tour, along Winter Park's waterways

3 acres (1 ha). The house and its lovely gardens showcase works spanning the career of the artist who specialized in the European figurative technique. The four galleries within the house also feature works by some other artists.

🎣 Winter Park Scenic Boat Tour
E end of Morse Blvd, Lake Osceola. 📞 *(407) 644-4056.* ⏰ *tours depart on the hour 10am–4pm daily.* ● *public hols.* 📠 w www.scenicboattours.com

Spend a very pleasant hour cruising along Winter Park's lovely lakes overhung with hibiscus and bamboo on this narrated pontoon boat ride. Running since 1938, this part-nature trip and part-local history lesson takes in landmarks such as Rollins College and huge lakeside mansions with green sweeping lawns, as well as cypress swamps where nature lovers can take a gander at birds such as herons and ospreys.

🏛 Zora Neale Hurston National Museum of Arts
227 E Kennedy Blvd, Eatonville. 📞 *(407) 647-3307.* ⏰ *9am–4pm Mon–Fri, 2–5pm Sun.* ● *public hols.* 🖼 🚻 w www.zoranealehurston.cc

One of the brightest stars of the Harlem Renaissance of the 1920s and 30s, writer, anthropologist, and folklorist Zora Neale Hurston was born in Eatonville in 1891. Many of her most famous writings – including the 1937 novel, *Their Eyes Were God* – reflected life in her hometown. This modest museum keeps her memory alive, offering maps for a self-guided walking

tour to the remaining literary landmarks of her neighborhood. There are exhibitions centered on Hurston and the Eatonville of days gone by. The museum also has rotating exhibits of a range of works by contemporary African-American artists.

🦅 Audubon Center for Birds of Prey
1101 Audubon Way, Maitland. 📞 *(407) 644-0190.* ⏰ *10am–4pm Tue–Sun.* ● *public hols.* 📠 *(donation requested).* 🚻 w www.audubonofflorida.org/conservation/cbop.htm

One of the largest bird rehabilitation centers in Southeastern US, this sanctuary for birds, created by Florida Audubon Society, is a great place to get up close and personal with eagles, owls, hawks, vultures, and other raptors. The center takes in about 700 birds annually and releases about 40 percent of them. Guests are not allowed to witness the rehabilitation process. Those birds that cannot survive being released

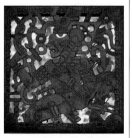

Decoration inspired by the Aztecs, at the Maitland Art Center

into the wild are kept here, living a pampered existence in this lovely lakeside location, while helping to educate visitors about wildlife issues and conservation. Guided tours are available for groups, and there is a wide-ranging volunteer program.

🏛 Maitland Art Center
231 W Packwood Ave, 6 miles (9.6 km) north of Downtown Orlando. 📞 *(407) 539-2181.* ⏰ *9am–4:30pm Mon–Fri, noon–4:30pm Sat & Sun.* ● *public hols.* 📠 *(donation requested).* 🚻 🚻 w www.maitartctr.org

Founded in the 1930s by artist André Smith, this was originally an artists' colony, with studios and living quarters. It is now an art museum and teaching center managed by the Maitland Historical Society. The studios are still used by working artists, and there are exhibitions of contemporary American arts and crafts as well as art classes taught by professional artists.

Set around courtyards and gardens, the buildings are interesting, with murals and carvings that make abundant use of Mayan and Aztec motifs.

🏛 Holocaust Memorial Resource & Education Center of Central Florida
851 N Maitland Ave, Maitland. 📞 *(407) 628-0555.* ⏰ *9am–4pm Mon–Thu, 9am–1pm Fri, 1–4pm Sun.* ● *public & Jewish hols.* 🖼 🚻 w www.holocaustedu.org

Set up with the aim of preventing the oppression of minority groups in future by learning from the Holocaust, this small museum's permanent exhibit has 12 segments, each introducing a major theme of the Holocaust. The museum features multimedia displays on the history of the Holocaust as well as photographs and artifacts.

There is also an extensive library on the subject, with more than 5,000 volumes and 500 videotapes, some of which contain oral histories of survivors of the Holocaust. The library also stocks a selection of juvenile books on this tragic event.

Audubon Center for Birds of Prey

S-32—Park Avenue and Municipal Zoo from the Band Shell on Lake Monroe, Sanford, Fla.

A postcard of Sanford, showing Lake Monroe

Sanford ❷

Seminole Co. 🚶 45,000. 🚗 🚌
ℹ️ 400 E 1st St, (407) 322-2212.
🔲 www.sanfordchamber.com

LOCATED TO THE north of
Orlando and on the south-
ern shores of Lake Monroe,
Sanford was founded in the
1870s by Henry S. Sanford,
near Fort Mellon, the US
Army post built
during the Seminole
Wars *(see p12)*. The
construction of a
railway station
thereafter added to
Sanford's prosperity
and the thriving
town soon became
a major inland port
thanks to the commercial
steamboat services, which also
brought the city's early tourists.
Restored downtown Sanford
dates from the 1880s, which
was the height of the steamboat era. Several of the lovely
old red brick buildings – a
rarity in Florida – are home to
antiques shops, and the area
can easily be explored on
foot in a couple of hours.
Today's visitors are more
likely to arrive on the Auto
Train *(see p196)* than by river,
but short pleasure cruises
are also available.

Sanford town sign

Mount Dora ❸

Lake Co. 🚶 11,000. 🚗
ℹ️ 341 Alexander St, (352) 383-2165.
🔲 www.mountdora.com

SET AMONG THE citrus groves
of Lake County, this town
is one of the prettiest Victorian
settlements left in the state.
Its name comes from both its
relatively high elevation of
184 ft (56 m) and the small
lake on which it sits. Mount
Dora was originally known as
Royellou, after Roy, Ella, and
Louis, the three children of
the first postmaster.
Mount Dora's attractive tree-
lined streets are laid out on
a bluff above the lakeshore.
Visitors can refer to the 3-
mile (5-km) historic
tour map, which is
available at the
town's chamber
of commerce.
The tour takes a
scenic route around
the quiet neighbor-
hoods of late 19th-
century clapboard
homes and the wonderfully
restored downtown historic
district, which has an array of
stores and antiques shops.
On Donnelly Street, you
will find the grand **Donnelly
House**, now a Masonic Hall.
A notable example of ornate
"steamboat architecture," the
building is aesthetically decorated with pinnacles and a
cupola. Nearby, the small
Royellou Museum – housed
in the old city jail – showcases local history exhibits.
Water sports and fishing are
on offer at Lake Dora.

🏛 **Royellou Museum**
450 Royellou Lane. [(352) 383-
0006. 🔲 1–5pm Thu–Sun. ● Jan 1,
Thanksgiving, Dec 25. 🔲 limited.

Blue Spring State Park ❹

Volusia Co. 2100 W French Ave,
Orange City. [(386) 775-3663.
🔲 8am–sundown daily. 🔲 🔲 🔲
www.floridastateparks.org/bluespring

ONE OF THE country's largest
first-magnitude artesian
springs, Blue Spring pours out
around 100 million gallons
(450 million liters) of water a
day. The temperature of the
water is at a constant 68°F
(20°C), and consequently
the park is a favorite winter
refuge for manatees. Between
the months of November and
March, when the manatees
escape from the cooler waters
of the St. Johns River, you can
see them from the park's elevated boardwalks. Activities
such as snorkeling and scuba
diving are available in the
turquoise waters of the spring
head, as is canoeing on St.
Johns. **Thursby House**, atop
one of the park's ancient
shell mounds, was built in
the late 19th century.

ENVIRONS: Just about 2 miles
(3 km) north as the crow flies
is wooded **Hontoon Island
State Park**. Reached by a free

Shingles and gingerbread decoration on Donnelly House, Mount Dora

Children playing in front of Thursby House, Blue Spring State Park

DeLeon Springs State Park ❻

601 Ponce DeLeon Blvd. DeLeon Springs. *(386) 985-4212.*
⬡ *8am–sundown daily.*
Ⓦ www.floridastateparks.org/deleonsprings

THE SPRINGS at this State Park were once believed to be the legendary fountain of youth. Today, they provide a pristine setting for various forms of outdoor recreation.

Swimming is one of the most popular activities here, with the springs being dammed to create a fine bathing area where the water remains at a pleasant 72°F (22°C). Numerous nature and hiking trails take visitors through beautiful, thickly wooded areas typical of Florida's habitat, and there are lovely picnic spots and pavilions. Fishing, boating, kayaking, and canoeing are permitted – you can rent kayaks and canoes at the park. At the **Old Spanish Sugar Mill** restaurant, guests can cook their own pancakes.

Adjoining the park is **Lake Woodruff National Wildlife Refuge**, a preserve for endangered birds and animals. Explore the lakes and marshes of the refuge in a canoe.

Lake Woodruff National Wildlife Refuge

2045 Mud Lake Rd, DeLeon Springs. *(386) 985-4673.*
⬡ *daylight hours daily.*

passenger ferry from Hontoon Landing, the island has an 80-ft (24-m) observation tower, picnic and camping areas, and a nature trail. Fishing skiffs and canoes can also be rented.

The original inhabitants of the park were the Timucua Indians. In 1955, a rare wooden owl totem was found here.

Hontoon Island State Park

2309 River Ridge Rd, DeLand. *(386) 736-5309.*
⬡ *8am–sundown daily.*

Southern Cassadaga Spiritualist Camp ❺

1325 Stevens St, Cassadaga. *(386) 228-3171.* ⬡ *10am–5pm daily. Office: 10am–noon Mon–Thu.*
Ⓦ www.cassadaga.org

FOUNDED BY A group of spiritualists in 1894 to study the philosophy, science, and religion of Spiritualism in greater depth, the Southern Cassadaga Spiritualist Camp is one of the oldest active religious communities in the United States. In 1991, the center was earmarked as a Historic District by the National Registry of Historic Places.

Spread over 57 acres (23 ha), the community is home to numerous certified and practicing healers, clairvoyants, mediums, and psychics, who offer healing sessions to those suffering from ailments of the body and the spirit. Visitors can arrange a session with any of the spiritual counselors for a specified fee. Accommodation is available on the premises. The center also organizes activities and classes on aspects of Spiritualism.

The Cassadaga Spiritualist Bookstore and Information Center has a vast collection of spiritual reading matter, CDs, and tapes, as well as gift articles such as crystals, jewelry, and ethnic artifacts.

The Old Spanish Sugar Mill amid the lush greenery and lakes of the DeLeon Springs State Park

Daytona Beach ❼

Volusia Co. 🏙 64,000. ✈ 🚌
ℹ️ 126 E Orange Ave, (386) 255-0415. 🌐 www.daytonabeach.com

The Daytona 500, held each February at Daytona International Speedway

Noisy Daytona Beach calls itself the "World's Most Famous Beach." This 23-mile (37-km) long beach is one of the few in Florida where cars are allowed on the sands, a hangover from the days when motor enthusiasts raced on the beaches: the first timed automobile runs took place just north of Daytona Beach, on the sands at Ormond Beach – the official "Birthplace of Speed" – in 1903.

Daytona is still a mecca for motorsports fans. The nearby **Daytona International Speedway** draws huge crowds, especially during the Speedweeks in February and the motorcycle racing events in March and October. Eight major racing weekends are held annually at the track, which can hold more than 110,000 spectators. The speed-way hosts NASCAR (National Association for Stock Car Auto Racing) meets – the Daytona 500 being the most famous – and sports car, motorcycle, and go-karting races. Events include charity bike-a-thons, vintage car rallies, superbike spectaculars, and production car tests. A tram tour around the speed-way track is available on days

A race car at Daytona International Speedway

when no races take place. Tickets for each Daytona 500 are usually sold out a year in advance, but visitors can relive the experience at DAYTONA USA, a popular attraction at the visitor center.

One of the main exhibits here is a film featuring spectacular in-car camera shots and behind-the-scenes action from a recent Daytona 500 race.

The beach, lined with a wall of hotels, bustles with frenzied activity. On offer are jet skiing, windsurfing, buggy rides, gondola sky-rides above Ocean Pier, and much else. The old-fashioned boardwalk on the seafront is nostalgic, with bandstands, arcades, go-karts, and cotton candy.

Downtown Daytona, known simply as "Mainland," lies across the Halifax River from the beach. The restored

downtown area is home to the **Halifax Historical Society Museum**. Located in a 1910 bank building, the museum is decorated with fancy pilasters and murals. Local history displays include a model of the boardwalk as it was in 1938.

Close by, **Jackie Robinson Ballpark** – named after the baseball legend – is the home field of the Daytona Cubs.

West of downtown, the excellent **Museum of Arts & Sciences** has exhibits that cover a range of subjects, from Florida prehistory to fine and decorative arts from 1640–1920. There is a notable Cuban and African art collection. The 1907 **Gamble Place**, run by the same museum, is a hunting lodge with period furnishings. Tours of the house require reservations, and also include the Snow White House – built in 1938 and an exact copy of the one in the 1937 Disney classic.

Daytona International Speedway
1801 W International Speedway Blvd. 📞 (386) 253-7223. 🕐 daily. ⬤ Dec 25. 🅿️ 🎫 ♿ 🌐 www. daytonainternationalspeedway.com
🏛 **Halifax Historical Society Museum**
252 S Beach St. 📞 (386) 255-6976. 🕐 10am–4pm Tue–Fri, 10am–noon Sat. ⬤ public hols. 🅿️ ♿ 🌐 www.halifaxhistorical.org
Jackie Robinson Ballpark
105 E Orange Ave. 📞 (386) 257-3172. 🌐 www.daytonacubs.com
🏛 **Museum of Arts & Sciences**
1040 Museum Blvd. 📞 (386) 255-0285. 🕐 9am–4pm Tue–Fri, noon–5pm Sat. ⬤ Thanksgiving, Dec 24, Dec 25. 🅿️ ♿ 🌐 www.moas.org

Cars cruising the hard-packed sands of Daytona Beach

Beaches of the East Coast

THE WIDE, SUN-SOAKED sandy beaches of Central Florida's Atlantic Coast, with their warm waters and an average daytime temperature of 73°F (23°C), attract millions of visitors annually. The 72 miles (116 km) of the Space Coast feature lovely beaches, several being contiguous with lush nature preserves. Most are on barrier islands, and range from the pristine white beaches of the Canaveral National Seashore and the Indian River, to boisterous resorts such as Cocoa Beach. To the north of the Space Coast are Ormond Beach and the highly popular Daytona Beach, both associated with automobile racing. Most of the East Coast beaches are family-friendly, with picnic areas and restrooms, and also offer a wide range of water sports.

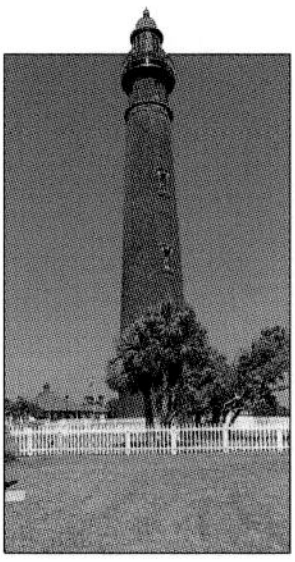

Ponce de Leon Inlet lighthouse

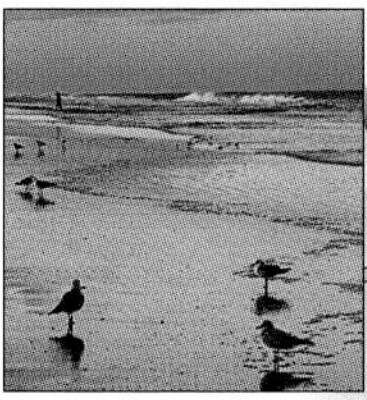

Ormond Beach ①
This resort offers small town charm along with water activities on its many rivers and lakes, as well as the ocean.

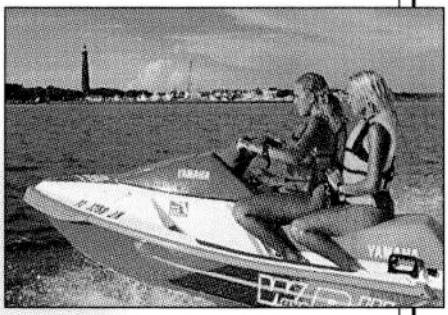

Daytona Beach ②
Proximity to an auto racing mecca, glittering nightspots, and a surfeit of water sports make this Florida's busiest beach.

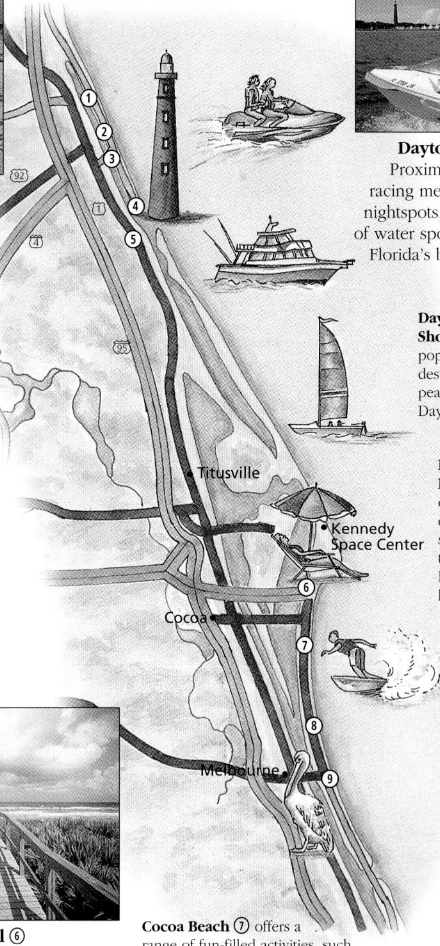

Daytona Beach Shores ③ is a popular family destination, more peaceful than Daytona Beach.

Ponce Inlet ④ is a vehicle-free beach with several nature trails. It also has an observation deck, and offers tours of its lighthouse.

Indian River Beaches ⑧ offer uncrowded stretches of sand and access to Merritt Island National Wildlife Refuge.

New Smyrna Beach ⑤ has a tranquil stretch of sand and gentle waves. Highlights include nature trails and quaint stores along the nearby streets.

Melbourne Beach ⑨ is a quiet spot, with superb sunsets and several beachfront parks.

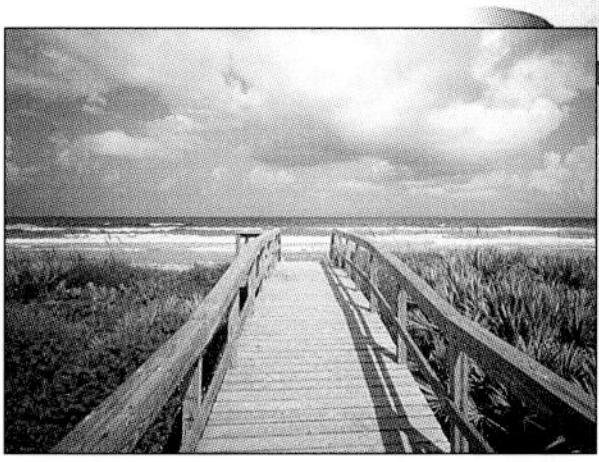

Playalinda at Canaveral ⑥
One of Florida's few nude beaches, it offers a great view of Kennedy Space Center's rocket launches *(see p126–9).*

Cocoa Beach ⑦ offers a range of fun-filled activities, such as surfing, scuba diving, and waterskiing, as well as dining and shopping options *(see p124).*

0 km 10
0 miles 10

Ocala National Forest ❽

Lake Co/Marion Co. ℹ️ *3199 NE Co. Rd, (352) 236-0288.* 🕐 *8am–sunset daily.* 🅿️ *to campsite & swimming areas.* ♿ ⛺ **Juniper Springs canoe rental** 📞 *(352) 625-2808.* 🔲 www.ocalacc.com/visitor-center/forestry.asp

The Jungle Cruise, one of the many attractions at Silver Springs

Locate between Ocala city and the St. Johns River, this is the world's largest pine forest, covering an area of 366,000 acres (148,000 ha). The forest is crisscrossed by spring-fed rivers and dozens of hiking trails. One of the last refuges of the endangered Florida black bear, it is also home to many more common animals such as deer and otter. Several birds, including barred owls, bald eagles, ospreys, the non-native wild turkey, and various species of waders – which frequent the river swamp areas – can all be spotted here.

The numerous hiking trails in the forest vary in length from boardwalks to short loop trails of under a mile (1.6 km) to a 66-mile (106-km) stretch of the cross-state National Scenic Trail. Bass fishing is popular on the many lakes scattered through the forest, and there are swimming holes, picnic areas, and campgrounds at recreation areas such as Salt Springs, Fore Lake, and Alexander Springs.

Canoes are easily available for rental. The 7-mile (11-km) canoe run down Juniper Creek from the **Juniper Springs Recreation Area** is one of the finest in the state. Book in advance as it is an extremely popular tourist destination. The Salt Springs Trail provides an excellent vantage point for bird-watching, and wood ducks congregate on Lake Dorr.

You can pick up guides and information at the main visitor center on the western edge of the forest, or at the smaller centers at Salt Springs and Lake Dorr, both on Route 19.

Silver Springs ❾

Marion Co. 5656 E Silver Springs Blvd. 📞 *(352) 236-2121.* 🕐 *10am–5pm daily.* 🅿️ ♿ limited. 🔲 www.floridastateparks.org/silverriver

Glass-bottomed boat trips at Silver Springs have been revealing the natural wonders of the world's largest artesian spring since 1878.

Today, Florida's oldest commercial tourist attraction offers not only the famous glass-bottomed boat rides but also jeep safaris and jungle cruises, which take you on a trip through the Florida outback. The early Tarzan movies starring Johnny Weismuller were filmed here.

Another popular attraction here is the Alligator & Crocodile Encounter at Cypress Island: this 5-acre (2-ha) area is home to 13 of the 23 species of alligators and crocodiles. Nearby, Wild Waters is a lively, family-oriented water park.

Environs: The **Silver River State Park**, 2 miles (3 km) southeast, offers a lovely walk through a hardwood hammock and cypress swamp area, leading to a swimming hole in a bend of the crystal-clear river.

FLORIDA'S BUBBLING SPRINGS

Most of Florida's 320 known springs are located in the upper half of the state. The majority are artesian springs, formed by waters forced up through deep fissures from underground aquifers (rock deposits containing water). Those that gush over 100 cu ft (3 cu m) per second are known as first-magnitude springs.

Filtered through the rock, the water is extremely pure and sometimes high in salts and minerals. These properties, plus the sheer beauty of the springs, have long attracted visitors for recreational and health purposes.

Juniper Springs in Ocala National Forest, adapted for swimmers in the 1930s

The gaping jaws of an alligator marking the entrance to Gatorland

🐾 Silver River State Park

1425 NE 58th Ave, Ocala. 🚗 *(352) 236-7148.* ⏰ *8am–sunset daily.* 🎫 ♿ 🅦 *www.floridastateparks.org/ silverriver*

Gatorland ❿

Orange Co. 14501 S Orange Blossom Trail, Orlando. 🚌 *(800) 393-5297.* 🚏 *Orlando.* 🚌 *Orlando.* ⏰ *9am–6pm daily.* 🎫 ♿ 🅦 *www.gatorland.com*

S PREAD OVER an area of 110 acres (44 ha), this park opened in the 1950s as a huge working farm, and has a special license to raise alligators for their hides and meat. Gatorland's breeding pens, nurseries, and rearing ponds are home to thousands of alligators that range in size from infants that fit into the palm of your hand to 12-ft (4-m) monsters. They can be observed from a boardwalk and tower as they bask in the shallows of a cypress swamp.

On sale at Gatorland

The shows are somewhat contrived but still fun. They include alligator wrestling and the Gator Jumparoo, in which huge alligators leap out of the water to grab chunks of chicken from the hands of the trainers. In addition, the park features close encounters and handling demonstrations of Florida's poisonous snakes.

The park's other highlights include an aviary, a bird breeding marsh, and a petting zoo. Gatorland's restaurant offers unique delicacies, such as Gator nuggets and ribs.

Kissimmee ⓫

Osceola Co. 🏚 *41,000.* 🚗 🚌 ℹ️ *1925 E Irlo Bronson Memorial Hwy, (407) 847-5000.* **Old Town** *5770 W Irlo Bronson Memorial Hwy.* 🚗 *(407) 396-4888.*

T HIS CATTLE boom town, whose name means "Heaven's Place" in the language of the Calusa Indians, had cows freely roaming its streets in the early 1900s. Now the only livestock visitors are likely to encounter are those that appear in the twice-yearly rodeos at Silver Spurs Arena, and the more down-to-earth rodeos held every Friday night at **Kissimmee Sports Arena & Rodeo** *(see p179)*. Most visitors headed for Walt Disney World often stop at Kissimmee, drawn by the many inexpensive motels strung along the busy, traffic-

One of the typically offbeat shops in Kissimmee's Old Town

ridden US 192. For those who wish to linger, Kissimmee's **Old Town** is a re-created pedestrian street of early 20th-century buildings with some unusual and eccentric shops, which offer psychic readings, tattoos, Irish linen, candles, and so forth. There is also an entertaining haunted house and a small fairground with antique equipment.

The **Flying Tigers Warbird Restoration Museum**, by the Kissimmee municipal airport, is enjoyably quirky. Some of its most regular visitors are old timers who remember piloting the World War II aircrafts that undergo repair here. Visitors can take a guided tour of the hangar and will learn about the finer points of airplane reconstruction. For a sizable fee, you can take a spin in a T-6 Navy Trainer.

🐎 Kissimmee Sports Arena & Rodeo

1010 Suhls Lane. 🚗 *(407) 933-0020.* ⏰ *for shows 8pm Fri.* 🎫 *Dec.* 🎫 ♿

🏛 Flying Tigers Warbird Restoration Museum

🚗 *(407) 933-1942.* ⏰ *9am–5:30pm Mon–Fri, 9am –5pm Sat & Sun.* 🎫 *Dec 25.* 🎫 ♿

A World of Orchids ⓬

Orange Co. 2501 Old Lake Wilson Rd, Kissimmee. 🚗 *(407) 396-1887.* ⏰ *9:30am–4:30pm Tue–Sun.* ⏰ *public hols.* 🎫 ♿

V ARIETIES OF gorgeous orchids bloom throughout the year in the rainforest setting – complete with streams and waterfalls – of this huge conservatory spread over 3,000 sq ft (279 sq m). Also showcased here are several species of tropical plants, including palms and bamboo, as well as exotic birds and small animals, such as Asian squirrels and chameleons. Rare species of colorful fish are on display in beautifully set-up aquaria. Visitors can enjoy nature walks and guided tours, and stop at the gift shop to carry home a couple of these spectacular plants. Plan to spend at least an hour in this lovely setting.

Fantasy of Flight ⓭

Polk Co. 1400 Broadway Blvd SE, Polk City. ☎ *(863) 984-3500.* 🚆 *Winter Haven.* 🚌 *Winter Haven.* ○ *9am–5pm daily.* ● *Thanksgiving, Dec 25.* 🖐 ♿ [W] www.fantasyofflight.com

THIS AVIATION center gains an advantage over similar attractions in Florida by being the only one to provide the very sensations of flying. The Fightertown section, for instance, allows visitors to ride in a World War II fighter aircraft simulator in a dogfight over the Pacific. While in the cockpit, you will be given a pre-flight briefing and receive advice from the control tower about takeoff, landing, and the presence of enemy aircraft.

Other attractions include a series of vivid walk-through exhibits, which take you into a World War II B-17 Flying Fortress during a bombing mission, and into World War I trenches in the middle of an air raid. A hangar holds an impressive collection of vintage airplanes in mint condition, such as the first widely used airliner in the US, the 1929 Ford Tri-Motor, which appeared in the film *Indiana Jones and the Temple of Doom*, and the Roadair 1, a combined plane and car that flew just once, in 1959.

Florida Southern College ⓮

Polk Co. 111 Lake Hollingsworth Dr, Lakeland. ☎ *(863) 680-4111.* 🚆 *Lakeland.* 🚌 *Lakeland.* ○ *daily.* ● *Jan 1, Jul 4, Thanksgiving, Dec 25.* **Visitor Center** ○ *10am–4pm Mon–Fri, 10am–2pm Sat, 2–4pm Sun.* ♿

LOCATED IN THE picturesque town of Lakeland, Florida Southern College has the world's largest collection of buildings designed by America's most eminent architect, Frank Lloyd Wright. Amazingly, the college president managed to persuade Wright to design the campus with the promise of little more than the opportunity to express his ideas, and payment when the money could be raised. Work began in 1938 on what Wright, already famous as the founder of organic architecture, termed his "child of the sun." His aim of blending the buildings with their natural surroundings was achieved by making special use of glass to bring outdoor light to the interiors. The original plan was for 18 buildings, but only seven had been completed by the time Wright died in 1959; five were finished or added later.

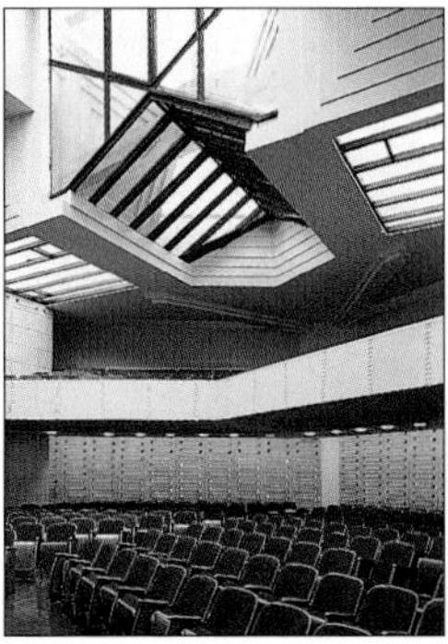

The light and spacious interior of the Annie Pfeiffer Chapel

The **Annie Pfeiffer Chapel** is a particularly fine expression of his ideas. Stained-glass windows break the monotony of the building blocks, and the entire edifice is topped by a spectacular tower in place of the traditional steeple. Wright called this tower a "jewel box."

On the whole, the campus has the light and airy feel that Wright sought to achieve. The buildings are linked to each other by the Esplanades – a covered walkway, stretching for 1.5-miles (2 km), in which light, shade, and variations in height draw attention from one building to the next.

You can wander around the campus at any time, but the interiors can be explored only during the week. The visitor center at **Thad Buckner Building** has drawings and furniture by Wright.

FLORIDA SOUTHERN COLLEGE

Annie Pfeiffer Chapel ⑥
Benjamin Fine Building ②
Emile Watson Building ①
J. Edgar Wall Waterdome ③
Lucius Pond Ordway Building ⑨
Polk County Science Buildings ⑧
Raulerson Building ④
Thad Buckner Building ⑤
William Danforth Chapel ⑦

KEY

Esplanades
[P] Parking
[i] Information

0 meters 100
0 yards 100

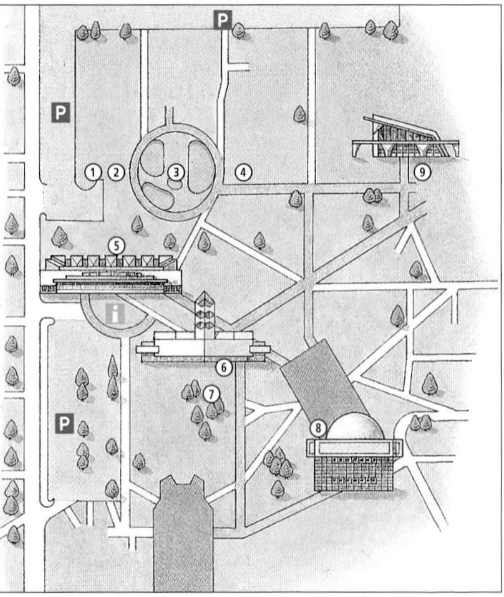

Dinosaur World ⓯

5145 Harvey Tew Rd, Plant City. 📞
(813) 717-9865. 🕐 *9am–6pm daily.*
♿ 🅿 🔖 🅦 *www.dinoworld.net*

Tyrannosaurus rex and around 150 other life-size dinosaurs tower over vegetation in the lush park setting of this outdoor museum. Made of styrofoam and metal, these realistic-looking and scientifically accurate models of prehistoric creatures are arranged in a chronological order through-out the park.

A museum displays fossils and other dinosaur-related objects. Other highlights include a film on the world of dinosaurs and a display that explains the elaborate process used by the park to create its dinosaurs.

Dinosaur World offers many hands-on activities for kids: at a fossil dig, they can use little shovels or dip their hands in the sand to come up with tiny treasures that are dinosaur related; at the Boneyard, they can hunt for dinosaur bones. Picnic areas abound, and there is a gift shop with fun but pricey products.

Cypress Gardens Adventure Park ⓰

Polk Co. 2641 South Lake Summit Dr, Winter Haven. 🚆 *Winter Haven.*
🕐 *daily.* ♿ 🔖
🅦 *www.cypressgardens.com*

Relying on the unlikely twin elements of flowers and waterskiing to attract the crowds, Florida's first theme park, Cypress Gardens, opened in 1936. Closed in 2003, the park was rescued by a grant from the state of Florida. The new park, which opened in 2004, seeks to combine the charm of the original with the excitement of various new thrill rides.

The reopened park retains the splendor of the beautiful botanical gardens, which feature 8,000 varieties of plants set beside a massive cypress-fringed lake. Also restored to their original glory are the amazing waterskiing

The colorful and beautifully landscaped flower beds of Cypress Gardens

and ice-skating stunt shows, the Wings of Wonder butterfly arboretum, topiary gardens, and animal exhibits. New attractions include a huge concert amphitheater and around 35 water, thrill, and roller coaster rides. A lovely carousel, a 100-ft (30-m) Ferris wheel, and bumper cars are other highlights.

Cypress Gardens is still undergoing reconstruction, with ever-more attractions being added to the park.

Bok Tower Gardens ⓱

Polk Co. 1151 Tower Blvd, Lake Wales. 📞 *(863) 676-1408.* 🚆 *Lake Wales.*
🚌 *Winter Haven.* 🕐 *8am–5pm daily.*
♿ 🔖 🅦 *www.boksanctuary.org*

Edward W. Bok arrived in the US from Holland in 1870 at the age of six, and subse-quently became an influential

The striking pink marble Singing Tower at Bok Tower Gardens

publisher. Shortly before his death in 1930, he presented 128 acres (52 ha) of beautiful woodland gardens to the American public "for the success they had given him."

Sitting at the highest spot in peninsular Florida – a dizzying 298 ft (91 m) above sea level – the gardens are spread around the **Singing Tower** that soars above the treetops and shelters Bok's grave at its base. Visitors are not allowed to climb the tower; but try to attend its 45-minute live carillon concert, which is rung daily at 3pm.

Yeehaw Junction ⓲

Osceola Co. Desert Inn, 5570 S Kenansville Rd, Yeehaw Junction. 📞 *(407) 436-1054.* 🕐 *daily.* 🔖
🅦 *www.desertinnrestaurant.com*

Located at the crossroads of US 60 and the Florida Turnpike, quaintly named Yeehaw Junction harks back to the Florida of a couple of centuries ago. It is known for its motel and restaurant, **Desert Inn**, which served as a watering hole for lumber-men and cowboys driving herds of cattle from the center of the state to the reservations and plantations on the coast. Now listed on the National Registry of Historical Places, the 1880s wooden building offers a fascinating look into the history of Cracker Country. The restaurant serves gator- and turtle-burgers, and also has a large outdoor area for festivals – mostly bluegrass music – and barbecues.

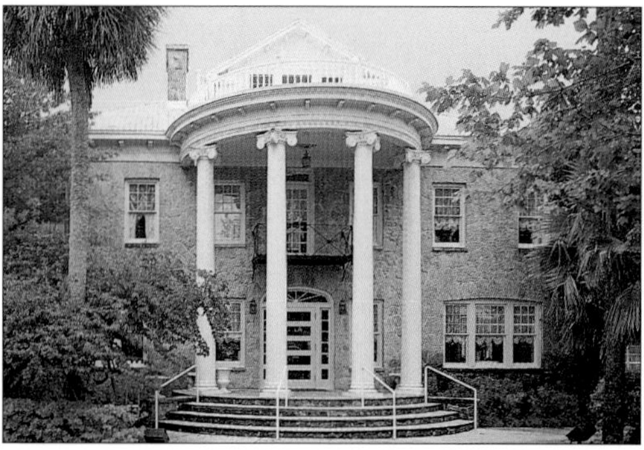

The grand Porcher House, on the edge of Cocoa's leafy historic district

Cocoa Beach 19

Brevard Co. 400 Fortenberry Rd. *(321) 459-2200.* *14,000.* *Cocoa.* www.ci.cocoa-beach.fl.us

LOCATED ON A barrier island adjoining the Atlantic Ocean, this is one of the most popular beaches on the Space Coast. Known as the East Coast's surfing capital, bustling Cocoa Beach hosts several surfing festivals during Easter and the Labor Day weekends. Motels, chain restaurants, and the odd strip joint characterize the main throughfare. The best-known attraction here is the **Ron Jon Surf Shop**, a neon palace-like store with a huge T-shirt collection and surfboards *(see p165)*.

Tour the Banana River Lagoon fringing Cocoa Beach to see marine and bird species in their natural habitat. Or go fishing at the dock at Ramp Road Park, one of the state's best fishing spots.

Ron Jon Surf Shop
4151 N Atlantic Ave. *(321) 799-8820.* *24 hrs daily.*

Cocoa 20

Brevard Co. *20,000.* *400 Fortenberry Rd, Cocoa Beach, (321) 459-2200.*

THE MOST APPEALING of the sprawling communities along the Space Coast mainland, the vibrant town of Cocoa is located close to the Indian River. Its historic district is an attractive enclave known as Cocoa Village – with buildings dating from the 1880s, replica gas streetlamps, and brick sidewalks. On Delannoy Avenue, on the eastern edge of the village, is the Classical Revival **Porcher House**, built of coquina stone in 1916 by a leading citrus plantation owner. Another not-to-miss site is the **Brevard Museum of History & Science**, which has nature trails that represent different ecosystems – pine sandhill, freshwater marsh, or hardwood hammock.

Brevard Museum of History & Science
2201 Michigan Ave. *(321) 632-1830.* *10am–4pm Mon–Sat, noon–4pm Sun.*

Valiant Air Command Warbird Museum 21

Brevard Co. 6600 Tico Rd, Titusville. *(321) 268-1941.* *Titusville.* *10am–6pm daily.* *Jan 1, Thanksgiving, Dec 25.* www.vacwarbirds.org

THIS MUSEUM is home to an enormous hangar that features an impressive collection of military aircraft from World War II and later, all restored to flying condition. The pride of the collection is a Douglas C-47 called Tico Belle, which became the official carrier for the Danish royal family at the end of the war. An air show is held in March each year.

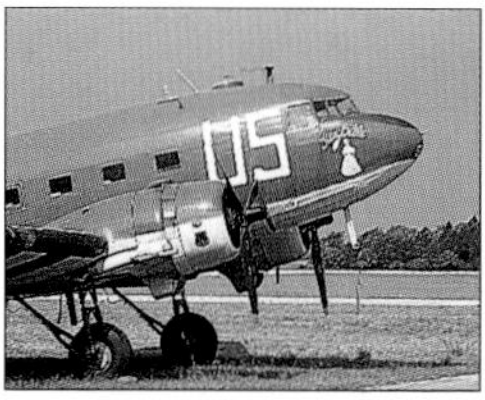

Tico Belle, the prize exhibit at the Warbird Air Museum

US Astronaut Hall of Fame® 22

Brevard Co. Junction of Rte 405 & US 1. *(321) 269-6100.* *Titusville.* *10am–8pm daily.* *Dec 25.* www.kennedyspacecenter.com/visitKSC/attractions/fame.asp

SET UP TO commemorate the country's astronauts, the facility showcases a fascinating collection of their personal memorabilia and other related artifacts. The center also offers interactive experiences in the

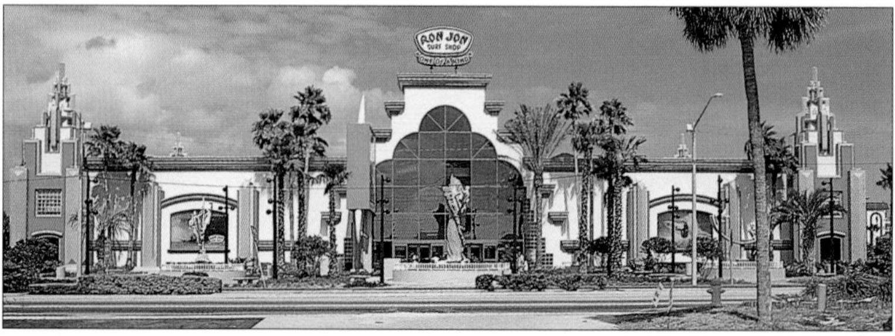

The Ron Jon Surf Shop in Cocoa Beach, with everything for the surfing or beach enthusiast

form of a simulated ride in a mock space shuttle. The US Space Camp, which is located on the same site, offers some specially designed courses for children interested in learning about space.

Canaveral National Seashore ㉓

Brevard Co. Rte A1A, 20 miles (32 km) N of Titusville or Rte 402, 10 miles (16 km) E of Titusville. ☎ (321) 267-1110.
🚌 Titusville. ⏰ Beaches 6am–8pm Apr–Oct, 6am–6pm Nov–Mar.
⬤ for shuttle launches. 🅿 ♿
🅦 www.nbbd.com/godo/cns

Spread over an area of 57,000 acres (23,000 ha), Canaveral National Seashore located on a barrier island, features an astounding range of fauna and a wide range of habitats, including marshes, saltwater estuaries, hardwood hammocks, and pine flat-woods. The bird life makes the greatest visual impact.

The park incorporates Florida's largest undeveloped barrier island beach – a magnificent 24-mile (39-km) stretch backed by barrier dunes. Apollo Beach, at the northern end, is accessible along Route A1A, while Playalinda Beach is reached from the south, along Route 402. Note that this is a popular spot for nude bathing.

Behind Apollo Beach, the Turtle Mound is a 40-ft (12-m) high midden of oyster shells created by Timucua Indians.

Merritt Island National Wildlife Refuge ㉔

Brevard Co. Route 406, 4 miles (6.5 km) E of Titusville. ☎ (321) 861-0667.
🚌 ⏰ sunrise–sunset daily. ⬤ for shuttle launches. 🅦 www.nbbd.com/godo/minwr

Experience an incredible variety of marine and wild-life at this expansive nature preserve adjoining Canaveral

SPACE COAST BIRD LIFE

The magnificent and abundant bird life of the Space Coast is best viewed early in the morning or shortly before dusk. Between November and March, in particular, the marshes and lagoons teem with migratory ducks and waders, as up to 100,000 arrive from colder northern climes.

Sandhill crane

Brown pelican

Royal tern

Black skimmer

An alligator in the wild

National Seashore. Covering an area of 140,000 acres (56,656 ha), the Merritt Island National Wildlife Refuge is a seaside haven for several endangered and threatened species of animals and birds, including manatees, sea turtles, Eastern indigo snakes, American alligators, otters, falcons, terns, ospreys, woodpeckers, owls, and many more. The refuge also provides sanctuary to thousands of plant species typical of Florida's ecosystems and habitats. By far the best way to explore the local wildlife is to follow the 7-mile (11-km) Black Point Wildlife Drive – a self guided tour through salt- and fresh-water marshes. An excellent leaflet, available at the track's start near the junction of

Routes 402 and 406, explains such matters as how dikes help control local mosquito populations – although it is a good idea to come armed with insect repellent in summer. Halfway along the drive, you can stretch your legs by following the 5-mile (8-km) Cruickshank Trail, which starts nearby and has an observation tower.

East along Route 402, toward Playalinda Beach, the Merritt Island Visitor Information Center offers educational displays and a short film about the refuge. A mile (1.6 km) farther east, the Oak Hammock and Palm Hammock trails have short boardwalks across the marshland for bird-watching and photography.

A large part of the refuge lies within Kennedy Space Center *(see pp126–9)* and is out of bounds to the public.

Scenic view from Black Point Drive, Merritt Island National Wildlife Refuge

Kennedy Space Center ㉕

NASA insignia

SITUATED ON MERRITT ISLAND Wildlife Refuge, just an hour's drive east of Orlando, the Kennedy Space Center is the only place in the Western Hemisphere from where humans are launched into space. It was from here, with the launch of *Apollo 11* in July 1969, that President Kennedy's dream of landing a man on the moon was realized. The center is the home of NASA (National Aeronautics and Space Administration), whose space shuttle *(see pp20–21)* can often be seen lifting off from one of the launch pads. With a scale and popularity comparable to Orlando's other theme parks, the Visitor Complex aims to both inform and entertain.

★ **Apollo/Saturn V Center**
A Saturn V rocket, of the kind used by the Apollo missions, is the showpiece here. There is also a reconstructed control room where visitors experience a simulated launch (see p129).

Spacemen
Staff dressed up as spacemen may put in a surprise appearance at any time, providing ideal photo opportunities for children.

Astronaut Encounter

Children's Play Dome

★ **Rocket Garden**
You can walk through a group of towering rockets, each of which represents a different period of space flight's history.

Nature's Technology Universe Theater

Exploration in the New Millennium

Entrance

STAR FEATURES

★ **Apollo/Saturn V Center**

★ **Rocket Garden**

★ **KSC Bus Tours**

★ **IMAX® Theater**

VISITOR COMPLEX

All visitors to the Kennedy Space Center must stop at the Visitor Complex, which was established in 1966 to offer bus tours of the area. It is now an extensive attraction with many exhibits.

★ KSC Bus Tours

A bus tour makes a circuit of the center's launch pads, passing the Vehicle Assembly Building and the "crawlerway," along which the shuttle is slowly maneuvered into position.

VISITORS' CHECKLIST

Brevard Co. Off Rte 405, 6 miles (9.5 km) E of Titusville. 🚉 *Titusville.* 🚌 *(321) 449-4444. Schedule of launches: (321) 867-4636.* ⏰ *9am–7pm daily.* ⬤ *Dec 25. The center closes occasionally due to operational requirements. Always call ahead to check.* ♿ 🍴 🏪 ♿ *all the exhibits are accessible; wheelchairs & strollers are available at Information Central.* 🌐 www.ksc.nasa.gov; www.kennedyspacecenter.com

★ IMAX® Theater

The IMAX® Theater runs films about space exploration. Footage from the shuttle missions offers some breathtaking views of Earth from space (see p128).

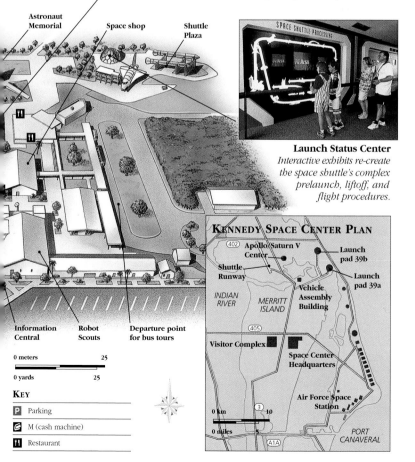

Launch Status Center
Interactive exhibits re-create the space shuttle's complex prelaunch, liftoff, and flight procedures.

Astronaut Memorial

Space shop

Shuttle Plaza

Information Central

Robot Scouts

Departure point for bus tours

0 meters 25

0 yards 25

KEY

🅿 Parking

💳 M (cash machine)

🍴 Restaurant

KENNEDY SPACE CENTER PLAN

(402) Apollo/Saturn V Center

Launch pad 39b

Shuttle Runway

Launch pad 39a

Vehicle Assembly Building

INDIAN RIVER

MERRITT ISLAND

(405)

Visitor Complex

Space Center Headquarters

Air Force Space Station

0 km 10

0 miles 5

(A1A)

PORT CANAVERAL

(3)

Exploring the Kennedy Space Center

Kids enjoy the Robot Scouts at the Imax® Theater

BUILT IN 1967 FOR astronauts and their families to view space center operations, today the Visitor Complex is host to more than 2 million tourists each year. The 131-sq-mile (340-sq-km) facility offers guests a full-day, comprehensive space experience, including excellent IMAX® films at the Visitor Complex, live-action shows, astronaut encounters, and the Apollo/Saturn V Center – the climax of the narrated, video-enhanced bus tour. The go-at-your-own-pace tour enables visitors to stop and explore each of the major destinations. One all-inclusive admission ticket takes visitors on the KSC Tour, both IMAX® space films, and all exhibits.

VISITOR COMPLEX

THE PLACE where everyone heads first is the **IMAX® Theater**, where two back-to-back IMAX® theaters put on stunning films on screens more than five stories high. For some people this is the highlight of their visit.

Top of the bill is *The Dream is Alive,* filmed by shuttle astronauts and narrated by Walter Cronkite. The film provides an insider's view, with in-flight footage gathered during a number of space missions; the thrills and basics of everyday life in space, and shows the awesome beauty of space flight. The other film on offer at the IMAX® Theater is *Space Station 3-D,* which

shows astronauts from Europe and America on board a space station. It provides great footage of those amazing views that only astronauts get to see.

The 300-seat Universe Theater at the Visitor Complex shows the inspirational film *Quest for Life,* which highlights the need for future space exploration to search for life in our galaxy. The **NASA Art Gallery**, inside the IMAX® Theater, offers more than 200 artworks by some famous artists, including Andy Warhol, Robert Rauschenberg, and Annie Leibovitz.

Kids will probably prefer to see the latest planetary explorer robots, and learn

about their interplanetary adventures as revealed in **Robot Scouts**. The **Astronaut Encounter** show offers visitors the rare opportunity of meeting a real astronaut.

In Shuttle Plaza, guests can climb aboard and enjoy a close-up view of **Explorer** – a replica of the space shuttle. The **Launch Status Center** alongside has displays of genuine flight hardware and rocket boosters, plus a number of shows illustrating various space-related topics. Nearby, a "Space Mirror" tracks the movement of the sun, reflecting its light onto the names inscribed on the **Astronaut Memorial**. This honors the 16 astronauts, from the *Apollo 1* to the Space Shuttle *Columbia* missions, who have died in the service of space exploration.

Exploration in the New Millennium offers a film, lecture, and informative exhibits on what the future holds for space exploration. Guests can see and touch a piece of a Mars meteorite.

The *Explorer*, a life-size replica of the space shuttle

TIMELINE OF SPACE EXPLORATION

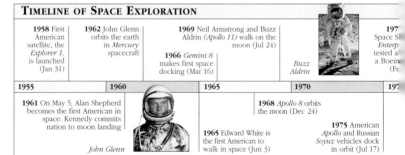

1955	1960	1965	1970	197

1958 First American satellite, the *Explorer 1,* is launched (Jan 31)

1962 John Glenn orbits the earth in *Mercury* spacecraft

1966 *Gemini 8* makes first space docking (Mar 16)

1969 Neil Armstrong and Buzz Aldrin (*Apollo 11*) walk on the moon (Jul 24)

Buzz Aldrin

197 Space S *Enterp* tested a a Boein (Fe

1961 On May 5, Alan Shepherd becomes the first American in space. Kennedy commits nation to moon landing

John Glenn

1965 Edward White is the first American to walk in space (Jun 3)

1968 *Apollo 8* orbits the moon (Dec 24)

1975 American *Apollo* and Russian *Soyuz* vehicles dock in orbit (Jul 17)

KSC Exhibits & Bus Tours

THE ENTRANCE GATE, modeled after the International Space Station, welcomes guests to the Visitor Complex. Once inside the complex, there is a fascinating walk-through exhibit, which shows visitors a comprehensive history of the major missions that provided the foundation for the space program. The all-glass rotunda leads to **Early Space Exploration**, which showcases key figures from the early days of rocketry. In the **Mercury Mission Control Room**, visitors view from an observation deck the actual components and consoles from which the first eight manned missions were monitored. Footage and interviews with some of the personnel are highlights of this area. Next to it are displays of some of the authentic *Mercury* and *Gemini* spacecraft, which enable visitors to relive some of the excitement and intensity of early space

The Vehicle Assembly Building, which dominates the flat landscape

exploration. KSC Tour buses leave every few minutes from the Visitor Complex and offer an exceptional tour of the space center's facilities. The tour encompasses two major facilities at the space center: the LC 39 Observation Gantry and the Apollo/Saturn V Center. The tour takes guests into secured areas, where guides explain the inner workings of each of the facilities. Visitors can take as long as they wish to explore each sight.

There are two additional special-interest tours that visitors can take at the center: **Cape Canaveral: Then & Now Tour**, which is a historic tour of the *Mercury*, *Gemini*, and *Apollo* launch pads; and the **NASA Up Close Tour**, which provides an insider's view of the entire space shuttle program. The NASA Up Close Tour includes within its ambit the International Space Station Center. Here, guests can walk through and peer inside the facility where each shuttle's components are assembled for launch.

Rockets on display at the Cape Canaveral Air Station

Space Center Tour

EACH SELF-GUIDED tour can take between two and six hours to fully explore the two facilities on the KSC Tour. Visitors can get a spectacular bird's-eye view of the gigantic launch pads from the 60-ft (18-m) observation tower at the first stop, the **LC 39 Observation Gantry**. Back on the ground, a film and exhibits tell the story of a NASA space shuttle launch and landing.

A commemmoration of the first moon landing of 1969, the spacious **Apollo/Saturn V Center** features an actual 363-ft (110-m) Saturn V moon rocket. Guests can view the historic launch of *Apollo 8*, the first manned mission to the moon, in the Firing Room Theater. They can follow this up by a film at the Lunar Theater, which shows actual footage of the moon landing. The only place in the world where guests can dine next to a genuine moon rock is also here, at the Moon Rock Café.

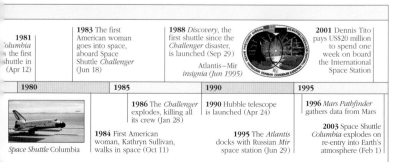

1981 Columbia is the first shuttle in (Apr 12)	1983 The first American woman goes into space, aboard Space Shuttle *Challenger* (Jun 18)	1988 *Discovery*, the first shuttle since the *Challenger* disaster, is launched (Sep 29) Atlantis–Mir insignia (Jun 1995)		2001 Dennis Tito pays US$20 million to spend one week on board the International Space Station
1980	**1985**	**1990**	**1995**	
Space Shuttle Columbia	1986 The *Challenger* explodes, killing all its crew (Jan 28) 1984 First American woman, Kathryn Sullivan, walks in space (Oct 11)	1990 Hubble telescope is launched (Apr 24) 1995 The *Atlantis* docks with Russian *Mir* space station (Jun 29)	1996 *Mars Pathfinder* gathers data from Mars 2003 Space Shuttle *Columbia* explodes on re-entry into Earth's atmosphere (Feb 1)	

Travelers' Needs

WHERE TO STAY

WITH AN extensive range of available accommodations and more than 100,000 hotel rooms in the area, Orlando caters to every budget and taste. A visitor can choose from neighborhood bed-and-breakfasts, off-the-beaten-track motels, resorts with in-room Jacuzzis and championship golf courses, ultra-luxurious penthouse suites, buildings shaped like giant guitars, and even rooms that overlook wandering herds of zebra and wildebeest. Outdoor enthusiasts, looking forward to sleeping under the stars, can access any of the

Logo of the Hard Rock Hotel

many campgrounds and trailer parks. If you are planning a long trip or are traveling in a big group, there are plenty of condos available for hire. The listings on pages 140–47 recommend a variety of places in Central Florida, all representing the best of their kind and in all the price ranges, from reasonable to extravagant. However, the prices tend to fluctuate depending on the season and the location. The Orlando/Orange County Convention & Visitors Bureau website can provide more detailed information on rooms and availability.

The opulent interior of the renowned Peabody Hotel, International Drive

HOTELS & RESORTS

MOST OF THE larger hotels and resorts in the area are fairly new or have been recently renovated. The smaller hotels, on the other hand, tend to be older and are well-established.

Widely prevalent and extremely popular, chain hotels have the advantage of at least being predictable – although prices vary depending on the location. Every chain is represented, from the high-end Radisson and Marriott hotels through the mid-range Holiday Inns to the budget Days Inn chain.

Resorts are large hotel complexes, usually set by the water and surrounded by acres of immaculately kept grounds. Prices are high, but these resorts provide various amenities, from swimming

pools and exercise rooms to shops and a wide range of world-class restaurants to choose from. With their well-equipped games rooms and special children's programs,

Disney's Palm Course, golfing paradise for amateurs and pros

these resorts can be a good option for families. Golf is a major attraction in Central Florida, and many resorts offer championship-level courses and instructors for private lessons. Themed resorts, designed around a particular era or activity such as sports or the films of the 1950s, are very popular.

Also designed to entertain are the traditional hotels, such as the Sheraton Safari with its African motif, the Red Horse Inn, decked out in Southwestern style, and the Doubletree Castle, with its towering spires and the Renaissance era music.

Only lacking the manicured acreage of the resorts, the grand hotels of Orlando are impressive in all other aspects. The Peabody Hotel, for instance, offers a fully-equipped athletic club with an Olympic-sized pool, tennis courts, and two excellent gourmet restaurants.

THE THEME PARK EXPERIENCE

WHEN THE DISNEY theme parks set up resorts right on their properties, it opened a whole new world of vacation possibilities *(see p135 & pp136–7)*. With several hotels literally within walking distance of a theme park or the Disney shopping area, the goal is to keep the attractions always in sight of

The brilliant exterior of the Hard Rock Hotel, Universal Studios

Universal Orlando is oriented more toward older children and adults than Disney. This is reflected in the main attractions of the two theme parks, and the "themes" of the three hotels on Universal property *(see p135 & p137)*. The Jurassic Park rides, The Amazing Adventures of Spider-Man, Back to the Future...The Ride, and Terminator 2: 3D are not for the Mickey Mouse-aged crowd. The lure of the Hard Rock Hotel, Portofino Bay, and the Royal Pacific Resort is also definitely adult oriented. The absence of any sports or recreational facilities here is more than made up by the shopping and dining options at Universal CityWalk. Placed between the two parks, it can make for an entertaining and exciting destination.

A relaxing massage at the Grand Floridian Resort & Spa

the entertainment-hungry visitor. Special package plans often include entry to the parks and transportation. Several shuttles and water-taxis connecting the parks and hotels are exclusively available for hotel guests.

In case parents equate theme parks with kid stuff, Disney property is also home to five 18-hole, PGA championship courses and training camps for the Atlanta Braves, the Orlando Rays, and the Tampa Bay Buccaneers ballteams. Recreational activities – such as surfing at the famous Typhoon Lagoon water park, golf, tennis, swimming, para-sailing, and horseback riding – are all included and within easy reach of the hotels.

Spa Hotels

Disney is the trendsetter of all things spa in Orlando, and hosts three world-class retreats on its property – the Saratoga Springs Resort & Spa, the Grand Floridian Resort & Spa with 900 rooms on an expansive 40-acre (16-ha) spread, and the 9,000-sq-ft (836-sq-m) Wyndham Palace Resort & Spa *(see pp141–42)*. Although all these are highly expensive stays compared to traditional hotels, the amenities provided here are difficult to

find anywhere else. Grand Floridian, in particular, offers beauty shops, facial, massage and water therapy, and a white-sand beach for relaxing.

The facilities at Westgate Lakes, just outside the Disney main gate on Lake Buena Vista, are typical of what local spas have to offer – personal attendants, facials, massages, steam rooms and saunas, whirlpools, and a full beauty salon. The Canyon Ranch Spa Club at the new Gaylord Palms Resort offers guests use of cardiovascular equipment, haircuts, and manicures along with body wraps and saunas. The internationally-renowned Mandara Spa from Indonesia has recently opened a center at Universal's Portofino Bay Hotel *(see p143)*.

The luxurious Grand Floridian Resort & Spa at Walt Disney World® Resort

The Hyatt Regency Hotel, Orlando International Airport

PLACES TO STAY AWAY FROM THE CROWDS

Hotels in Downtown Orlando and in smaller suburbs can offer high-end accommodations at much lower prices *(see pp143–7)*. Conveniently located inside the Orlando International Airport, Hyatt Regency is a good choice for travel-weary tourists and is only 16 miles (26 km) from Disney. Visitors using the Orlando-Sanford International Airport have a choice of several three- and four-star hotels in Sanford and Lake Mary. You can be far from the crowds at these hotels, and at the same time, within fairly easy reach of the theme parks. The attractive Park Plaza Hotel, in upscale Winter Park, has "garden suites" and bougainvillea-draped balconies. The Art Deco Westin Grand Bohemian Hotel in Downtown Orlando has 250 rooms as well as a AAA Four Diamond Award-winning restaurant.

BED-AND-BREAKFASTS

Travel to the north and east of Orlando for cosy and affordable B&Bs. Old-world hospitality and homes with antique furnishings are on offer here. Thurston House in Maitland is a Queen Anne Victorian home with fruit trees and lovely flower gardens. Higgins House, a quaint Victorian inn near the St. Johns River, is close to Sanford. If you're looking for a snug, romantic getaway, Mount Dora Historic Inn is a great option. The Courtyard at Lake Lucerne is a group of four historic buildings, built between 1883 and 1945, in Downtown Orlando. The PerriHouse Bed & Breakfast Inn is close to the Walt Disney World Resort and is surrounded by orange groves. All B&Bs offer short- and long-term stays, and guests often eat together in an informal atmosphere. The ambience and the personal touch of the hosts usually make up for the absence of the amenities offered by a full-service hotel.

Higgins House, a B&B near St. Johns River

CONDO RENTALS

Renting a condominium is a popular alternative to hotels and resorts. This is specially true for long-term stays or large family groups. One and two bedroom apartments tend to be near the theme parks; the larger homes are farther away.

Weekly apartments, townhouses, and full-size home rentals can cost the same as or less than a medium-rate hotel room. However, the in-house kitchens, private pools, and multiple bedrooms are very convenient and are good value for money. Most places require security deposits in advance, and also ask for cleaning fees. There is usually a minimum stay requirement too. If you wish to cancel your reservation, it is a good idea to notify the owners well in advance as the cancelation fees at most condos are fairly high.

A condo rental in Orlando, set amid lush green gardens

An elegant dining area setting at an Orlando lodging

How to Reserve

Rooms at the Disney and the Universal resorts can be booked when you buy the theme park tickets. Tickets can be purchased either by phone or online. The closer it is to busy season, the harder it might be to book a first-choice room, but rarely are resorts or larger hotels sold out. Online brokers such as **Priceline** and **Travelocity** can usually secure rooms, but many hotels hold back rooms for their telephone or website reservations. If a late check-in is expected, notify the hotel in advance. Many multi-day packages are also available from the theme parks as well as through travel agents.

Prices & Seasons

Room rates vary greatly, depending on the season and location. The busiest and most expensive periods are the holidays during November–April and summer vacation (June–August). Most hotels, even the high-priced chains, will often negotiate a lower rate if asked, but won't volunteer it. Be sure to ask for any special rates that might be available for senior citizens, students, frequent flyers, or corporate clients. Many resorts and non-park hotels offer packages that include theme park admissions and free shuttle services. Disney hotels will sometimes upgrade a room at no extra charge during "off-season," if asked.

Hidden Extras

Room rates are generally quoted exclusive of both sales tax and the so-called resort tax. These add up to 11 percent in Orlando and 12 percent in Kissimmee. The cost of making a phone call from a hotel room can be exorbitant. Some hotels offer free local phone calls from rooms, but most will add a surcharge for local calls or when dialing toll-free numbers. Using the hotel's dial-up service for Internet access could also incur a per-minute charge. Many hotels charge for valet parking services too.

Traveling with Children

Most hotels provide cribs, fold-away cots, and other facilities for children. The theme park resorts pay extra attention to children, offering baby-sitting services, child-friendly rooms, and fun-filled activities. Specially designed guided tours for children include the popular Hidden Mickey tours where kids search eagerly for the concealed Disney icon.

Kids checking in at a children-friendly hotel, Orlando

DIRECTORY

Theme Park Hotels

Walt Disney World Resorts
W http://disneyworld.disney.go.com/wdw/resorts/resortOverview

Downtown Disney Hotels
W www.downtowndisneyhotels.com

Universal Orlando Resorts
W www.UniversalOrlando.com

Hotel Rentals

Hotel Locators
W www.hotellocators.com

Orlando.com
W www.orlando.com

Just Orlando Hotels
W www.justorlandohotels.com

Travelocity
W www.travelocity.com

Hotwire.com
W www.hotwire.com

Priceline
W www.priceline.com

Bed-and-Breakfasts

AAA Auto Club South
W www.aaasouth.com

Florida Bed & Breakfasts Inns
W www.florida-inns.com

Bed & Breakfasts Online
W www.bbonline.com/fl/orlando.html

Condo & Apartment Rentals

Villas of the World
W www.villasoftheworld.com

CheapTickets.com
W http://cheaptickets.skyauction.com

Florida Homes & Condos
W www.disneycondo.com

Staying at the Theme Parks

WHEN WALT DISNEY started buying untouched Florida wilderness in the late 1960s, he began a multi-billion dollar industry that would change the culture of sleepy citrus town Orlando forever. Currently, the area in and around the theme parks has several thousands of hotel, motel, and resort rooms – and many more are being created – for the never-ending stream of tourists flocking each year to Disney World, Universal Orlando, and SeaWorld. The descriptions on these pages highlight accommodations on theme park property or those located nearby.

A giant replica of Woody at All Star Movie Resort, WDW Resort

WALT DISNEY WORLD® RESORTS

DISNEY PROPERTY has the largest collection of resorts in Orlando, with offerings to suit every pocket and taste (*see p135 & pp140–42*).

The opening of Walt Disney World's Pop Century Resort in 2003 – with 2,880 rooms – was the largest single hotel opening in Disney's history. It joined the ranks of the 23 resort hotels directly owned by the parks. Dedicated to American fashions and fads, Pop Century features icons and relics from the 1950s to the 1990s, such as a larger-than-life Rubik's Cube and Sony Walkman, as well as giant bowling pins and yo-yos. All-Star Resorts, the triple-treat of movie, sports, and music-themed hotels, are the least expensive of all on-site lodgings.

The Animal Kingdom Lodge is advantageously located on the western edge of Disney's newest theme park. Most of its 1,293 rooms include balconies overlooking three savannas, and provide breathtaking views of more than 200 grazing animals and birds, including giraffes, zebra, ibis, and ostriches. Guest rooms include a Royal Suite, with a domed ceiling, a kitchen and a dining room, and sweeping porches. The resort is also host to two of the best restaurants on Disney property.

The two massive hotels that make up the Swan and Dolphin resorts offer almost 2,270 rooms, including 191 special suites themed to Italian, Egyptian, Japanese, and Southwest decor.

Disney's Port Orleans Resort echoes the majestic mansions and row houses of romantic Louisiana. The Beach Club Resort transports Nantucket Bay to Orlando with access to the 25-acre (10-ha)

Visitor enjoying the slide at Old Man Island, Port Orleans Resort

Crescent Lake facility, where canopy and paddleboats are available, as well as the Stormalong Bay water park for the kids.

HOTELS AT WALT DISNEY WORLD® RESORT

DOWNTOWN DISNEY hosts seven excellent hotels on its property. Those closest to most of the attractions include Best Western Lake Buena Vista, literally a brisk walk from the Downtown Disney shopping and entertainment area; Hilton, the only hotel to offer "Extra Magic Hour," which allows guests staying at the hotel to enter the Disney theme parks one hour prior to the general opening; Doubletree Guest

Rooms offering views of wild animals grazing, Animal Kingdom Lodge

Holiday Inn Family Suites Resorts, near Walt Disney World® Resort

HOTELS & MOTELS NEAR THE PARKS

M OST PLACES TO STAY form concentric rings around both Disney and Universal, diminishing in price the farther away they get from Main Street. But some of the most affordable hotels are just beyond the front door of the parks. The two AmeriSuites hotels, with rooms at less than a third of the price at the Hard Rock Hotel, are under a mile (1.6 km) from Universal. The Caribe Royale All-Suites Resort, virtually right outside Disney's doors, and with 1,200 rooms and 120 villas, manages to be less expensive than many of the resorts on Disney property.

Bargains can be found within sight of the parks, many offering amenities such as pools and restaurants. There are thousands of hotels in the area. Sand Lake Road, north of Interstate 4, has several miles of motels and hotels of all ranges, many offering free shuttles to the parks and concierge service for tickets to other attractions. To the south of I-4 is International Drive, a long stretch of commercial properties and outlet malls, with places to stay that range from seedy no-name motels to five-star resorts. To the north and east are the grand hotels of Downtown Orlando and smaller motel chains on Colonial Drive.

Suites, with on-site ticket sales and free shuttles to the parks; Holiday Inn, a 323-room hotel featuring a 14-story atrium; Hotel Royal Plaza, with tennis courts and spa; Wyndham Palace, featuring the award-winning Arthur's 27 restaurant and Disney character breakfasts; and last but not the least, Grosvenor Resort, a British-themed complex which offers special packages for meals and theme park admission. The 626-room Grosvenor is heavily steeped in Florida amenities, including Disney character meals for the kids and a huge Aquatic Center with heated swimming pools, a thermal spa, and beach volleyball. Each hotel has at least one full-service restaurant.

UNIVERSAL ORLANDO RESORTS & HOTELS

H OTELS ON Universal grounds are located along the perimeter of the two parks – the Islands of Adventure and Universal Studios Florida. Most of the hotels offer themed vacation packages in keeping with Universal's somewhat more adult image *(see p135 & p143)*. The Royal Pacific takes its cue from a tropical island paradise, offering a lagoon-style swimming pool and sand beach, transportation by water taxi to the parks, an orchid-draped courtyard, and five restaurants, including Emeril's Hawaiian-inspired Tchoup Chop. The Portofino Bay Hotel is a faithful re-creation of a seaside resort in Italy, with cobble streets and

outdoor cafés, bocce ball courts, and a full spa and fitness center. For those with rock star dreams, the Hard Rock Hotel features rock memorabilia in every room, an "exclusive" seventh-floor Club level with a lounge and music library, and an underwater audio system in the pool. The hotel's Graceland Suite, a tribute to Elvis, is of gigantic proportions.

All these three hotels are pet-friendly, with special rooms and a room-service menu for four-legged guests.

The Universal Express service, offered by all the hotels, allows guests access to all the park rides without having to wait in long lines. In addition, it also provides priority seating at the hotel restaurants, of which there are many to choose from.

Universal's Portofino Bay Hotel, a replica of an Italian seaside resort

Camping & Trailer Parks

THOSE WITH AN OUTDOOR spirit and the desire to sleep under the stars can find accommodations in Central Florida that range from a tent in the woods to modern, almost luxurious RV camps, complete with swimming pools and clubhouses. Visitors can choose from a wide range of campsites – on state land and private Kampgrounds of America (KOA) parks, and even right on Disney property. Depending on the season, pitching a tent can be fairly inexpensive or can cost as much as a good hotel. RV parks can help tourists on a tight budget save thousands of dollars. In fact, many regular visitors reserve special spots in these parks for years.

Campers picnicking at Disney's Fort Wilderness Resort & Campground

CAMPING

OFFERING THE finest campsite amenities, Disney World stakes out 700 camping spaces at the **Fort Wilderness Resort & Campground** (see p73), with sites ranging from spartan to luxurious. This pet-friendly resort offers charcoal

Boating in scenic heaven, Wekiwa Springs State Park

grills, electric golf carts, cable TV hook-ups, and campfire singalongs. Prices here range from $40 to $80 per night; cabins cost $200 to $300.

Other camping sites also have cabins, priced from $30 to $70 depending on season, which can sleep four to eight people. Many of the Disney-centric campgrounds are located just off US Route 192 in Kissimmee.

Campsites are to be found all across Central Florida. The **East Lake Fish Camp** in Kissimmee combines outdoor living with Florida's fresh-water bounty, offering some of the best bass in the world.

Of all local campgrounds, **Wekiwa Springs State Park** is the most rustic, and most typical of authentic Florida. Open year-round, it is located on the Wekiva River, with 8,000 acres (3,237 ha) of wild scenery that has remained unchanged for centuries.

RV PARKS

RV CAMPS ARE very popular with cross-country travelers, especially visitors from the far North. Most camps offer all the amenities of resort living, including pools and fitness centers, clubhouses and movie theaters, laundry facilities, cable television and electrical hook-ups, as well as the splendor of the great Florida outdoors. RV site rates vary and can range from $30 a night to almost $400 per month. Permanent spots are also available for those who choose to return every year.

Just 5 miles (8 km) from Disney is the largest RV and trailer park in the area, the **Encore RV Resort**. Located in Clermont, it is host to 467 sites with electrical, water, and sewage hook-ups, two heated pools, a fitness center with a Jacuzzi, shuffleboard courts, tennis courts, laundry, cable TV and telephone services, and social activities such as bingo and dances.

KOA Kissimmee/Orlando is Orlando's nearest KOA Campground. It is just 5 miles (8 km) from Disney, 6 miles (9.6 km) from SeaWorld, and 8 miles (13 km) from Universal. Patio sites with picnic tables, casual furniture, and Mexican chimineas are on offer here.

The **Tropical Palms Fun Resort** in Kissimmee offers campers access to swimming pools, private cottages with air conditioning and kitchens, watercraft rentals, picnic areas, and nearby restaurants.

Picturesque cabins at Orlando SW/ Fort Summit KOA Campground

DIRECTORY

RV & CAMPING CENTERS

Florida Association of RV Parks and Campgrounds
1340 Vickers Rd,
Tallahassee.
(850) 562-7151.
W www.floridacamping.com

Florida Department of Environmental Protection (State Parks)
3800 Commonwealth Blvd,
Tallahassee.
(850) 245-2157.
W www.dep.state.fl.us/parks

KOA Campgrounds
(406) 248-7444.
W www.koa.com

Passport America
(800) 283-7183.
W www.passport-america.com

RV on the Go
2650 Holiday Trail,
Kissimmee.
W www.rvonthego.com

CAMPSITES

Canoe Creek Campground
4101 Canoe Creek Rd, St. Cloud.
(407) 892-7010.

Citrus Valley Campground
2500 US Hwy 27 S, Clermont.
(352) 394-4051.

Cypress Cove Nudist Resort & Spa
4425 S Pleasant Hills Rd,
Kissimmee.
(407) 933-5870.

East Lake Fish Camp
3705 Big Bass Rd,
Kissimmee.
(407) 348-2040.

Orlando SW/Fort Summit KOA
Lake Buena Vista, Orlando.
(800) 424-1880.

Fort Wilderness Resort & Campground
4510 N Fort Wilderness Trail,
Lake Buena Vista, Orlando.
(407) 824-2900.

Gator RV Resort
5755 E Irlo Bronson Hwy,
Rte 192/441, St. Cloud.
(407) 892-8662.

KOA Kissimmee/Orlando Campground
2644 Happy Camper Place,
Kissimmee.
(407) 396-2400.

Orange Blossom RV Resort LLC
3800 W Orange Blossom Trail,
Apopka.
(407) 886-3260.

Orange Grove Campground
2425 Old Vineland Rd, Kissimmee.
(407) 396-6655 .

Orlando Lake Whippoorwill KOA
12345 Narcoossee Rd,
Orlando.
(407) 277-5075.

Outdoor World – Orlando Resort
13800 SR 545,
Winter Garden.
(407) 239-8774.

Sanlan Ranch Campground
3929 US Hwy 98 S, Lakeland.
(800) 524-5044.

Southport Park Campground & Marina
2001 W Southport Rd,
Kissimmee.
(407) 933-5822.

Stage Stop Campground
14400 W Colonial Dr,
Winter Garden.
(407) 656-8000.

Tropical Palms Fun Resort
2650 Holiday Trail,
Kissimmee.
(800) 647-2567;
(407) 396-4595.

Twelve Oaks RV Resort
6300 State Route 46,
W Sanford.
(800) 633-9529.

Wekiwa Springs State Park
1800 Wekiwa Circle, Apopka.
(407) 884-2008.

Yogi Bear's Jellystone Park Camp Resort
8555 W Irlo Bronson Hwy (US 192),
Kissimmee.
(407) 239-4148.

RV PARKS

Aloha RV Park
4648 S Orange Blossom Trail,
Kissimmee.
(407) 933-5730.

Camp City of Orlando RV Resort
5150 Boggy Creek Rd,
St. Cloud.
(407) 892-5171.

Encore RV Resort
9600 Hwy 192,
West Clermont.
(888) 558-5777.

Fairview Mobile Court
4462 Edgewater Dr,
Orlando.
(407) 293-8581.

Great Oak RV Resort
4440 Yowell Rd,
Kissimmee.
(407) 396-9092.

Merry D RV Sanctuary
4261 Pleasant Hill Rd,
Kissimmee.
(407) 870-0719.

Paradise Island RV Resort
2900 S US Hwy 27,
Haines City.
(863) 439-1350.

Ponderosa RV Park
1983 Boggy Creek Rd,
Kissimmee.
(407) 847-6002.

Secret Lake RV Resort
8550 W Irlo Bronson Hwy
(West 192),
Kissimmee.
(407) 396-6101.

Sherwood Forest RV Park
5300 W Irlo Bronson Hwy,
Kissimmee.
(407) 396-7431.

Choosing a Hotel

THE HOTELS IN THIS GUIDE have been selected across a wide price range for their good value, facilities, and location. This chart highlights some of the factors that may influence your choice. Hotels are listed by region, beginning with the Walt Disney World Resort. All the entries are listed alphabetically within each price category.

Hotel	Credit Cards	Children's Facilities	Swimming Pool	Restaurant	Number of Rooms
WALT DISNEY WORLD® RESORT					
ANIMAL KINGDOM: *Disney's All-Star Movie Resort* $$ 1991 W Buena Vista Dr. ☎ *(407) 939-7000.* [FAX] *(407) 939-7111.* Low prices and pop-culture icons make this a very popular resort. Disney movie symbols, such as giant Dalmatians and the 25-ft (7.6-m) Buzz Lightyear, are sure to capture the interest of the video generation.	AE DC MC V	●	■	●	1900
ANIMAL KINGDOM: *Disney's All-Star Music Resort* $$$ 1801 W Buena Vista Dr. ☎ *(407) 939-6000.* [FAX] *(407) 939-7222.* The theme is music, music, and more music. From the bedspreads to the walk-through jukebox, the resort creates a musically charged ambience. The rooms are pleasant.	AE DC MC V	●	■		1920
ANIMAL KINGDOM: *Disney's All-Star Sports Resort* $$$ 1701 W Buena Vista Dr. ☎ *(407) 939-5000.* [FAX] *(407) 939-7333.* Overwhelmingly sports-oriented, the hotel will prove to be a delight for sport fans. The resort shares most of its facilities, including the huge pools, with the neighboring All-Star Music Resort.	AE DC MC V	●	■		1920
ANIMAL KINGDOM: *Holiday Inn Hotel & Suites Maingate* $$$ 5678 W Irlo Bronson Hwy. ☎ *(407) 396-4488.* [FAX] *(407) 396-1296.* Children rule here – there is even a kids' check-in desk. Clowns form an important part of the hotel's entourage and are also in charge of activities at a children's camp, 3 miles (5 km) outside Walt Disney World.	AE DC MC V	●	■		614
ANIMAL KINGDOM: *Disney's Pop Century Resort* $$$$ 1050 Century Dr, Lake Buena Vista. ☎ *(407) 938-4000.* [FAX] *(407) 938-4040.* One of Disney's most popular hotels. Massive yo-yos and a giant Sony Walkman form part of the decor in the themed rooms. Kids love the huge food court and the room service pizza.	AE DC MC V	●	■	●	2880
ANIMAL KINGDOM: *Animal Kingdom Lodge* $$$$$ 2901 Osceola Parkway, Bay Lake. ☎ *(407) 934-7639.* [FAX] *(407) 938-4799.* An exceptional resort, the 5-story African *kraal* was hand-thatched by African artisans, and the lobby is worth a visit even if you're staying elsewhere. Balcony suites overlook a 30-acre (12-ha) savanna with wildlife on display.	AE DC MC V	●	■	●	1293
DISNEY-MGM STUDIOS: *Coronado Springs Resort* $$ 1000 W Buena Vista Dr, Lake Buena Vista. ☎ *(407) 939-1000.* [FAX] *(407) 939-1001.* Located between Disney's Animal Kingdom and Disney-MGM Studios, the resort consists of three themed villages, Casitas, Ranchos, and Cabanas. Has American Southwest-style bungalows and a huge pool.	AE DC MC V	●	■	●	2112
DOWNTOWN DISNEY: *Sheraton Safari* $$ 12205 Apopka-Vineland Rd. ☎ *(407) 239-0444.* [FAX] *(407) 239-4566.* [W] *www.sheratonsafari.com* An "African Safari" theme runs through the hotel. Kids love playing on the giant water slide and in the wading pools. The resort also offers 90 "Safari Suites" with kitchenettes and a parlor.	AE DC MC V	●	■	●	489
DOWNTOWN DISNEY: *Best Western* $$$ 2000 Hotel Plaza Blvd, Lake Buena Vista. ☎ *(407) 828-2424.* [FAX] *(407) 828-8933.* [W] *www.orlandoresorthotel.com* @ *reservations@orlandoresorthotel.com* Set in a lush garden atmosphere, this upscale, full-service hotel has guest rooms with private, furnished balconies offering views of Lake Buena Vista and the Walt Disney World Resort area.	AE DC MC V	●	■	●	325
DOWNTOWN DISNEY: *Grosvenor Resort* $$$ 1850 Hotel Plaza Blvd, Lake Buena Vista. ☎ *(407) 828-4444.* [FAX] *(407) 828-8192.* An elegant hotel with a colonial theme. The resort features pleasant rooms and is host to a wide range of facilities.	AE DC MC V	●	■	●	626

		Price categories / Legend		CREDIT CARDS	CHILDREN'S FACILITIES	SWIMMING POOL	RESTAURANT	NUMBER OF ROOMS

Price categories for a standard double room per night in high season, including tax and service charges:

$ under $60
$$ $60–$100
$$$ $100–$150
$$$$ $150–$200
$$$$$ over $200

CHILDREN'S FACILITIES
A child-friendly hotel, with cribs, high chairs, and other facilities that may include a baby-sitting service and special children's programs.

SWIMMING POOL
The hotel has a swimming pool for use by residents.

RESTAURANT
The hotel has a restaurant or dining room open to both residents and non-residents unless otherwise stated.

NUMBER OF ROOMS
The hotel has the listed number of rooms available for prospective guests.

Listing	Credit Cards	Children's Facilities	Swimming Pool	Restaurant	Number of Rooms
DOWNTOWN DISNEY: *PerriHouse Bed & Breakfast Inn* $$$ 10417 Vista Oaks Court. (407) 876-4830. FAX (407) 876-0241. www.perrihouse.com birds@perrihouse.com A quiet and secluded country inn on a 16-acre (6-ha) nature preserve adjacent to Walt Disney World. Perfect for families. Comfortable rooms feature cherry and oak furnishings.	AE DC MC V	●	▥		8
DOWNTOWN DISNEY: *Blue Tree Resort* $$$$ 12007 Cypress Run Rd. (407) 238-6000. FAX (407) 239-0680. Rental condo resort on 16 manicured acres (6 ha), a mile from Disney property. Tennis, volleyball, basketball, and miniature golf on the premises are on offer at this country club setting. Accommodations are available for two to six guests.	AE DC MC V	●	▥		275
DOWNTOWN DISNEY: *Doubletree Guest Suites* $$$$ 2305 Hotel Plaza Blvd, Lake Buena Vista. (407) 934-1000. FAX (407) 934-1015. www.doubletreeguestsuites.com The only all-suite hotel actually on Disney property. A full-service hotel offering one- or two-bedroom suites with dining areas, separate living rooms, and kitchen facilities.	AE DC MC V	●	▥	●	229
DOWNTOWN DISNEY: *Hilton in the Walt Disney World® Resort* $$$$ 1751 Hotel Plaza Blvd, Lake Buena Vista. (407) 827-4000. FAX (407) 827-3890. Surrounded by 23 acres (9 ha) of landscaped grounds and within walking distance of Downtown Disney Marketplace. The only Downtown Disney hotel to offer Disney's Extra Magic Hour, which allows guests to enter Disney theme parks one hour prior to opening.	AE DC MC V	●	▥	●	810
DOWNTOWN DISNEY: *Hotel Royal Plaza* $$$$ 1905 Hotel Plaza Blvd, Lake Buena Vista. (407) 828-2828. FAX (407) 827-6338. www.royalplaza.com Get ready to be pampered. On offer are rooms with whirlpool tubs and balconies with breathtaking views, a fully equipped fitness center, and preferred tee times at five Disney championship golf courses. Free shuttles are also available to all Disney theme parks.	AE DC MC V	●	▥	●	394
DOWNTOWN DISNEY: *Port Orleans Resort – Riverside* $$$$ 1000 W Buena Vista Dr, Lake Buena Vista. (407) 934-6000. FAX (407) 934-5777. An antebellum, Southern-style resort, with Dixie mansions lining a picturesque, Mississippi-style waterway. Two unique vacation villages, Magnolia Bend and Alligator Bayou, comprise this hotel.	AE DC MC V	●	▥	●	2048
DOWNTOWN DISNEY: *Disney's Old Key West Resort* $$$$$ 1510 N Cove Rd. (407) 827-7700. FAX (407) 827-7710. This popular resort is remarkably successful in re-creating the atmosphere of Old Key West. Ceiling fans, picket fences, and palm trees form part of the decor. Recreational facilities abound.	AE DC MC V	●	▥	●	761
DOWNTOWN DISNEY: *Disney's Saratoga Springs Resort & Spa* $$$$$ 1960 Broadway, Lake Buena Vista. (407) 827-1100. FAX (407) 827-1151. This luxurious resort offers full-day programs of skin therapy, soothing body treatments, and workouts in the health club of the Victorian-style spa. The Artist's Palette restaurant is one of the best on Disney property.	AE DC MC V		▥	●	2005
DOWNTOWN DISNEY: *Wyndham Palace Resort & Spa* $$$$$ 1900 Buena Vista Dr, Lake Buena Vista. (407) 827-2727. FAX (407) 827-3472. If you're looking for a relaxing and refreshing experience, this is the place to be. The rooms are done up in calming earthy tones. The resort features a host of restaurants and facilities.	AE DC MC V	●	▥	●	1014
EPCOT: *Disney's Caribbean Beach Resort* $$$$ 900 Cayman Way. (407) 934-3400. FAX (407) 934-3288. Five cheerful "villages" with attractive rooms are situated around a lake where waterbirds congregate. Pools and artificial white sand beaches dot the property and contribute to a tropical feel.	AE DC MC V	●	▥		2112

For key to symbols see back flap

Price categories for a standard double room per night in high season, including tax and service charges:

$ under $60
$$ $60–$100
$$$ $100–$150
$$$$ $150–$200
$$$$$ over $200

CHILDREN'S FACILITIES
A child-friendly hotel, with cribs, high chairs, and other facilities that may include a baby-sitting service and special children's programs.

SWIMMING POOL
The hotel has a swimming pool for use by residents.

RESTAURANT
The hotel has a restaurant or dining room open to both residents and non-residents unless otherwise stated.

NUMBER OF ROOMS
The hotel has the listed number of rooms available for prospective guests.

	CREDIT CARDS	CHILDREN'S FACILITIES	SWIMMING POOL	RESTAURANT	NUMBER OF ROOMS
EPCOT: *Disney's Beach Club Resort* $$$$$ 1800 Epcot Resorts Blvd. (407) 934-8000. FAX (407) 354-1866. Echoing the style of New England's grand hotels of the 1870s, this resort has exquisite rooms, extensive facilities, and one of the best restaurants in Walt Disney World.	AE DC MC V	●	▦	●	621
EPCOT: *Disney's BoardWalk Inn* $$$$$ 2101 N Epcot Resorts Blvd. (407) 939-5100. FAX (407) 939-5150. This elegant inn re-creates the ambience of an old-world bed-and-breakfast. Floral rugs and hardwood floors form the decor and the rooms are quite pleasant.	AE DC MC V	●	▦		378
EPCOT: *Disney's BoardWalk Villas* $$$$$ 2101 N Epcot Resorts Blvd. (407) 939-5100. FAX (407) 939-5150. Opened in 1996, these villas were designed as New England-style "seaside" cottages. Known for their comfortable lodgings, the villas are an ideal option for families.	AE DC MC V	●	▦		532
EPCOT: *Disney's Yacht Club Resort* $$$$$ 1700 Epcot Resorts Blvd. (407) 934-7000. FAX (407) 934-3450. Styled like a posh Cape Cod yacht club, with brass fittings and charts on the walls, this lavish resort shares its wide range of facilities with the neighboring Beach Club.	AE DC MC V	●	▦		630
EPCOT: *Walt Disney World Dolphin* $$$$$ 1500 Epcot Resorts Blvd. (407) 934-4000. FAX (407) 934-4099. Famous for its architecturally arresting structure, the urbane Dolphin caters primarily to a business clientele.	AE DC MC V	●	▦	●	1510
EPCOT: *Walt Disney World Swan* $$$$$ 1200 Epcot Resorts Blvd. (407) 934-3000. FAX (407) 934-4499. Topped by two swans, 5-stories high, this hotel offers colorful rooms and some of the best dining in the park. The swan theme is evident throughout.	AE DC MC V	●	▦	●	758
FORT WILDERNESS: *Disney's Wilderness Lodge* $$$$$ 901 Timberline Dr. (407) 824-3000. FAX (407) 824-3232. An isolated, romantic "mountain retreat" with wooden floors and crackling fires. This is the ideal place to unwind.	AE DC MC V	●	▦		728
MAGIC KINGDOM: *Shades of Green on Walt Disney World® Resort* $$$ 1950 W Magnolia Palm Dr. (407) 824-3400. FAX (407) 824-3665. W www.shadesofgreen.org Leased by the Department of Defense, the resort is only for retired and active military personnel and their families, as well as members of the reserves and the National Guard.	AE DC MC V	●	▦	●	586
MAGIC KINGDOM: *Disney's Contemporary Resort* $$$$$ 4600 N World Dr. (407) 824-1000. FAX (407) 824-3539. This slick, lively resort is connected to both Epcot and the Magic Kingdom by the monorail. Offers Art Deco-style rooms.	AE DC MC V	●	▦	●	1008
MAGIC KINGDOM: *Disney's Grand Floridian Resort & Spa* $$$$$ 4401 Grand Floridian Way. (407) 824-3000. FAX (407) 824-3186. Verandas, oak beds, and Victorian-style opulence offer a taste of old Florida. Indulge yourself with the many facilities provided for your enjoyment.	AE DC MC V	●	▦	●	900
MAGIC KINGDOM: *Disney's Polynesian Resort* $$$$$ 1600 Seven Seas Dr, Lake Buena Vista. (407) 824-2000. FAX (407) 824-3174. Located right on the monorail line passing through the Disney theme parks. Waterfalls, gardens, a tropical lagoon swimming area, and a white sand beach offer a peek into the *Pirates of the Caribbean* fantasy.	AE DC MC V	●	▦	●	855

OTHER THEME PARKS

SeaWorld: *Hilton Garden Inn Orlando SeaWorld International Center* $$$
6850 Westwood Blvd. (407) 354-1500. FAX (407) 354-1528.
A splash away from SeaWorld, this is a mid-priced Hilton for business travelers. Offers free, high-speed Internet access in every room and a 24-hour business center. The lobby has a 24-hour convenience mart.
AE DC MC V — 233

SeaWorld: *Renaissance Orlando Resort at SeaWorld* $$$$
6677 Sea Harbor Dr. (407) 351-5555. FAX (407) 351-9991.
Has huge rooms and a 10-story landscaped tropical atrium lobby. Five restaurants, sports facilities, a 2-story aviary, and an Olympic-sized pool echo the "large" theme of this resort.
AE DC MC V — 778

SeaWorld: *Residence Inn Orlando SeaWorld/International Center* $$$$
11000 Westwood Blvd. (407) 313-3600. FAX (407) 313-3611.
W www.residenceinnseaworld.com This all-suite hotel is just a brisk walk away from SeaWorld. Free shuttles to the theme park are also available. Also offers high-speed Internet access in rooms.
AE DC MC V — 350

Universal Orlando: *Hawthorn Suites Universal Studios* $$$$
7601 Canada Ave. (407) 581-2151. FAX (407) 581-2152. W www.hawthorn.com
A free one-mile (1.6-km) shuttle away from Universal and near the Sand Lake Road restaurant row, this simple hotel is a good place to rest and recuperate when the theme park excitement is over.
AE DC MC V — 143

Universal Orlando: *Portofino Bay Hotel & Resort* $$$$$
5601 Universal Blvd. (407) 503-1000. W www.loewshotels.com
Enjoy a ride on the scheduled gondola taxis at this re-created Italian fantasy resort. Stylish rooms and all the facilities you could need are available here.
AE DC MC V — 750

Universal Orlando: *Hard Rock Hotel®* $$$$$
5800 Universal Blvd. (407) 503-7625. FAX (407) 503-7655. W www.loewshotels.com
Designed along the lines of a California Mission-style hotel, this resort is very popular with tourists. Hosts the largest heated pool in Orlando.
AE DC MC V — 650

Universal Orlando: *Royal Pacific Resort* $$$$$
6300 Hollywood Way. (407) 503-3000. FAX (407) 503-3202.
A new resort, it boasts Emeril's newest restaurant on the premises. A beautiful orchid garden and pools follow a tropical theme, and hotel guests get special access to Universal rides.
AE DC MC V — 1000

ORLANDO & CENTRAL FLORIDA

Cape Canaveral: *Radisson Resort at the Port* $$$
8701 Astronaut Blvd. (321) 784-0000. FAX (321) 784-3737. W www.radisson.com
Ceiling fans and wicker give this resort a Caribbean feel. Just a ten-minute drive from the Kennedy Space Center, it offers convenient sightseeing opportunities.
AE DC MC V — 285

Celebration: *Celebration Hotel* $$$$$
700 Bloom St. (407) 566-6000. FAX (407) 566-1844. W www.celebrationhotel.com
This popular hotel, situated in the heart of the Disney-built town of Celebration, overlooks a lake. Offers superior service and a superb restaurant, with hardwood floors, ceiling fans, and rocking chairs on the porch.
AE MC V — 115

Cocoa: *Econo Lodge Space Center* $$
3220 N Cocoa Blvd, US 1. (321) 632-4561, (888) 721-9423. FAX (321) 631-3756.
Nothing spectacular, but adequate and clean. Located just 8 miles (13 km) from the Kennedy Space Center.
AE DC MC V — 150

Cocoa Beach: *Comfort Inn & Suites Hotel & Conference Center* $$$
3901 N Atlantic Ave. (321) 783-2221. FAX (321) 783-0461.
W www.comfortinncocoabeach.com Positioned just a hop, skip, and jump from the beach. The inn opens onto a palm-shaded, pool-side area with barbecue grills.
AE DC MC V — 170

Cocoa Beach: *Inn at Cocoa Beach* $$$$$
4300 Ocean Beach Blvd. (321) 799-3460. FAX (321) 784-8632.
W www.theinnatcocoabeach.com The patios and balconies at this quaint bed-and-breakfast offer a beautiful view of the sea. The room decor ranges from modern to traditional.
AE DC MC V — 50

Price categories for a standard double room per night in high season, including tax and service charges:

$ under $60
$$ $60–$100
$$$ $100–$150
$$$$ $150–$200
$$$$$ over $200

CHILDREN'S FACILITIES
A child-friendly hotel, with cribs, high chairs, and other facilities that may include a baby-sitting service and special children's programs.

SWIMMING POOL
The hotel has a swimming pool for use by residents.

RESTAURANT
The hotel has a restaurant or dining room open to both residents and non-residents unless otherwise stated.

NUMBER OF ROOMS
The hotel has the listed number of rooms available for prospective guests.

	Price	CREDIT CARDS	CHILDREN'S FACILITIES	SWIMMING POOL	RESTAURANT	NUMBER OF ROOMS
CYPRESS GARDENS: *Best Western Admiral's Inn* 5665 Cypress Gardens Blvd. ((863) 324-5950. FAX (863) 324-2376. The beautiful Cypress Gardens are just a step away from this charming inn. Offers comfortable (though not fancy) rooms. 🚶♿📶🛎️🅿️🔳🚭📺	$$	AE DC MC V	●	▥	●	156
DAYTONA BEACH: *Coquina Inn Bed & Breakfast* 544 S Palmetto Ave. ((386) 254-4969. W www.coquinainndaytonabeach.com @ CoquinaBnB@aol.com This 1912 home, on a quiet tree-lined street in the historic district, has beautifully furnished rooms with oak floors and ceiling fans. The elaborate breakfast is a delight. 📶🛎️🅿️🚭	$$	AE DC MC V				4
DAYTONA BEACH: *Inn on the Beach* 1615 S Atlantic Ave. ((386) 255-0921. FAX (386) 944-0182. W www.innonthebeach.com This budget oceanfront hotel has spacious kitchen facilities in the rooms, a sundeck, and swimming pools for both adults and kids. 🚶♿📶🛎️🅿️🚭	$$	AE DC MC V	●	▥		195
DAYTONA BEACH: *Adam's Mark* 100 N Atlantic Ave. ((386) 254-8200. FAX (386) 253-0275. W www.adamsmark.com/daytonabeach Overlooking the beach boardwalk, this is Daytona's most stylish resort. It has several restaurants, a health club, a disco, and a playground for children. 🚶♿📶🛎️🅿️🔳🚭📺	$$$$	AE DC MC V	●	▥	●	742
DAYTONA BEACH: *Bahama House* 2001 S Atlantic Ave. ((800) 571-2000. FAX (386) 248-0991. W www.daytonabahamahouse.com This friendly Bahamas-themed establishment offers bleached-wood furnishings and kitchen facilities in the rooms; some units have Jacuzzis. Plenty of children's activities too. 🚶♿📶🛎️🅿️🚭	$$$$$	AE DC MC V	●	▥		95
DOWNTOWN ORLANDO: *The Courtyard at Lake Lucerne* 211 N Lucerne Circle E. ((407) 648-5188. FAX (407) 246-1368. W www.orlandohistoricinn.com This well-run B&B is situated in a quiet garden beside Lake Lucerne. It comprises four historic houses, one of which is the oldest in town. 🅿️🔳	$$$$	AE DC MC V			●	30
DOWNTOWN ORLANDO: *Eō Inn & Urban Spa* 227 N Eola Dr. ((407) 481-8485. FAX (407) 481-8495. W www.eoinn.com This has a tailored, urban decor, with "smart rooms" for the business traveler and a full day spa with massages and facials for the hedonist. Hosts the trendy Panera café and the views of Lake Eola are breathtaking. 🚶📶🛎️🔳🚭📺	$$$$	AE DC MC V			●	17
DOWNTOWN ORLANDO: *The Veranda* 115 N Summerlin Ave. (& FAX (407) 849-0321. The only B&B in the fashionable Thornton Park area near Lake Eola, it consists of five historic buildings centered around a courtyard dating back to the early 1900s. 🚶📶🛎️🅿️🚭	$$$$	AE DC MC V				12
DOWNTOWN ORLANDO: *Westin Grand Bohemian* 325 S Orange Ave. ((866) 663-0024. FAX (407) 313-9001. W www.grandbohemianhotel.com Almost decadently luxurious, this hotel showcases classic and contemporary works by locally and internationally renowned artists. 📶🔳🕐🚭📺🏋️	$$$$$	AE DC MC V	●	▥	●	286
INTERNATIONAL DRIVE: *Adam's Mark Orlando* 1500 Sand Lake Rd. ((407) 859-1500. FAX (407) 855-1585. W www.adamsmark.com/orlando/ An ideal combination of luxury, low prices, and a location inside the Florida Mall. From the single-bed rooms to the two bi-level presidential suites, there is something for everyone. 🅿️🚶📶🛎️🔳🚭📺	$$	AE DC MC V	●	▥	●	510
INTERNATIONAL DRIVE: *Best Western MovieLand* 6233 International Dr. ((407) 351-3900. FAX (407) 352-5597. W www.bestwesternmovieland.com Within splashing distance of Wet 'n' Wild and just a mile away from Universal Orlando. The large rooms and the low prices make this hotel a tempting proposition. 🚶♿📶🔳🚭📺	$$	AE DC MC V		▥	●	261

INTERNATIONAL DRIVE: *Red Horse Inn* $$ AE DC MC V   159
5825 International Dr. (*407*) *351-4100.* FAX (*407*) *996-4599.*
W *www.redhorseorlando.com* A slice of old-time Orlando, this Florida cowboy-themed hotel offers a "cowboy Continental" breakfast with homemade biscuits and gravy, and range-inspired decor in all the rooms.

INTERNATIONAL DRIVE: *Best Western Plaza International* $$$ AE DC MC V   672
8738 International Dr. (*407*) *345-8195.* FAX (*407*) *352-8196.*
Ideally located, this hotel is just a ten-minute drive away from Walt Disney World; SeaWorld is even closer. The family suites are good for kids.

INTERNATIONAL DRIVE: *Doubletree Castle Hotel* $$$ AE DC MC V   216
8629 International Dr. (*407*) *345-1511.* FAX (*407*) *248-8181.*
This pink, fairy-tale hotel has gargoyles in the lobby, a massive pool, and freshly baked chocolate chip cookies. Offers complimentary shuttles to all area attractions.

INTERNATIONAL DRIVE: *Westgate Lakes Resort & Spa* $$$ AE DC MC V   2738
10000 Turkey Lake Rd. (*407*) *345-0000.* FAX (*407*) *355-2982.*
W *www.westgateresorts.com* A lakeside location and a complete spa highlight this resort. Offers water sports, bicycle rentals, a children's playground, tennis and volleyball courts, and a bar and grill near the eight heated pools.

INTERNATIONAL DRIVE: *Caribe Royale All-Suites Resort* $$$$ AE DC MC V   1338
8101 World Center Dr. (*407*) *238-8000.* FAX (*407*) *238-8050.* W *www.cariberoyale.com*
Set on 45 tropical acres (18 ha), this is one of Orlando's premier conference centers and ideal for families too. The Fun Family Vacation Package offers passes to both Disney and Universal and daily transportation.

INTERNATIONAL DRIVE: *Embassy Suites Jamaican Court* $$$$ AE DC MC V   246
8250 Jamaican Court. (*407*) *345-8250.* FAX (*407*) *352-1463.*
Three-room suites and free Internet access make this a popular hotel for both families and business travelers. Offers a complimentary breakfast and free shuttle service to both Universal and SeaWorld.

INTERNATIONAL DRIVE: *Rosen Centre Hotel* $$$$ AE DC MC V   1334
9840 International Dr. (*800*) *800-9840.* FAX (*407*) *996-0865.* W *www.rosencentre.com*
Next to the Orange County Convention Center, this Florida-themed hotel is designed for both relaxation and business. The restaurant and microbrewery are first rate, as are the spa and the personal tour guides.

INTERNATIONAL DRIVE: *Sheraton Studio Hotel* $$$$ AE DC MC V   302
5905 International Dr. (*800*) *327-1366.* FAX (*407*) *248-0266.*
W *www.sheratonstudiocity.com* Located right in the heart of International Drive, this hotel provides convenient access to all the area's attractions.

INTERNATIONAL DRIVE: *Marriott's Royal Palms & Imperial Palms* $$$$$ AE DC MC V   169
8404 Vacation Way. (*407*) *238-6200.* FAX (*407*) *239-6247.*
Two grand hotels on one property, the Imperial Palms has 46 three-bedroom suites and two villas, while the Royal Palms has 123 two-bedroom suites. Hosts two excellent restaurants and an on-site golf course.

INTERNATIONAL DRIVE: *The Peabody Orlando* $$$$$ AE DC MC V   891
9801 International Dr. (*407*) *352-4000.* FAX (*407*) *363-1505.*
W *www.peabodyorlando.com* Winner of the AAA Four Diamond award for 17 years, its Dux signature restaurant has received AAA's Four Diamond award for 15 consecutive years (*see p155*).

KISSIMMEE: *Days Inn, Days Suites at Old Town* $$ AE DC MC V   604
5820 W Irlo Bronson Hwy. (*407*) *396-7900.* FAX (*407*) *396-1789.* W *www.thhotels.com*
Just 2.5 miles (4 km) from WDW, the resort offers four pools, a children's play-ground, and a picnic area for your enjoyment and relaxation.

KISSIMMEE: *Oak Plantation Vacation Resort Apartments* $$$ AE DC MC V   242
4090 Enchanted Oaks Circle. (*407*) *465-3873.*
A gated community and self-catered rental apartments 20 minutes from the theme parks. Oak trees line the 16-acre (6-ha) facility, with shops and restaurants within walking distance.

KISSIMMEE: *Windsor Palms Resort* $$$$ AE DC MC V
2300 Wyndham Palms Way. (*407*) *390-1991.* W *www.windsorpalmsresort.com*
Privately owned homes for rent. Two- to three-bedroom condominiums and three-bedroom town homes accommodate as many as 16 people. Features pools, exercise rooms, and an on-site movie theater.

Price categories for a standard double room per night in high season, including tax and service charges:

$ under $60
$$ $60–$100
$$$ $100–$150
$$$$ $150–$200
$$$$$ over $200

CHILDREN'S FACILITIES
A child-friendly hotel, with cribs, high chairs, and other facilities that may include a baby-sitting service and special children's programs.
SWIMMING POOL
The hotel has a swimming pool for use by residents.
RESTAURANT
The hotel has a restaurant or dining room open to both residents and non-residents unless otherwise stated.
NUMBER OF ROOMS
The hotel has the listed number of rooms available for prospective guests.

	CREDIT CARDS	CHILDREN'S FACILITIES	SWIMMING POOL	RESTAURANT	NUMBER OF ROOMS
KISSIMMEE: *Emerald Island Resort* $$$$$ 2751 Emerald Island Blvd. (800) 359-4827. W www.emerald-island.com Privately owned rental homes on a 300-acre (12-ha) wildlife conservation area. Located close to Disney, it offers trails for walking, jogging, or biking.	AE DC MC V	●	■		30
KISSIMMEE: *Gaylord Palms™ Resort & Convention Center* $$$$$ 6000 W Osceola Parkway. (407) 586-2000. FAX (407) 586-1999. W www.gaylordhotels.com Indulge yourself at this themed resort, host to five restaurants, two pools, two bars, and three separate Florida-style residences. Four acres (1.6 ha) of overhead glass and ancient trees vie for the wow factor.	AE DC MC V	●	■	●	1406
KISSIMMEE: $$$$$ *Orlando World Center Marriott Resort & Convention Center* 8701 World Center Dr. (407) 239-4200. FAX (407) 238-8777. This resort is surrounded by 200 acres (81 ha) of lush tropical landscaping. A guest-friendly staff, six restaurants, an on-site golf course, and a spa round out the offerings.	AE DC MC V	●	■	●	2000
LAKE MARY: *Marriott Orlando Lake Mary* $$$$$ 1501 International Parkway. (407) 995-1100. FAX (407) 995-1150. Close to Sanford International Airport, this resort offers well-kept rooms and splendid service, which caters to both the business and the leisure traveler. Boasts the world-class restaurant, Bistro 1501.	AE DC MC V	●	■	●	283
LAKE WALES: *Chalet Suzanne Country Inn* $$$$$ 3800 Chalet Suzanne Drive. (863) 676-6011. FAX (863) 676-1814. W www.chaletsuzanne.com One of the few high-end hotels in the area, outside of Disney property, to have an award-winning restaurant for the past 28 years. Also one with a canning plant, where they manufacture their famous soups. Offers guided tours.	AE DC MC V	●	■	●	30
MAITLAND: *Thurston House* $$$ 851 Lake Ave. (407) 539-1911. FAX (407) 539-0365. W www.thurstonhouse.com @ thurstonbb@aol.com Built in 1885 and restored in 1991, the period Queen Anne Victorian farmhouse sits on a beautiful lakefront. All four rooms have a queen-sized bed, a desk with a phone, a TV, and a reading area.	AE MC V	●			4
MOUNT DORA: *Mount Dora Historic Inn* $$$ 221 E Fourth Ave. (352) 735-1212. FAX (352) 735-9743. W www.mountdorahistoricinn.com Built in the 1880s as a romantic hideaway, the B&B is just a short drive from Orlando. Filled with period antiques, the house offers a full gourmet breakfast and special event rates.	AE DC MC V				4
MOUNT DORA: *Simpson's Bed & Breakfast* $$$ 441 N Donnelly St. (352) 383-2087. FAX (352) 383-0119. W www.simpsonsbnb.com In the heart of historic downtown, this former boarding house is now an all-suite B&B. Each multi-room suite offers sitting areas and a different themed decor, and comes complete with a mini-kitchen and bath.	AE DC MC V				6
MOUNT DORA: *Darst Victorian Manor* $$$$ 495 Old Hwy. 441. (352) 383-4050. FAX (352) 383-7653. W www.bbonline.com/fl/darstmanor/ Two blocks from Mt. Dora's antiques shop center and 20 miles (32 km) north of Orlando, this Victorian house overlooks Lake Dora. Offers both a single, ground-floor room and a three-room Queen Victoria suite with a sitting room and a remote control fireplace.	AE MC V				6
MOUNT DORA: *Lakeside Inn* $$$$ 100 N Alexander St. (352) 383-4101. FAX (352) 385-1615. W www.lakeside-inn.com Built in 1883 and refurbished a century later, this resort is ideal for a period of peaceful solitude. The inn is extremely popular with anglers, bird-watchers, and antiques-hunters.	AE DC MC V	●	■	●	89

MOUNT DORA: *Magnolia Inn Bed & Breakfast* $$$$ 347 E Third Ave. ☎ *(352) 735-3800.* [FAX] *(352) 735-0258.* [W] *www.magnoliainn.net* @ *info@magnoliainn.net* A slice of the Old South, the inn was built in 1926 and features four quaintly decorated rooms in the main house and a separate carriage house suite. A minimum two-night stay is mandatory on weekends. ❄ 🍃 🚭	*AE DC MC V*				5
OCALA: *Holiday Inn* $$$ 5751 E Hwy. 40, Silver Springs Blvd, Silver Springs. ☎ *(352) 236-2575.* [FAX] *(352) 236-2576.* This budget inn offers clean and comfortable rooms. Recreational facilities, such as a heated pool, tennis courts, and an exercise center, are also available. 🔒 ♿ ⇅ ❄ 🗨 🍃 ⧗ 🚭 🏋 🐕	*AE DC MC V*	●	■	●	103
OCALA: *Seven Sisters Inn* $$$$ 820 S E Fort King St. ☎ *(352) 867-1170.* [FAX] *(352) 867-5266.* [W] *www.sevensistersinn.com* Located near the Ocala State Forest, this Victorian B&B getaway was built in 1888. It is listed on the National Register of Historic Places. Jacuzzis, Victorian soaking tubs, and fireplaces are available in most rooms. A gourmet breakfast and afternoon tea are also on offer. ❄ 🍃 🚭	*AE DC MC V*		■		13
ORLANDO INTERNATIONAL AIRPORT: *Holiday Inn Select* $$$$ 5750 TG Lee Blvd. ☎ *(407) 851-6400.* [FAX] *(407) 240-3717.* Located just outside the airport grounds and 8 miles (13 km) from downtown, this is perfect for that late-night flight. A heated outdoor pool, sauna, and the hot whirlpool offer comfort to those travel-tired muscles. Wireless Internet access is also available throughout the hotel. ♿ ⇅ 🍃 ⧗ 🚭 🏋	*AE DC MC V*	●	■	●	288
ORLANDO INTERNATIONAL AIRPORT: *Hyatt Regency* $$$$$ 9300 Airport Blvd. ☎ *(407) 825-1234.* [FAX] *(407) 856-1672.* [W] *www.orlandoairport.hyatt.com* Roll out of a long flight and find comfort close at hand. This upscale hotel offers first-rate amenities such as a well-stocked airport shopping mall right outside, a pool, and a fitness center. 🔒 ♿ ⇅ ❄ 🍃 ⧗ [24] 🚭 🏋	*AE DC MC V*	●	■	●	483
SANFORD: *The Higgins House Bed & Breakfast* $$$ 420 S Oak Ave. ☎ *(407) 324-9238.* [FAX] *(407) 324-5060.* [W] *www.higginshouse.com* Within a 30-minute drive to Downtown Orlando, this 1894 Victorian inn overlooks a park near beautiful Lake Monroe and the St. Johns River. A Victorian garden, decks, and a hot tub compete with Continental breakfast for the finest amenities. 🔒 ❄ 🗨 🍃 🚭	*AE DC MC V*				3
TITUSVILLE: *Casa Coquina Bed & Breakfast* $$$ 4010 Coquina Ave. ☎ *(321) 268-4653.* [FAX] *(321) 268-3959.* [W] *www.casacoquina.com* @ *info@casacoquina.com* An ideal place for those looking to add the Space Coast and Cape Canaveral to their vacation plans. The second-story deck overlooks the Indian River and is the perfect spot for watching a shuttle launch. A large, comfortable home-away-from-home. ♿ ❄ 🗨 🍃 🚭	*AE DC MC V*				5
WINTER GARDEN: *Orange County National Golf Center & Lodge* $$$ 16301 Phil Ritson Way. ☎ *(407) 656-2626.* [FAX] *(407) 656-7262.* [W] *www.ocngolf.com* Set on 922 acres (373 ha) of rolling hills, this getaway resort has surprisingly inexpensive rates. The special Stay and Play package rates offer guests large, well-kept suites and 18 holes of golf daily on the two on-site championship courses. 🔒 ♿ ⇅ ❄ 🗨 🍃 🚭 🏋	*AE DC MC V*		■	●	50
WINTER HAVEN: *The Lemmon Drop Inn Bed & Breakfast* $$ 663 Ave I NW. ☎ *(863) 293-9229.* [W] *www.bbonline/fl/lemmondrop* This quaint little inn is located about 30 miles (48 km) from Orlando. Hosts just three rooms. The Hemingway Room has a private bath, while the Cat Room and the Ben Hogan Room share a bath. Perfect for those looking for a quiet and private getaway. ❄ 🍃 🚭 🐕	*AE DC MC V*				3
WINTER PARK: *Fairfield Inn* $$ 951 Wymore Rd. ☎ & [FAX] *(407) 539-1955.* Owned by Marriott, the inn is well-kept and convenient for those looking for more than just theme park distractions. Only 3 miles (5 km) from the shops, restaurants, and museums in downtown Winter Park, it's still within 20 minutes of Disney. ♿ ⇅ 🗨 🚭	*AE DC MC V*	●	■		135
WINTER PARK: *Park Plaza* $$$$ 307 Park Ave S. ☎ *(407) 647-1072.* [FAX] *(407) 647-4081.* [W] *www.parkplazahotel.com* Wooden flooring and rooms furnished with antiques and oriental rugs characterize the decorative theme of this hotel. A restaurant next door provides a convenient option for eating out. ♿ ❄ 🚭	*AE DC MC V*				27

For key to symbols see back flap

WHERE TO EAT

A FOOD LOVER'S paradise, the joy of Florida is in the rich and abundant fresh produce it has to offer. From juicy tropical fruits to mouthwatering seafood, every restaurant is overflowing with Florida's natural bounty. Catering to every palate and budget, the region's restaurants range from small cafés to

Stone crab claws

trendy diners to five-star resorts. A vast immigrant population and the constant flow of tourists contributes to a wide variety of ever-changing food choices. See the listings on pages 150–57. Intimate suppers by candlelight, and themed dinners ensure that the dining experience is as much about entertainment as sustenance.

Mexican food at its best – Chili's Grill & Bar, I-Drive

TYPES OF RESTAURANTS

ORLANDO IS A multi-cultural city offering a wide range of cuisines. The large number of Thai and Vietnamese residents guarantees a bounty of high-quality Asian restaurants. Mexican and Cuban eateries are also plentiful and, since this is the South, barbecue is never far away. African, Irish, Lebanese, Pakistani, Polish, and Indian – foods from all over the world are joyfully served to cater to all tastebuds. Almost every regional American cuisine is represented, from Maine to New Orleans, while a breed of innovative chefs has combined Florida's finest local produce with zesty Caribbean flavors to create what is called New Florida or "Floribbean" cuisine. Sushi is available in every supermarket, and every street corner has a pizza joint. "Natural" supermarkets, Whole Foods, and Chamberlain's offer organic meals.

Restaurants of every size and shape serve seafood. In one Florida institution, the "raw bar," you can enjoy deliciously fresh raw oysters or clams and steamed shrimp.

RESERVATIONS

RESERVATIONS ARE usually not required at smaller restaurants; some do not accept them at all. But it would be a good idea to make advance reservations at larger places in upscale areas such as Sand Lake Road, International Drive, and the theme parks, particularly on weekends. Guests staying at the Disney World and Universal resorts get preferred seating at the attraction-owned restaurants.

DINING ON A BUDGET

THERE ARE SEVERAL ways to reduce your food budget. Most restaurants offer huge and inexpensive breakfasts. Bargain meals are plentiful away from the hotels and theme parks, particularly at the large number of Indian,

Vietnamese, and Thai eateries. Several seafood and Chinese all-you-can-eat buffets can be found along I-Drive. Southern barbecue is also affordable. Check online for discount coupons, which can usually cut a meal bill by 25 percent or more.

Some restaurants will cook your own fish for a reduced price. In addition, many state parks have barbecues where you can grill your catch or any other food that you care to bring along. Delis and supermarkets are good for picnic provisions.

EATING OUT LATE

MOST RESTAURANTS close at 10pm since Floridians prefer to eat early – usually between 7 and 9pm. Some restaurants, however, do stay open until 11pm. The Globe, on Wall Street in Downtown Orlando, serves food until 2am. Diners such as Denny's, the B-Line on International Drive, and the 5 & Diner near

The highly acclaimed Emeril's Restaurant at Universal Orlando

Ran Getsu of Tokyo, an exclusive Japanese restaurant near the Sand Lake Road, I-Drive area

the University of Central Florida, are open 24 hours. Mexican food lovers can drive north on State Road 436 to Beto's, which never closes.

CELEBRITY DINING

THE NEW WORD in Orlando dining is "celebrity." Names that would generally be found attached to big-city restaurants or appearing on the Food Network are popping up all over Central Florida. Emeril Lagasse, who set up Emeril's at Universal and the Tchoup Chop at the Royal Pacific Resort, is now joined by Todd English, who operates Olives in New York and now bluezoo at Disney's Dolphin Hotel. Norman Van Aken founded Norman's at the Ritz-Carlton, and innovative chef Melissa Kelly has set up Primo at the JW Marriott. Wolfgang Puck and Roy Yamaguchi own signature restaurants, and a trio of French superstars – Paul Bocuse, Gaston Lenotre, and Roger Verge – run Les Chefs de France at Epcot.

DINING DISTRICTS

LIKE MUSHROOMS in the damp Florida summer, restaurants sprout in groups in Orlando. The Sand Lake Road "Restaurant Row," near the theme parks, is home to corporate-owned, high-end eateries such as Seasons 52, Bonefish Grill, Roys, and Timpano's, as well as standalone destinations Essence of India, Anaelle & Hugo, and Vines. To the west, Bistro 1501 at the Orlando Marriott Hotel offers fine dining in

Lake Mary. The ViMi district of Colonial Drive is home to scores of Vietnamese, Thai, and Chinese restaurants. Old favorites such as Little Saigon and Shin Jung are next to the newcomers Lemongrass Bistro and Pho Hoa. Thornton Park in downtown is host to HUE, Napasorn Thai, the Japanese eatery Ichiban, lunchtime favorite Dexters, and upscale Arthur's 27 and Harvey's Bistro. Nearby College Park draws diners with Jade Bistro, Restaurant K, Babbo Wine Bar, Edgewater Grill with a taste of the Mediterranean, and the hip tapas eatery Taste.

THEME PARK DINING

SOME OF THE finest dining in Orlando can be found at the parks, including the AAA Five-Diamond Award winner, Victoria & Albert's, at the Grand Floridian Resort & Spa, and the award-winning Palm at Universal's Hard Rock Hotel.

You can be fairly certain that anything consumed, from hot dogs to haute cuisine, at any of the theme parks will be somewhat on the expensive side. However, more often than not, the food is worth it.

The parks are full to the brim with themed restaurants. The Coral Reef Restaurant at Epcot has an 8-ft (2.5-m) high glass wall panorama of the 5.7 million gallon (21.5 million liter) Living Seas aquarium. Delfino Riviera at Universal's Portofino Bay Hotel transports diners to a full-scale replica of Italy's Portofino harbor. Also at Universal, CityWalk treats sports-loving guests to NBA City for basketball-themed goodies, and racing meals at the NASCAR Café. Disney's Rainforest Café features hourly thunderstorms amid animatronic gorillas. The parks are also home to the Hard Rock Café, House of Blues, and Planet Hollywood.

Chef's table at Victoria & Albert's, Disney's Grand Floridian Resort & Spa

Choosing a Restaurant

THE RESTAURANTS in this guide have been selected for their good value, exceptional food, or interesting location. This chart highlights some of the factors that may influence your choice, such as the style of food and whether you can opt to eat outdoors. All the entries are listed alphabetically within each price category.

WALT DISNEY WORLD® RESORT	CREDIT CARDS	CHILDREN'S FACILITIES	EARLY BIRD SPECIALS	LATE OPENING HOURS	BAR
ANIMAL KINGDOM: *Boma – Flavors of Africa* $$ Disney's Animal Kingdom Lodge, Bay Lake. ☎ *(407) 939-3463.* Tables laden with spicy African dishes – flavored with delicious combinations of tamarind, cumin, cinnamon, hot chilies, cilantro, and papaya – invite exploration at the overwhelming dinner and breakfast buffets in Disney's colorful, Dark-Continent-themed resort hotel. ♿ [V] 🍷	AE DC MC V	●			■
ANIMAL KINGDOM: *Jiko – The Cooking Place* $$$$ Disney's Animal Kingdom Lodge, Bay Lake. ☎ *(407) 939-3463.* [FAX] *(407) 938-4799.* Pan-African splendor surrounds you in this gorgeous restaurant overlooking acres of savanna where wild animals roam. Traditional food from all over the continent includes a tasty, slow-cooked Moroccan stew and flatbread with yogurt and onions baked in open *jiko* ovens. ♿ [V] 🍷	AE DC MC V				■
DISNEY-MGM STUDIOS: *Sci-Fi Dine-In Theater* $$$ Lake Buena Vista. ☎ *(407) 560-3359.* The theme is drive-in movies and the menu offers burgers, fries, pasta, ribs, and outrageous milk shakes. Although expensive, the experience of sitting in a replica 1950s auto while watching old sci-fi movies is nostalgic for old-timers and fun for kids. ♿ [V] ⛱ 🍷	AE DC MC V	●			■
DISNEY-MGM STUDIOS: *Hollywood Brown Derby* $$$$$ Lake Buena Vista. ☎ *(407) 560-5376.* Re-creating the fabled Brown Derby of 1930s Hollywood, the Art Deco interior echoes the retro menu, including a world-famous Cobb Salad. Seafood and steaks in fusion style and acclaimed desserts (try the grapefruit cake) round out the offerings. Known for the best mixed drinks in the park. ♿ [V] ⛱ 🍷	AE DC MC V	●		●	■
DOWNTOWN DISNEY: *Dakshin* $$$ 12541 Suite Rd 535. ☎ *(407) 827-9080.* A South Indian haven for lovers of seafood and vegetarian wonders. Lobster curry, delicacies from Goa and Mangalore, and a separate dinner menu offering delicious Indian crepes are on offer. The weekend brunch is worth a visit. Attentive service provides help if you're not sure what to eat. ♿ [V]	AE MC V	●			■
DOWNTOWN DISNEY: *Planet Hollywood® Orlando* $$$ 1506 E Buena Vista Dr. ☎ *(407) 827-7827.* Located within a purple neon globe, this has large video screens and masses of movie memorabilia. The fare is mainstream, with meaty burgers and tasty pizzas. ♿	AE MC V	●		●	■
DOWNTOWN DISNEY: *Wolfgang Puck® Café* $$$ Downtown Disney W Side, Lake Buena Vista. ☎ *(407) 938-9653.* [FAX] *(407) 828-0090.* The familiar fire-roasted pizzas, pastas, and grilled foods are quite good. The loud, frenzied atmosphere adds energy and vitality to the place. A separate, fine-dining restaurant is located upstairs. ♿ [V] 🍷	AE DC MC V	●		●	■
DOWNTOWN DISNEY: *Arthur's 27* $$$$$ Wyndham Palace, 1900 Buena Vista Dr. ☎ *(407) 827-3450.* The fabulous view and the appetizing food are the trademarks of this restaurant on the 27th floor. Some of Orlando's finest "Floribbean" cuisine is on offer here. ♿ 🍷 ♫ ● *Sun, Mon & Tue.*	AE DC MC V	●			■
EPCOT: *Cape May Café* $$ Disney's Beach Club Resort. ☎ *(407) 939-3463.* The buffet breakfast proceedings here are conducted by Admiral Goofy. At dinner, a bell announces the start of the clam bake buffet, which offers a tempting array of food to choose from. ♿ ● *L.*	AE MC V	●			

Price categories include a three-course meal for one, a glass of house wine, and all unavoidable extras including service and tax.
$ under $20
$$ $20–$30
$$$ $30–$45
$$$$ $45–$60
$$$$$ over $60

Credit Cards
Indicates which credit cards are accepted: AE American Express; DC Diners Club; MC MasterCard; V VISA.

Children's Facilities
Small portions and high chairs available, and there may also be a special children's menu.

Early Bird Specials
Meals offered at a discounted price if you eat early, usually before 7pm.

Late Opening Hours
Indicates that the restaurant is open until late in the evening.

	Credit Cards	Children's Facilities	Early Bird Specials	Late Opening Hours	Bar
Epcot: *Flying Fish Café* $$$ Disney's Boardwalk, Lake Buena Vista. ☎ *(407) 939-3463.* Another reason to visit the free Disney Boardwalk area aside from the view of nightly fireworks. Service is superb – the waiters seem to anticipate your needs while they serve creative American seafood cuisine. The daily specials synchronize with what's in season. ♿ [V] 🍷	AE DC MC V	●		●	■
Epcot: *Gulliver's Grill* $$$ Walt Disney World Swan Hotel. ☎ *(407) 934-1609.* Try the tastes of BROBDINGNAG, the legendary land of giants, amidst beautiful plants at this lovely restaurant. Well-prepared American cuisine is on offer here. ♿ [V] 🍷	AE DC MC V	●	■		
Epcot: *Yachtsman Steakouse* $$$ Disney Yacht Club Resort. ☎ *(407) 939-3463.* This eatery is open all day for "down home" favorites' including fish, steak, and pasta, all to be enjoyed in nautical surroundings. The scrumptious desserts available at the dinner buffet are not to be missed. ♿	AE MC V	●			■
Epcot: *Shula's* $$$$ Walt Disney World Dolphin Hotel. ☎ *(407) 934-1609.* If you're looking for steaks, this is the place to be. One of the resort's best steakhouses, they are also known for their fine selection of seafood. ♿	AE MC V	●			■
Epcot: *Les Chefs de France* $$$$$ Epcot World Showcase, Walt Disney World. ☎ *(407) 939-3463.* Haute cuisine doesn't get much higher than a restaurant created by Bocuse, Lenotre, and Verge, three masters of French cooking. From appetizers to classics like duck a l'orange, every dish is a definition of the art. Epcot admission necessary. ♿ [V] ⛱ 🍷	AE MC V				■
Fort Wilderness: *Artist Point* $$$ Disney's Wilderness Lodge, Lake Buena Vista. ☎ *(407) 939-3463.* [FAX] *(407) 824-0265.* From the size of the plate to the size of the portions, everything here is big. The innovative, Northwestern-themed menu offers exotic items such as sautéed elk sausage. The service and setting are spectacular. ♿ [V] 🍷	AE DC MC V	●			■
Fort Wilderness: *Whispering Canyon Café* $$$ Disney's Wilderness Lodge, Lake Buena Vista. ☎ *(407) 939-3463.* Strap on your six-guns and settle in for an all-you-can-eat campfire cookout buffet in a highly realistic Wild West setting. The café is also open for frontier-style breakfasts. ♿ [V]	AE MC V	●			■
Magic Kingdom: *Cinderella's Royal Table* $$ Cinderella's Castle. ☎ *(407) 934-4000.* Prime rib and chicken for adults and Disney characters for the kids – this is the traditional Character Breakfast taken to the ultimate. Little girls love to get a glimpse of Cinderella during their meal. Advance reservations – sometimes three to four months in advance – are mandatory. ♿	AE DC MC V	●			
Magic Kingdom: *California Grill* $$$ Disney's Contemporary Resort. ☎ *(407) 939-3463.* This stylish restaurant hosts an open-plan kitchen that serves creative West Coast fare such as smoked salmon pizza and grilled pork with polenta. The view from here is much to be admired. ♿ 🍷	AE MC V	●			■
Magic Kingdom: *Chef Mickey's* $$$ Disney's Contemporary Resort. ☎ *(407) 939-3463.* Enjoy the antics of your beloved Disney characters as you eat. Very family-oriented, the restaurant offers breakfast and dinner buffets and is a favorite with children. ♿ 🍷 ● *L.*	AE MC V	●			

<table>
<tr><td colspan="2">

Price categories include a three-course meal for one, a glass of house wine, and all unavoidable extras including service and tax.
$ under $20
$$ $20–$30
$$$ $30–$45
$$$$ $45–$60
$$$$$ over $60

</td><td colspan="2">

CREDIT CARDS
Indicates which credit cards are accepted: AE American Express; DC Diners Club; V VISA.
CHILDREN'S FACILITIES
Small portions and high chairs available, and there may also be a special children's menu.
EARLY BIRD SPECIALS
Meals offered at a discounted price if you eat early, usually before 7pm.
LATE OPENING HOURS
Indicates that the restaurant is open until late in the evening.

</td></tr>
</table>

	CREDIT CARDS	CHILDREN'S FACILITIES	EARLY BIRD SPECIALS	LATE OPENING HOURS	BAR
MAGIC KINGDOM: *Narcoossee's* $$$ Disney's Grand Floridian Resort & Spa, Lake Buena Vista. (407) 939-3463. This restaurant is located in an octagonal chalet alongside the Seven Seas Lagoon. The meat and fish dishes are delicious and are served along with fresh local vegetables. ♿ ● *L*.	AE MC V	●			■
MAGIC KINGDOM: *Ohana* $$$ Disney's Polynesian Resort, Lake Buena Vista. (407) 939-3463. This buzzing, open-plan dining room is the setting for Polynesian-style cuisine. Fixed-price dinners include meat and shellfish roasted over a fire pit and served on 3-ft (1-m) long skewers. ♿ ♬ ● *L*.	AE MC V	●			
MAGIC KINGDOM: *Citrico's at the Grand Floridian* $$$$ Disney's Grand Floridian Resort & Spa, Lake Buena Vista. (407) 939-3463. FAX (407) 824-2458. This delightful eatery offers international fare, with a focus on slow-roasted meats. Influenced by French cuisine, everything from breads to desserts is exquisite – even the view of the drama in the open kitchen. Expensive but worth it. ♿ 🍽 🍷 ● *Mon & Tue.*	AE DC MC V				■
MAGIC KINGDOM: *Disney's Spirit of Aloha Dinner Show* $$$$ Disney's Polynesian Resort, Lake Buena Vista. (407) 939-3463. Tropical appetizers and "Island" ribs are the highlight of this Polynesian diner. The food is served alongside music and dances of Tahiti, Samoa, Tonga, New Zealand, and Hawaii. Great fun for both kids and adults who like the hula. ♿ ♬ 🍷 🎪	AE DC MC V	●			
MAGIC KINGDOM: *Victoria & Albert's* $$$$$ Disney's Grand Floridian Resort & Spa, Lake Buena Vista. (407) 824-1089. Reservations are a must at this lavish and extremely popular restaurant. The six-course, fixed-price menu is superlative, and you're waited on by a butler and a maid. Ask for the chef's table, the most exclusive one in the house. ♿ ♬ 🍽 🍷 ● *L*.	AE MC V			●	

OTHER THEME PARKS

	CREDIT CARDS	CHILDREN'S FACILITIES	EARLY BIRD SPECIALS	LATE OPENING HOURS	BAR
SEAWORLD: *Atlantis* $$$ 6677 Sea Harbor Dr. (407) 351-5555. Located in the Renaissance Orlando resort *(see p143)*. The Mediterranean seafood menu is accompanied by live harp music, crystal chandeliers, and European-quality service. Almost a theme park on its own, it serves chargrilled steaks for those not enamored of fish. ♿ ♬ 🍷	AE DC MC V				■
SEAWORLD: *Sharks Underwater Grill* $$$ 7007 SeaWorld Dr. (407) 351-3600. Enjoy Caribbean and Florida-style seafood inches away from more than 50 sharks at SeaWorld. The menu is upscale and the food as fresh as getting it directly from the tank. Admission to SeaWorld is required. ♿ 🍷	AE DC MC V	●			■
SEAWORLD: *Primo* $$$$$ 4040 Central Florida Parkway. (407) 393-4444. Organic cuisine at the enormous JW Marriott Orlando. From free-range lamb to homemade sausage, care is taken with every ingredient and the result is deliciously successful. Prices are in the very high range, but if you're looking for a special meal, Primo is the place to be. ♿ 🍷	AE DC MC V			●	■
UNIVERSAL ORLANDO: *Grill Kabob* $$ 4642 Kirkman Rd. (407) 578-0585. The glorious menu features Afghani, Lebanese, Moroccan, Indian, and Pakistani dishes. Moroccan versions of familiar Indian dishes offer flavor without heat. Entire sections are devoted to kormas, tikkas, and spicy kabobs. The special all-you-can-eat lunch buffets are a real bargain. ♿ 🍷	AE DC MC V	●			

UNIVERSAL ORLANDO: *Hard Rock Café Orlando* $$
6050 Universal Blvd. ((407) 351-7625.
This massive restaurant in CityWalk overflows with pop memorabilia.
The sundaes are great, and the live music in the concert hall makes it an
extremely popular hangout. ᴘ ♫ *Fri & Sat.*

	AE				
	DC	●		●	▦
	MC				
	V				

UNIVERSAL ORLANDO: *Emeril's Restaurant Orlando* $$$
6000 Universal Blvd. ((407) 224-2424.
Savor the casual, contemporary atmosphere, the warm and spicy colors,
and first-class service in this Universal CityWalk restaurant. Highlighting the
"bam" cuisine of Emeril Lagasse, the menu offers flawlessly prepared items
such as the andouille-crusted Texas redfish. ᴘ ▼ ♀

	AE				
	DC	●		●	▦
	MC				
	V				

UNIVERSAL ORLANDO: *Jimmy Buffett's Margaritaville* $$$
6000 Universal Blvd. ((407) 224-2155. FAX (407) 224-2133.
Soak up Key West flavor and Jimmy Buffet tunes at Margaritaville in the
heart of glitzy CityWalk. There's more flash in the colorful atmosphere than
in the food at this noisy and crowded spot, but the ocean of margarita
varieties will satisfy your drink-and-be-merry craving. ᴘ ♫

	AE				
	DC	●		●	▦
	MC				
	V				

UNIVERSAL ORLANDO: *Delfino Riviera* $$$$
Portofino Bay Hotel, 5601 Universal Blvd. ((407) 503-1415.
Upscale, award-winning Italian food captivates both the body and soul,
with a setting overlooking a re-created Portofino Bay. The menu ranges
from venison osso buco to citrus-cured sturgeon over a bed of fennel and
greens. An excellent choice for a romantic dinner. ᴘ ▼ ♀ ● *Sun & Mon.*

	AE				
	DC	●		●	▦
	MC				
	V				

UNIVERSAL ORLANDO: *Palm Restaurant* $$$$
5800 Universal Blvd. ((407) 503-7256. FAX (407) 503-2383.
The first Palm was opened in New York circa 1926, and the Orlando
branch within the Hard Rock Hotel *(see p143)* features a mixture of fine,
uncomplicated dishes and slight near-misses. Steaks are enormous. Unlike
most Universal eateries, free valet parking is right at the door. ᴘ ♈ ⊞ ♀

	AE				
	DC	●		●	▦
	MC				
	V				

ORLANDO & CENTRAL FLORIDA

COCOA BEACH: *The Mango Tree Restaurant* $$$$$
118 N Atlantic Ave. ((321) 799-0513.
This gourmet restaurant serves local dishes, with seafood as its specialty.
Situated just yards from the Atlantic Ocean, there is a tropical garden with
waterfowl, Japanese carp, and lush foliage. ᴘ ♫ ▼ ⊞ ♀ ● *Mon.*

	AE				
	MC	●			▦
	V				

DAYTONA BEACH: *Aunt Catfish* $$
4009 Halifax Dr. ((386) 767-4768.
This popular eatery located on the Intracoastal Waterway is especially
renowned for its fried catfish and other Southern-style dishes such as crab
cakes and clam strips. Also open for Sunday brunch. ᴘ ⊞

	AE				
	MC	●	▦	●	▦
	V				

DAYTONA BEACH: *Down the Hatch* $$
4894 Front St, Ponce Inlet. ((386) 761-4831.
A family-oriented restaurant that serves fresh fish and a few meat dishes. It
is set right by the waterside – you can watch the boats unload their catch at
the end of the day. ᴘ ⊞ ♫ *Wed–Sun.* ● *Thanksgiving, Dec 25.*

	AE				
	MC	●	▦		▦
	V				

DOWNTOWN ORLANDO: *Little Saigon* $
1106 E Colonial Dr. ((407) 423-8539. FAX (407) 425-3283.
Located at the intersection of Mills Avenue and Colonial Drive, this
restaurant has been serving Vietnamese food for more than a decade. The
menu offers appetizers, noodle dishes, and stir-fries, with choices of pork,
beef, seafood, and vegetables. The combo plates are a good deal. ᴘ ▼

	AE				
	DC	●			
	MC				
	V				

DOWNTOWN ORLANDO: *Dexters of Thornton Park* $$
808 E Washington St. ((407) 648-2777.
Spacious, light, and airy, with seating at the bar or on barstools at elevated
tables. Sandwiches and pastas – small and large portions – are staples.
You'll also find the urban-professional set ordering wines both by the bottle
and "on tap." ᴘ ▼ ⊞ ♀

	AE				
	DC	●		●	▦
	MC				
	V				

DOWNTOWN ORLANDO: *Jade Bistro* $$
2425 Edgewater Dr. ((407) 422-7968.
Veteran sushi chefs join seasoned restaurant owners for a truly delightful
combination. The pan-Oriental cuisine is excellent and often exceeds
expectations. Athough not entirely Japanese, Chinese, or Thai, it still
manages to excel in all these areas. ᴘ ▼ ⊞ ♀

	DC				
	MC	●		●	▦
	V				

Price categories include a three-course meal for one, a glass of house wine, and all unavoidable extras including service and tax.

$ under $20
$$ $20–$30
$$$ $30–$45
$$$$ $45–$60
$$$$$ over $60

CREDIT CARDS
Indicates which credit cards are accepted: AE American Express; DC Diners Club; MC MasterCard; V VISA.

CHILDREN'S FACILITIES
Small portions and high chairs available, and there may also be a special children's menu.

EARLY BIRD SPECIALS
Meals offered at a discounted price if you eat early, usually before 7pm.

LATE OPENING HOURS
Indicates that the restaurant is open until late in the evening.

	Credit Cards	Children's Facilities	Early Bird Specials	Late Opening Hours	Bar
DOWNTOWN ORLANDO: Babbo Wine Bar & Café $$$ 1710 Edgewater Dr. (407) 649-9770. A throwback to restaurants in Naples, this café features dishes straight from the trattorias of Southern Italy, such as a savory baked gnocchi and tortellini alla Campagnola. The select, individual pizzas are hand-tossed and crispy-delicious. Wine bar serves 110 wines, 52 by the glass. _Sun._	AE MC V	●			▩
DOWNTOWN ORLANDO: Edgewater Grill $$$ 2306 Edgewater Dr. (407) 425-1801. The main street of College Park is the setting for this modern Mediterranean bistro. Serves lots of root vegetables, tomatoes, and beans that accompany thick cuts of meat, grilled seafood, and roasted chicken. The high-quality cooking fills both plates and appetites. _Sun._	AE DC MC V			●	▩
DOWNTOWN ORLANDO: Il Pescatore $$$ 651 N Primrose Dr. (407) 896-6763. FAX (407) 896-6735. A simple setting for food that's truly Italian through and through. Traditional house specialties like trippa del Pescatore (tripe in tomato sauce) make this spot unique. Choosing between the various pasta sauces is pleasingly difficult. _Sun & Mon._	AE DC MC V			●	
DOWNTOWN ORLANDO: K Restaurant & Wine Bar $$$ 2306 Edgewater Dr. (407) 872-2332. FAX (407) 872-7988. The former Café Allegre reaches a grand level of food and service, creating dishes that are both simple and elegantly delicious. From salads to starters to the main course, everything hits the right note, surpassing the restaurant's already sterling reputation. _Sun & Mon._	AE DC MC V			●	▩
DOWNTOWN ORLANDO: Lake Eola Yacht Club $$$ 407 E Central Blvd. (407) 851-6980. Dine on extraordinarily good entrées either indoors or outdoors, with a beautiful view of Lake Eola's landmark fountain. The menu leans toward seafood and lighter dishes. The food is satisfying for the most part, and service is tripping-over-themselves friendly. _Mon._	AE DC MC V			●	▩
DOWNTOWN ORLANDO: Napasorn Thai $$$ 56 E Pine St. (407) 245-8088. The young yet experienced owners wander slightly from traditional Thai food, but manage to serve up well-prepared dishes, the basil duck standing out. The reasonably good sushi bar combines to make it a most enjoyable destination. _Fri._	AE DC MC V	●		●	▩
DOWNTOWN ORLANDO: Harvey's Bistro $$$$ 390 N Orange Ave. (407) 246-6560. FAX (407) 246-6561. The reputation for reasonably priced, beautifully presented dishes, served in a lively but elegant atmosphere is well-earned. It remains one of downtown's best options for American bistro cuisine. A suitable place for special events. _Sun._	AE DC MC V			●	▩
DOWNTOWN ORLANDO: Gargi's $$$$$ 1414 N Orange Ave. (407) 894-7907. A local favorite for more than 20 years, the new location right on Lake Ivanhoe affords spectacular sunset views of Downtown Orlando. Enjoy a romantic evening with offerings of old-world service and classic traditional Italian food. Take the wine suggestions as gospel.	AE DC MC V	●		●	▩
INTERNATIONAL DRIVE: Cedar's Restaurant $$ 7732 W Sand Lake Rd. (407) 351-6000. FAX (407) 355-0607. Cedar's spin on traditional Lebanese food has a lightness of texture and flavor that is both refreshing and inviting. Use the puffy, hot pitas to scoop up baba ghanoush, a smooth roasted eggplant and garlic purée with a wonderfully smoky taste. The lunch buffet is a bargain.	AE DC MC V	●		●	

INTERNATIONAL DRIVE: *The Crab House* $$$ 8291 International Dr. (407) 352-6140. Choose from no less than nine crab dishes at this informal restaurant. The seafood salad bar is loaded with freshly shelled oysters, shrimp, marinated mussels, and crawfish, and other seafood dishes.	AE DC MC V	●			■
INTERNATIONAL DRIVE: *Hanamizuki Japanese Restaurant* $$$ 8255 International Dr. (407) 363-7200. FAX (407) 363-1006. Deceptively situated in a bland I-Drive strip mall, this sushi restaurant is both elegant and expensive. The minimalist decor combines with a menu of surprising depth and intrigue to create a flawlessly integrated and refreshing experience. Locals swear the sushi is the best in town. *Sun.*	AE DC MC V	●		●	■
INTERNATIONAL DRIVE: *Bonefish Grill* $$$$ 7830 W Sand Lake Rd. (407) 355-7707. FAX (407) 355-7705. Moderately priced seafood and a pleasant atmosphere are on offer here. The bar is popular, and appetizers such as the saucy shrimp and the mussels Josephine are superb, perhaps better than the multiple-choice fish entrées. The seafood offerings change with availability.	AE DC MC V	●		●	■
INTERNATIONAL DRIVE: *Roy's Restaurant* $$$$ 7760 W Sand Lake Rd. (407) 352-4844. FAX (407) 352-3733. This upscale restaurant, set up by celebrity chef Roy Yamaguchi, is a curious fusion of Pacific Rim cuisines, with an emphasis on Hawaiian ingredients, such as the shutome swordfish in a Thai curry sauce. Both the menu and the wine list offer a wide variety of selections.	AE DC MC V				■
INTERNATIONAL DRIVE: *Ruth's Chris Steak House* $$$$ 7501 W Sand Lake Rd. (407) 226-3900. FAX (407) 226-3108. Within a gentlemen's club ambience, the menu and service are both delivered with excellence. The New Orleans-based chain serves only aged meats from corn-fed Hereford cows, seared on a 1,800-degree grill – so tender, a knife isn't necessary. For expense accounts and special occasions.	AE DC MC V			●	■
INTERNATIONAL DRIVE: *Season's 52* $$$$ 7700 W Sand Lake Rd. (407) 354-5212. The concept is of fresh seasonal food. So a favorite dish made with pears from Oregon might not be available the next time you go, but something as impressive will be. The satisfying and occasionally unusual combinations of regional and global ingredients make the food enjoyable.	AE DC MC V	●		●	■
INTERNATIONAL DRIVE: *Timpano Italian Chophouse* $$$$ 7488 W Sand Lake Rd. (407) 248-0429. FAX (407) 248-1945. This re-creates big-city dining with the allure of 1950s New York nightclubs. The result is extraordinary quality and impeccable service. The veal saltimbocca – thin cutlets served with prosciutto ham and provolone in a subtle garlic and sage sauce – is exceptionally brilliant.	AE DC MC V			●	■
INTERNATIONAL DRIVE: *Dux at the Peabody Hotel* $$$$$ 9801 International Dr. (407) 345-4550. Awash with swanky atmosphere, this upscale restaurant nestled inside the Peabody Hotel *(see p145)* offers a menu that changes with the seasons, and includes soups, fish courses, meats, and desserts. But don't ask for duck because it isn't on the menu.	AE DC MC V			●	■
KISSIMMEE: *Magic Mining Steaks & Seafood Company* $$ 7736 W Hwy 192. (407) 396-1950. Ribs, steaks, chicken, more ribs, and anything that will fit on a grill. Kids will adore the Gold Mine decor with its styrofoam rock walls, full-scale electric train that runs throughout the restaurant, and video game "depot." After the meal, parents can enjoy the two 18-hole golf courses on the roof.	AE DC MC V	●			
KISSIMMEE: *Phoenician Restaurant* $$ 2920 Vineland Rd. (407) 397-2230. A Turkish delight sheltered in a strip mall off the busy US 192. The tabbouli and hummus are made fresh daily, the shish kabob is sizzling hot and the coffee is bracingly strong. Authentic couscous for non-meat-eaters, and a great pastry shop next door.	AE MC V	●			
KISSIMMEE: *Pacino's Italian Ristorante* $$$ 5795 W Hwy 192. (407) 396-8022. Charbroiled food is the focus of this comfortable and friendly family restaurant. If you would rather eat in the comfort of your room, there's a free delivery service to any nearby hotel.	AE DC MC V	●			■

Price categories include a three-course meal for one, a glass of house wine, and all unavoidable extras including service and tax.
$ under $20
$$ $20–$30
$$$ $30–$45
$$$$ $45–$60
$$$$$ over $60

CREDIT CARDS
Indicates which credit cards are accepted: AE American Express; DC Diners Club; MC MasterCard; V VISA.
CHILDREN'S FACILITIES
Small portions and high chairs available, and there may also be a special children's menu.
EARLY BIRD SPECIALS
Meals offered at a discounted price if you eat early, usually before 7pm.
LATE OPENING HOURS
Indicates that the restaurant is open until late in the evening.

	CREDIT CARDS	CHILDREN'S FACILITIES	EARLY BIRD SPECIALS	LATE OPENING HOURS	BAR
MAITLAND: *Bucca de Beppo* $$ 1351 S Orlando Ave. (407) 622-7663. FAX (407) 622-5317. Think big, big, and bigger at this fun, family-style restaurant, with foot-long lasagnes, sandwiches that last a week, and pizzas as big as the table. A good place for those who like to take food home with them; the doggie bags have handles. Reservations are highly recommended. V	AE DC MC V	●			▦
MAITLAND: *Enzian Theater* $$$ 1300 S Orlando Ave. (407) 629-1088. FAX (407) 629-6870. Nachos and hummus with avant-garde films, pasta and salads with thrillers, tiramisu and ice cream with musicals. The premier film and dinner destination, the Enzian shows first-run indie movies with a small but varied menu of dinner and snack items to enjoy while watching the show. V	AE DC MC V				▦
MOUNT DORA: *Windsor Rose English Tea Room* $$ 142 W Fourth Ave. (352) 735-2551. FAX (352) 735-1709. The place to go for high tea, as well as a nice shepherd's pie. The *pièce de résistance* is the Queen Victoria cake, crowned by powdered sugar and filled with strawberry preserves and cream cheese. The gift shop next door will sell the bone china cup you just drank from. V	AE DC MC V	●			
MOUNT DORA: *Goblin Market* $$$ 331 N Donnelly St. (352) 735-0059. FAX (352) 735-1122. A creative, casual gourmet outlet, tucked away in a downtown alleyway. Offers high quality seafood and little flourishes such as a flavorful crab bisque served with a small crystal pitcher of sherry. V ● Sun & Mon.	AE DC MC V				
OCALA: *Arthur's* $$ Ocala/Silver Springs Hilton, 3600 SW 36th Ave. (352) 854-1400. Arthur's is well known for its delicious lunch and dinner buffets. Different specials are on offer every day, and the lavish brunch on Sundays is an assured treat.	AE DC MC V	●	▦		▦
PLANT CITY: *Branch Ranch Dining Room* $$$ 5121 Thonotosassa Rd. (813) 752-1957. Southern food served in a restaurant that's been around since 1956. Handmade from traditional recipes, the baked ham, pole beans, fried green tomatoes, and buttermilk biscuits are delicious. V	AE DC MC V	●			▦
SANFORD: *Da Vinci* $$$ 107 Magnolia Ave. (407) 323-1388. A slightly funky and as yet undiscovered restaurant nestled in renovation-in-progress downtown Sanford. The traditional dishes are offset by Mediterranean-inspired creations. Well worth the trip. V ● Sun.	AE DC MC V			●	▦
TITUSVILLE: *Dixie Crossroads* $ 1475 Garden St. (321) 268-5000. FAX (321) 268-3933. A traditional Florida fish camp offering fresh and filling no-frills seafood. Serves huge portions of fried, steamed or broiled catfish, shrimp, scallops, and mullet, and the best corn fritters in town. V	AE DC MC V	●			▦
TITUSVILLE: *New York, New York* $$ 5401 Riveredge Dr. (321) 264-2585. Outdoor Florida dining at its casual best, NYNY sits on the Indian River Lagoon and serves full service dinners, light snacks, sandwiches, and bar food. Very popular for sports events, it hosts pool tables, darts, and karaoke in the Tiki Bar. V	AE DC MC V	●		●	▦
WINTER PARK: *Brooklyn Pizza* $ 1881 W Fairbanks Ave. (407) 622-7499. The best place for genuine New York pizza. Trading on a family tradition going back 40 years, Brooklyn Pizza delivers the kind of handmade, authentic pies you had as a kid, along with subs and baked dinners. V	AE DC MC V	●			

WINTER PARK: *Briar Patch* $$$
252 Park Ave. [(407) 628-8651. FAX (407) 628-8028.
A perennial favorite of the strolling lunch crowd on Park Avenue. What
keeps old fans and curious newcomers coming back is the front porch
coziness and the creative menu items. Long lines at breakfast and
lunchtimes on weekends – and many who are willing to wait. & V 🏠
AE MC V

WINTER PARK: *Café Aragon* $$$
2415 Aloma Ave. [(407) 671-2222. FAX (407) 671-2290.
The emphasis is on the cuisine from the northern region of Spain that
inspired the name of the outlet. Café Aragon excels at traditional, simple
dishes served elegantly. Lots of sweet garlic highlight the pollo al ajillo
(chicken) and the bistec de Palomilla (steak). &
AE DC MC V

WINTER PARK: *The Cheesecake Factory* $$$
520 N Orlando Ave. [(407) 644-4220. FAX (407) 644-4330.
Huge, towering interiors with portions that are almost as large. More than
30 varieties of mouthwatering cheesecake complement the meal, though
you can pick up a piece at the take-out counter for later too. Wonderful
from beginning to end. & V 🍷
AE DC MC V

WINTER PARK: *Fiddler's Green* $$$
544 W Fairbanks Ave. [(407) 645-2050. FAX (407) 645-1152.
One of the largest selections of draft ales, lagers, and stouts in the area.
Serves traditional Irish fare and ambitious offerings such as grilled
salmon with champagne sauce. This pub proves that a focus on flavor,
presentation, and service can spell "gourmet" for Irish cuisine. & 🎵 V
AE DC MC V

WINTER PARK: *Thai Place* $$$
501 N Orlando Ave. [(407) 644-8449. FAX (407) 644-8232.
One of the best Thai restaurants, with dark walls and glittery artwork. The
food is always as good as you remember it. The fragrant tom kha gai, the
salad with peanut dressing, and a choice of chicken, seafood, beef, or pork
in a variety of sauces is excellent. & V ⬤ *Sun.*
AE DC MC V

WINTER PARK: *Allegria Wine Bar & Café* $$$$
115 E Lyman Ave. [(407) 628-1641. FAX (407) 628-1249.
Allegria offers a joyous Italian experience just off Park Avenue. Savor the
house antipasto (cheeses, polenta, sausage in red pepper sauce) over a glass
of wine. The pollo Rosario, chicken topped with sundried tomatoes, shrimp,
and pink garlic-vodka sauce, beats all. & V 🏠 🍷 ⬤ *May–Aug: Mon & Tue.*
AE DC MC V

WINTER PARK: *Limoncello Ristorante* $$$$
702 Orange Ave. [(407) 539-0900.
A chef from Sorrento, owner from Rome, and food from the Italian gods.
Handmade pasta dishes like gnocchi Porto Cervo, deeply satisfying seafood
dishes, and impeccable service make this place a winner and ensure a
memorable experience. & V 🏠 🍷 ⬤ *Sun.*
AE MC V

WINTER PARK: *Shiki Japanese Cuisine* $$$$
525 S Park Ave. [(407) 740-8018.
A modest spot where the elements of Japanese cuisine – artistic presentation
and interior design – come together gracefully. Sushi, sashimi, and service
that is restrained but casual and friendly. & V
AE DC MC V

WINTER PARK: *Blackfin Seafood Grill & Bar* $$$$$
460 N Orlando Ave. [(407) 691-4653. FAX (407) 691-0240.
A surprising daily menu change awaits you at the freshest fish restaurant
around. Set in the very trendy Winter Park Village mall, Blackfin has
attentive service, a reasonable wine list, and a team of chefs who know
their seafood. A great place for seafood lovers. & 🎵 🏠 🍷
AE DC MC V

WINTER PARK: *Chef Justin's Park Plaza Gardens* $$$$$
319 S Park Ave. [(407) 645-2475.
The Park Plaza Hotel renamed its venerable restaurant after local star chef
Justin Plank, a veteran of Wolfgang Puck. Ambitious dishes are served in a
classy Continental atmosphere. Check out the beautiful people, sit at the
intimate bar, or go all-out at the patio restaurant in the back. & V 🏠 🍷
AE DC MC V

WINTER PARK: *Fleming's Steak House* $$$$$
933 N Orlando Ave. [(407) 699-9463.
A high-end steakhouse with an emphasis on the wine. Offers aged, hand-
cut beef in huge, thick-as-a-brick servings and family-style side dishes,
giant seafood entrées, and enormous desserts. & 🍷 ⬤ *Mon.*
AE DC MC V

SHOPPING IN CENTRAL FLORIDA

SHOPPING IS ONE of the major forms of entertainment for visitors to Central Florida. Indoor malls with more than 100,000 sq ft (9,300 sq m) of shopping compete with discount outlet centers, traditional department stores and chain outlets sit side-by-side with unique local shops, and rows of antiques stores are within miles of boutique clothing stores and art galleries. Almost any national retailer can be found on International Drive or in Florida Mall, the state's largest shopping center, while

A typical Florida souvenir

specialty shops sell a wide selection of items, such as antiques, electronics, and sports equipment. Prices range from bargain basement cheap to haute-couture expensive. The theme parks have combined shopping, dining, and entertainment in two massive spending belts running right through their properties, where restaurants and circuses sell souvenirs and souvenir stores offer free magic shows. For listings of malls and factory outlets, see pages 160–61. Shopping districts are described on pages 162–3.

Shops and boutiques along the Park Avenue strip, Winter Park

SALES TAX

SALES TAX ON clothing is 6 percent in Orange County (Orlando) and 7 percent in Osceola County (Kissimmee), where Walt Disney World is actually situated, so park souvenirs are at the higher rate.

SHOPPING SEASONS

ALTHOUGH ACTUAL weather seasons don't vary very much in Central Florida, fashion seasons still turn four times a year. This has led to massive sales in late spring and early fall on clothing and household items.

BOUTIQUE SHOPPING CENTERS

SITTING ON THE grounds of the first outdoor shopping center in the area, **Winter Park Village** is home to a

wide variety of sleek boutique shops that cater to the latest styles. Fashion can be found at the Ann Taylor Loft store, career-wear at Camille La Vie, and fine men's clothing at Jos. A. Bank. Many young hipsters

New Metropolis, a posh furniture store in Winter Park

have filled their homes from New Metropolis, the "Urban Chic" furniture store, while their well-off parents were buying fine linens at Angela Neel. The center offers not only clothing, home furnishings, and jewelry stores, but also several fine restaurants, a large Borders bookstore, and, uniquely, condominium lofts above some of the shops.

The Mall at Millenia might also be called a boutique, as it is the only place in Orlando to shop for Jimmy Choo shoes, Max Azria handbags, Betsey Johnson clothing, and Giorgio's of Palm Beach accessories.

DEPARTMENT STORES

DEPARTMENT STORES are still a way of life in Orlando, even with a wealth of smaller specialty shops in malls and neighborhoods. Regional chains such as **Dillard's**, **Bealls**, and **Burdines-Macy's** dominate the department store scene in Central Florida, offering not only shopping mall outlets but stand-alone stores and discount outlets as well. The Bealls outlets in particular dominate the retail shopping segment, offering discounts on overstock and discontinued goods from the larger stores, and special outlet-only goods and merchandise.

But with the advent of upscale giant malls such as the Mall at Millenia and

An outlet of the exclusive and up-market Saks Fifth Avenue, Orlando

the Florida Mall, national chains are developing a larger presence. Fans of big-city favorites Bloomingdales, Macy's, Nordstrom, Saks Fifth Avenue, and Neiman Marcus can find outlets alongside the more traditional and budget-conscious JC Penney, Sears, and Lord & Taylor in the big malls. For essentials, you need look no further than the no-frills supermarkets such as Target, K-Mart, and Wal-Mart, which can be found anywhere.

Photographic equipment available at a bargain price

SHOPPING FOR BARGAINS

Discount stores and factory outlets carry all kinds of general merchandise, with electronic equipment, household goods and clothing being

the biggest draw. Inexpensive designer clothes, sometimes out of season, turn up at local outlets of the TJMaxx, Marshalls, and **Stein Mart** chains at substantial savings over retail. Consignment clothing outlets such as **Deja Vu** and **Orlando Vintage Clothing Co** have deals on pre-owned clothes from modern times back to the 1920s.

Shops in the outlet malls have big savings on electronics such as discontinued or factory-second cameras, video equipment, and portable stereos. Then there are the late spring and the fall clearance sales that turn even the high-priced department stores into bargain basements.

DIRECTORY

Bealls
8205 S John Young Parkway,
Orlando, FL 32819.
(407) 370-9557.
Osceola Square Mall,
4081 W Vine St,
Kissimmee, FL 34741.
(407) 847-4301.

Burdines-Macy's
3505 E Colonial Dr,
Orlando, FL 32803.
(407) 896-5300.

Deja Vu
1825 N Orange Ave,
Orlando, FL 32804.
(407) 898-3609.

Dillard's
3403 E Colonial Dr,
Orlando, FL 32803.
(407) 896-1211.

Orlando Vintage Clothing Co
2117 W Fairbanks Ave,
Winter Park, FL 32789.
(407) 599-7225.

Stein Mart
7506 Dr. Phillips Blvd,
Orlando, FL 32819.
(407) 363-5770.
2530 E Colonial Dr,
Orlando, FL 32803.
(407) 895-2581.

Winter Park Village
510 N Orlando Ave,
Winter Park, FL 32789.
W www.shopwinterparkvillage.com

One of Florida's many factory outlets, advertising its bargain prices

Shopping Malls

SHOPPING MALLS ARE a quintessential feature of the shopping scene in Florida, where the indoor, air-conditioned mall was invented. They provide all kinds of facilities from movies to restaurants, some even offering personal shoppers and child-minding services. Most malls are conveniently located, often visible from the highway, and in Central Florida range from the Seminole Towne Center on the banks of the St. Johns River to the enormous Florida Mall near the attractions.

Each mall has its own style, some designed as outdoor pavilions, others fully enclosed for all-weather shopping. The discount outlet malls tend to attract large crowds of out-of-town shoppers on the weekends, while the upscale centers fill up during sales. The local Sunday *Orlando Sentinel (see p191)* is a source of sale flyers for the malls. Hotels offer discount cards for most stores, and malls themselves have frequent-shopper programs.

The very posh interior of the Mall at Millenia

The huge food court at the Florida Mall

THE FLORIDA MALL

SPRAWLING OVER an area of 200,000 sq ft (18,580 sq m) the Florida Mall is the largest shopping location in Central Florida. It is anchored by the big names of the US

shopping industry – Burdines, Dillard's, JC Penney, Saks Fifth Avenue, Sears, Nordstrom, and Lord & Taylor department stores. With more than 250 specialty stores, it's difficult to imagine a category this shopping oasis doesn't cover. Check with guest services for a free discount coupon book.

The Florida Mall is so popular that many local hotels run shuttles to it. It is particularly favored by teens, having an enormous food court and several clothing stores aimed at the younger generation.

For visitors exhausted after hours of shopping, the Adams Mark hotel has an entrance right on the main Mall concourse. Other hotels in the vicinity include the Howard Johnson, Archway Inn, Best Western Florida Mall, and Florida Mall Hotel.

THE MALL AT MILLENIA

UPSCALE AND BEYOND, the luxury Mall at Millenia offers valet parking, a full service concierge and personal shopper service, and a foreign currency exchange. With its own exit on Interstate 4, the Millenia has Bloomingdales, Macy's, and Neiman Marcus department stores, along with flagship stores from Louis Vuitton, Gucci, Tiffany, Chanel, Apple Computer, Lancel, Tommy Bahama, Burberry, Cartier, St-John, and Cole Haan. Also featured are California Pizza Kitchen, McCormick & Schmick, Brio Tuscan Grille, P.F. Chang's China Bistro, Cheesecake Factory, and Panera Bread.

The atypical food court has more full-service restaurants than many Orlando

The dazzling façade of the Mall at Millenia, one of Orlando's swankiest malls

neighborhoods. Dramatic architectural highlights and dancing fountains add to the glitz of many stores unique to the Orlando area, such as Bang & Olufsen, Japanese Weekend Maternity, Metropolitan Museum of Art Store, and home furnishings specialist Z Gallerie.

DISCOUNT SHOPPING MALLS

ONE OF THE most popular malls, the giant **Belz Factory Outlet Mall** draws as many people as Universal Orlando on a good day. With 700,000 sq ft (6,500 sq m) of outlet shopping, the largest discount center in the country takes up two fully enclosed malls and four strip centers, requiring its own shuttle buses to cover it all. Factory seconds and overruns cover the spectrum of shopping, from 15 different shoe stores to camera and electronic equipment, vitamins to bibles, and jewelry to music. Cooks find discounts on professional knives, while souvenir hunters head for the Universal Studios outlet. Designer labels, such as Geoffrey Beane and Tommy Hilfiger, are all available, along with Mikasa and Pfaltzgraff dishware. Up the road from the primary Belz location are the **Lenox Factory Store**, where you can buy discounted china and crystal, and **Off 5th-Saks Fifth Avenue Outlet**, with trendy yet affordable apparel.

Orlando Premium Outlets, near SeaWorld, caters to the upscale shopper, offering

Orlando Premium Outlets, which stocks designer brands

deep discounts on Coach, Burberry, DKNY, Fendi, Nike, Giorgio Armani, and Versace. More than 100 designer brands end up here, from shoes and handbags to apparel and jewelry, as well as a vast selection of housewares and home furnishings.

Located on the busy US 192 Highway, the **Kissimmee Manufacturers Outlet** leans more toward home and luggage fashions, and offers Cannon, Tourister, and Fieldcrest discounts.

On the low end of the bargain scale are flea markets, dealing in a mixture of new discount merchandise and recycled bargains. The largest example is **Flea World**, located between Orlando and Sanford. More than 1,700 vendors man booths of antiques, clothing, used books, jewelry, and several more odd assortments of items than can be listed.

The Nike Factory Store at Belz Factory Outlet Mall, Orlando

Shopping Districts

R ETAIL STORES CONGREGATE along the high-traffic areas of Orlando, alongside Disney and Universal, and near the large hotels. Aside from the shopping area following the village green of Winter Park, districts tend to be outside of central areas, Downtown Orlando having little shopping of its own. But follow the traffic, and on roads heading southwest to the theme parks and farther west toward the Coast, shopping becomes a journey of discovery. Here, antiques stores and art galleries stand cheek-by-jowl with souvenir stands, and hand-painted furniture is as easily obtainable as a pair of sunglasses.

The Mercado shopping center at International Drive

ORLANDO SHOPPING DISTRICTS

N ORTH ORANGE is a high-traffic strip heading directly out of downtown toward Winter Park. Antiques stores sell tiny knickknacks, huge, almost mall-sized stores hawk fine furniture, and several stores cater to home improvement via decorative

stone and tile. One of the last great bastions of vinyl and used CDs is **Rock & Roll Heaven**. **Flo's Attic** is the rambling two-story home of fine – and not so fine – furniture, while comic book fans looking to redecorate can visit **Boom-Art** for furniture in a pop art style.

A few blocks away from North Orange Street is Mills Avenue, affectionately known as Rainbow Row. This area has more antiques malls, a smattering of art galleries, and several gay-friendly stores.

The **Orlando International Airport** (see p192) has become a major shopping stop, with two Disney Store outlets alongside a Universal Studios store, a wet-looking shop from SeaWorld, and the Warner Brothers Studio Store in the main concourse.

International Drive rewards shoppers by having row upon row of stores catering to every taste. There are brand-name shops and designer

Tile with flamingos

outlet stores, many of which target clothing, shoe, and home decor bargain hunters. Tommy Hilfiger and Armani hold sway at **Pointe Orlando**, an open-air shopping complex replete with palm trees and fountains. The complex also offers several shaded spots where tired shoppers can rest awhile.

Also on International Drive is **The Mercado** shopping center, a quirky place, with marionettes at Puppets Unlimited and spy cameras at Spy USA. It has some good restaurants and a food court.

WINTER PARK SHOPPING DISTRICTS

U PSCALE Park Avenue in Winter Park caters to the well-to-do, on a 10-block strip of shops, restaurants, art galleries, and even a museum or two. **Bari Men's** features fine suits, **Nicole Miller** and **Talbots** handle upscale women's clothing, and Banana Republic and The Gap take care of everyone else. Stores such as Williams-Sonoma and Caswell-Massey supply kitchen and makeup tables, while **Restoration Hardware** and Pottery Barn fill the home. **Park Ave CDs** is a mainstay of new music from smooth jazz to the outer reaches of rock.

Winter Park offers contemporary work from 150 local artists in the Scott Laurent Gallery (see pp164–5), while

A wide variety of shops lined up at Orlando International Airport

Visitors crowding a street at Downtown Disney's West Side

Timothy's Gallery handles art furniture and home decor. The exemplary gift shop at the **Charles Hosmer Morse Museum of American Art** offers reproductions and apparel based on the museum's collection of Louis Comfort Tiffany artworks.

An expansive outdoor shopping plaza, Winter Park Village *(see pp158–9)* offers an all-round experience, with its many – and varied – clothing shops, home decor and furniture stores, jewelry outlets, a bookstore, fine dining, and a state-of-the-art movie theater.

SHOPPING AT THE THEME PARKS

SOUVENIRS ARE not the only expensive things visitors can buy at the theme parks. **Universal CityWalk** *(see pp98–9)* is a center for music and funky dining, but shopping also rules, with a San Francisco-style rambling hill that houses establishments such as the Art Deco jewelry store Silver, and Glow!, which sells only stuff that glows in the dark. The

Universal Studios store sells movie memorabilia, while All Star Collectibles offers autographed sports photos and merchandise. After dinner, wander through Cigarz At Citywalk for, yes, cigars, or pick up a realistic – but fake – diamond ring at Elegant Illusions.

Downtown Disney's West Side *(see pp74–5)* is the home of $3,000 sunglasses at Celebrity Eyeworks and a $30,000 guitar at the Guitar Gallery. West Side's Virgin Megastore is the largest CD outlet in the city of Orlando. Autograph hunters flock to Starabilia's for framed signatures of the stars. There are also gift shops attached to the House of Blues, Planet Hollywood, and Cirque du Soleil in West Side.

Downtown Disney's Marketplace *(see p75)*, right next door, is home to the LEGO Imagination Center, with giant Lego dinosaurs towering outside. Disney toys abound in stores at the Marketplace, from the Hasbro Once Upon A Toy store to the World of Disney superstore.

Souvenirs from Universal Studio

DIRECTORY	Pointe Orlando	Nicole Miller	THEME PARKS
ORLANDO	9101 International Dr, Orlando, FL 32819. 📞 *(407) 248-2838.* 🌐 www.pointeorlandofl.com	312 Park Ave S, Winter Park, FL 32789. 📞 *(407) 628-0400.*	**Downtown Disney's Marketplace** 10,000 Lake Buena Vista Blvd, Lake Buena Vista, FL 32831. 📞 *(407) 824-4321.*
Boom-Art 1821 N Orange Ave, Orlando, FL 32804. 📞 *(407) 281-0246.*	**Rock & Roll Heaven** 1814 N Orange Ave, Orlando, FL 32804. 📞 *(407) 896-1952.*	**Park Ave CDs** 528 Park Ave S, Winter Park, FL 32789. 📞 *(407) 629-5293.*	
Flo's Attic 1800 N Orange Ave, Orlando, FL 32804. 📞 *(407) 895-1800.*	**WINTER PARK**	**Restoration Hardware** 400 Park Ave S, Winter Park, FL 32789. 📞 *(407) 622-1050.*	**Downtown Disney's West Side** Buena Vista Dr, Lake Buena Vista, FL 32830. 📞 *(407) 939-6244.*
The Mercado 8445 S International Dr, Orlando, FL 32819. 📞 *(407) 345-9337.* 🌐 www.themercado.com	**Bari Men's** 309 Park Ave N, Winter Park, FL 32789. 📞 *(407) 539-7044.*		
Orlando International Airport One Airport Blvd, Orlando, FL 32827. 📞 *(407) 825-2001.*	**Charles Hosmer Morse Museum of American Art** 445 Park Ave, Winter Park, FL 32789. 📞 *(407) 645-5311.*	**Talbots** 180 Park Ave N, Winter Park, FL 32789. 📞 *(407) 629-6444.* 🌐 www.talbots.com/	**Universal CityWalk** 1000 Universal Studios Plaza, Orlando, FL 33612. 📞 *(407) 224-2691.*

Specialty Shops

WHILE BARGAINS ON clothing is the big retail draw, Central Florida holds its own on more eclectic shopping as well. Indoor and outdoor antiques malls are widespread and popular, cheap electronics hold sway in outlet centers, and Florida's fresh produce can be found in neighborhood farmers' markets almost every day of the week. Work by local artists fills galleries and restaurants alike, and the tourist trade hungers for theme park souvenirs. Orlando's temperate climate means that outdoor sports are a year-round undertaking, which makes sports items a big shopping draw.

Antique Row on Orange Avenue, Orlando

ANTIQUES

THE MECCA OF antiques in Central Florida is a one-hour drive away from a town called Mount Dora (*see p116*). The picturesque village on a chain of lakes has the largest collection of antiques dealers and stores in Southern USA. The most dramatic shopping experience is at **Renninger's Antique Center**, with more than 180 shop sites in a 40,000 sq ft (3,716 sq m) air-conditioned building. Open on weekends, the collection of furniture, dolls, silver, and jewelry is difficult to surpass. Dealers here specialize in Art Deco items, World's Fair collectibles, Mission and Arts & Crafts furniture, and art pottery. The area also hosts one of the largest antiques fairs in the US (*see p25*). This extravagant

event takes place four times a year. There are 20 more antiques shops on the streets of Mount Dora, including **Uncle Al's Time Capsule** for collectible books and souvenirs, and **Southern Exotics Antiques** with a collection of restored architectural details. The North Orange and Mills Avenue areas, in Downtown Orlando, are antiques strips worth exploring. **Eclectics** takes on furniture from several eras while **Iron Gate Antiques** handles new and restored iron furniture and fences. **Victoria's Treasure Shop** is a mini-mall of antiques dealers.

ART GALLERIES

A GROWING local arts community means an increasing supply of items for the **Scott Laurent Gallery** in Winter Park, which specializes in local work. **Gallery on Virginia** displays work from an Orlando artists' guild, while **OVAL on Orange** is owned by a visual artists group, bringing emerging work to Downtown Orlando. Nearby, **Grand Bohemian Gallery** offers the work of artists from all over the world. Most downtown restaurants feature paintings for sale by new artists on their walls.

FARMERS' MARKETS

TUESDAY MEANS the **Sanford Tuesday Morning Farmers' Market** starting at 7am; and every Wednesday at 5:30am there's the **Volusia County Farmers' Market**. On Thursday nights the all-organic **College Park Growers Market** brings farm-grown vegetables, herbs, and flowers to the area. Saturday is a fresh treasure-trove for shopping in **Winter Park Farmers' Market** and the **Downtown Orlando Farmers' Market**, and Sunday means greens at the **Celebration Sunday Farmers' Market** from 9am.

GIFTS & SOUVENIRS

A POPULAR GIFT for Florida's visitors are fresh citrus fruits, including the varieties grown in Central Florida such as pink, red, and white grapefruit, Hamlin and Valencia oranges, and tangerines. Not the giant fruit producer it once was, Orlando still has some groves where one can buy fruit or have it shipped directly. Disney and the theme parks have turned merchandising into a fine art, and shopping for souvenirs is a major activity. From concession stands within the parks to shopping arcades such as Universal's CityWalk and Disney's West Side to the authorized **SeaWorld Store** at Orlando International Airport and the Universal clearance store at Belz Factory Outlets, it's hard to escape branded gifties. Shops all along International Drive sell

The bounty at Winter Park Farmers' Market

discounted Disney clothing and merchandise. Local museums have stores, such as the **Orlando Science Center Store**, with gifts geared toward current exhibits.

ELECTRONICS OUTLETS

BECAUSE OF THE large influx of foreign tourists, many electronics shops along International Drive and in the outlet malls carry camcorders and video equipment suited for international customers. Sony, Panasonic, Bose, and others have factory outlet shops for bargains on overruns and reconditioned goods. Bang & Olufsen, Sound Advice, and Absolute Sound offer premium equipment not found in the chain outlets.

Ron Jon Surf Shop, one of the best-known sports retailers

SPORTS EQUIPMENT

WHILE AN HOUR from either coast and any ocean, several retailers in Orlando sell scuba equipment and surfboards. The largest of these is **Ron Jon Surf Shop**, a 40-year tradition in Cocoa

Beach that opened an outlet in Orlando in 2003 – it features a huge collection of surfboards and swimwear. **Jet Ski Orlando** handles the power water sports toys, while **Play It Again Sports** recycles used golf, tennis, and exercise equipment.

DIRECTORY

ANTIQUES

Eclectics
1510 N Mills Ave,
Orlando, FL 32803.
 (407) 898-1968.

Iron Gate Antiques
1722 N Mills Ave,
Orlando, FL 32803.
(407) 896-0181.

Renninger's Antique Center
20651 US Hwy 441,
Mt Dora, FL 32757.
(352) 383-8393.

Southern Exotics Antiques
116 W 5th Ave,
Mount Dora,
FL 32757.
(352) 735-2500.

Uncle Al's Time Capsule
140 E 4th Ave,
Mount Dora,
FL 32757.
(352) 383-1958.

Victoria's Treasure Shop
361 E Michigan St,
Orlando,
FL 32806.
(407) 849-9719.

ART GALLERIES

Gallery on Virginia
1003 Virginia Dr,
Orlando, FL 32803.
(407) 898-8343.

Grand Bohemian Gallery
325 S Orange Ave,
Orlando, FL 32801.
(407) 581-4801.

OVAL on Orange
29 S Orange Ave,
Orlando, Florida 32801.
(407) 648-1819.

Scott Laurent Gallery
348 Park Ave N,
Winter Park,
FL 32789.
(407) 629-1488.

Timothy's Gallery
212 Park Ave N,
Winter Park, FL 32789.
(407) 629-0707.

FARMERS' MARKETS

Downtown Orlando Farmers' Market
8am–2:30pm Sat.
Magnolia Ave & Central
Blvd, Orlando, FL 32801.
(321) 689-2798.

Celebration Sunday Farmers' Market
Oct–Jun: 9am–3pm.
Celebration &
Mulberry Aves,
Celebration, FL 34747.
(407) 892-1135;
(407) 566-1234.

College Park Growers Market
Oct–Jun: 6pm–9pm Thu.
Edgewater Dr,
Orlando, FL 32804.
(407) 649-3148.

Sanford Tuesday Morning Farmers' Market
8am–2pm Tue.
Magnolia Square,
Sanford,
FL 32772.
(407) 814-8120.

Volusia County Farmers' Market
5:30am–5pm Wed.
3090 E New York Ave,
Deland, FL 32724.
(386) 734-1614.

Winter Park Farmers' Market
7am–1pm Sat.
New England & New York
Aves.
Winter Park, FL 32789.
(407) 599-3358.

GIFTS & SOUVENIRS

Ollieanna Groves
PO Box 940067,
Maitland, FL 32794.
(407) 644-8803.

Orlando Science Center Store
777 E Princeton St,
Orlando, FL 32803.
(407) 514-2230.

SeaWorld Store
Orlando International
Airport,
West Hall,
One Airport Blvd,
Orlando, FL 32827.
(407) 825-2642.

SPORTS EQUIPMENT

Jet Ski Orlando
6801 S Orange Ave,
Orlando, FL 32809.
(407) 859-3006.

Play It Again Sports
2823 S Orange Ave,
Orlando, FL 32806.
(407) 872-3351.

Ron Jon Surf Shop
5160 International Dr,
Orlando, FL 32819.
(407) 481-2555.

ENTERTAINMENT IN CENTRAL FLORIDA

THEME parks are just one of the many forms of entertainment available to tourists in Central Florida. This region is home to a wide and varied assortment of theater, dance, and music venues, as well as popular nightspots and bars. The classics are well represented in Orlando by the Philharmonic Orchestra, the Orlando Opera Company, and the several classical music festivals held each year. A thriving Shakespearean company caters to theater patrons, presenting world-class stage productions.

Advertisement for the
Florida Film Festival

The annual Florida Film Festival brings independent movie-making closer to home, and offers a launch pad to student filmmakers from local universities who get the opportunity to screen their films alongside professionals. Local theaters such as Enzian regularly showcase an array of art films. Apart from the cultural activities, Orlando also offers nighttime entertainment with nightclubs and dinner shows in Downtown Disney *(see pp74–5)*, Universal CityWalk *(see pp98–9)* and Downtown Orlando.

Scene from a performance in progress, Orlando Opera Company

SOURCES OF INFORMATION

THE TWO MOST popular and reliable sources for current and new entertainment listings are the calendar sections of the *Orlando Sentinel*, which is included in Friday's edition of the daily paper, and the free *Orlando Weekly*, which is available on Thursdays. Both can be accessed online as well. You can also check the websites of MSN's City Guide as well as Digital City Orlando *(see p189 & p191)* for any additional information.

THEATER

ORLANDO HAS a surprisingly rich theater community, and a wide variety of offerings. The not-to-miss event is the **Orlando International Fringe Festival** *(see p23)*, which takes place in May each

year. The festival brings more than 60 companies from around the world together for an exciting ten days of almost continuous theatrical activities. A wide range of productions as well as plays of every imaginable kind are showcased here.

Actors dressed in character,
Orlando-UCF Shakespeare Festival

The **Bob Carr Performing Arts Center** hosts a Broadway series of touring shows with productions such as *The Producers* and *Les Miserables*. With actors constantly drawn to Orlando for work at the theme parks, the local theater has a large pool of talent that organizes shows at the Mad Cow Theatre *(see p109)* and the award-winning **Theatre Downtown**. The **Orlando Broadway Dinner Theater** also serves a prime-rib buffet along with performances of *Camelot* and *A Chorus Line*.

The University of Central Florida, Rollins College, and Valencia Community College all have their own individual and unique theater programs. The colleges have full seasons of productions that are open to the public.

At one time only a seasonal theater, the famous Orlando-UCF Shakespeare Festival *(see p107)* now produces the classics throughout the year. The theater has a state-of-the-art center with three indoor stages, but the late spring performances are generally held at the 900-seat outdoor Lake Eola Amphitheater, located in Downtown Orlando.

CLASSICAL MUSIC & DANCE

ORLANDO'S PUBLIC radio station, WMFE (90.7 FM), broadcasts classical music almost continuously. Broadcasting more than two dozen

Dancers from the Orlando Ballet performing on stage

performances a year on the radio, the highly gifted **Orlando Philharmonic** orchestra also performs more than 100 times each season. They also provide the accompaniment to **Orlando Ballet**, one of the oldest and most renowned professional dance companies in the Southern United States. The Central Florida Ballet, a popular dance company in Orlando, also gives several performances through the year. The **Orlando Chorale**, a 40-voice choir, is a community chorus presenting vocal work in an extensive classical repertoire.

Classical music festivals, such as the **Festival of Orchestras** concert series, features five or more internationally acclaimed symphony orchestras each year, including the National Orchestra of France and the New York Philharmonic. The Rollins College **Winter Park Bach Festival** offers performances from the famous Bach Festival Choir and Orchestra.

DINNER SHOWS

Dinner theater is a popular concept in Central Florida. You can partake of an appetizing dinner while watching an entertaining show. Take a short trip into the Middle Ages as jousting knights fill the arena in front of you at the **Medieval Times Dinner & Tournament** show *(see p170)*. **Pirates Dinner Adventure** is a Broadway-style show alive with swashbuckling stunts and songs. **Arabian Nights Dinner Attraction** is a show that combines magnificent Arabian stallions with gypsy stunt riders and a Wild West show. The newest attraction in Orlando, **Dolly Parton's Dixie Stampede Dinner & Show**, is a country hoedown featuring animal races and Civil War rivalries with lots of music and dancing.

Neon sign of Southern Nights

Disney is also home to two dinner shows with large-scale extravaganzas: Hoop-Dee-Doo Musical Revue at the Fort Wilderness Resort, with a country buffet and Western entertainment, and Disney's Spirit of Aloha *(see p75)*, an evening of hula, fire dancing, and a luau feast at the popular Polynesian Resort.

NIGHTCLUBS & BARS

While clubs and bars are found everywhere, from the theme parks to the coast, the hub of nighttime entertainment is Downtown Orlando. **The Social** is the ideal destination for everything from rock music to the weekly Phat-n-Jazzy show. Most clubs have DJs and places such as **The Club at Firestone** are perennial hot spots with nights of Latin, hip-hop, and dance music. **Alpha Bar** and **Central Station Bar** are smaller and more intimate downtown dance clubs, while Tabu is a former movie theater turned disco. Clubs such as **Parliament House** and **Southern Nights** form an east-west bracket of downtown for gay nightlife. The fun usually ends at 2am when bars stop serving liquor.

An exciting chariot race at the central arena, Arabian Nights Dinner Attraction show

The colorful and illuminated exterior of CityJazz, CityWalk

LIVE MUSIC AT THE THEME PARKS

UNIVERSAL'S CityWalk and Disney's Pleasure Island are two exciting hot spots for adults. **CityJazz** presents both the Down Beat Hall of Fame jazz museum and live music from top jazz talents. Nearby, **Bob Marley – A Tribute to Freedom** plays reggae music. Both **Hard Rock Live** at CityWalk and **House of Blues** at Disney's West Side are enormous world-class venues, featuring famous bands from around the globe.

The **Pleasure Island Jazz Company** showcases local and national jazz performers. Disney also features the Epcot Flower & Garden Festival from April to June *(see p22)*, with a Flower Power concert of stars from the 1960s. Held annually, the Blues Festival at Pleasure Island features live performances on several stages,

Live concert performance, Hard Rock Live, CityWalk

and Universal celebrates Mardi Gras in spring with concerts by stars such as Cyndi Lauper and the Black Eyed Peas.

LIVE MUSIC AWAY FROM THE PARKS

THE ECLECTIC nature of Orlando's music scene is reflected at **Will's Pub**, which offers musical acts from heavy metal and punk to soft rock. **Kate O'Brien's** and **Scruffy Murphy's Irish Pub** are downtown pubs showcasing Irish folk music performers.

The Orange Avenue strip in Downtown Orlando offers hip-hop and avant-garde rock in underground clubs such as Tanqueray's. The hip **Ballard & Corum** offers great live music along with a full bar. The **Café Annie** features special Brazilian and Middle Eastern band nights. April brings music lovers to downtown's Florida Music Festival.

The **Copper Rocket** in Maitland is a local favorite for folk and rock bands. Winter Park's **Chapters on Park** plays everything from funk-jazz to Beatles cover bands. R Bistro hosts pop and jazz bands, while singers at the popular **Red Fox Lounge** croon love songs.

CHILDREN'S ENTERTAINMENT

APART FROM Mickey Mouse and the theme parks, there is plenty to entertain kids. The **DisneyQuest** *(see p75)* indoor interactive video arcade lets guests design and ride their own thrill ride.

Children learn how to draw Disney characters and can record CDs at the Radio Disney Song Maker.

The popular Gatorland *(see p121)*, features 110 acres (44 ha) of live alligators, crocodiles, and scenes from Old Florida. A highlight of the park is the Gator Jumparoo where the reptiles leap into the air to be fed by the trainers.

WonderWorks *(see p112)*, set in an "upside-down" building on International Drive, has interactive science exhibits such as virtual roller coasters and a simulated earthquake.

CRUISES & BOAT TRIPS

WITH THOUSANDS of lakes, rivers, springs, and swamps, Florida's waters are a prime source of entertainment. One of the oldest continuing attractions is the Winter Park Scenic Boat Tour *(see p115)*, a one-hour cruise through three lakes interconnected by 12 miles (19 km) of canals, which takes you past mansions and the sights of natural, unspoiled Florida. Other boat tours in the area navigate beautiful Lake Tohopekaliga in Kissimmee, up the north-flowing St. Johns River on the Beresford Lady paddle wheeler, or along the vast Intracoastal Waterway that separates Daytona from the Florida mainland. Trips on an authentic Florida airboat guide sightseers along ancient swampland, and dayboats can be hired out of Port Canaveral for fishing trips.

A family enjoying the day out on a relaxing boating trip

DIRECTORY

THEATER

Annie Russel Theatre
Rollins College, 1000 Holt Ave, Winter Park.
§ *(407) 646-2501.*
w *www.rollins.edu/ theatre/annie.html*

Bob Carr Performing Arts Center
401 Livingston St, Orlando.
(407) 849-2577.
w *www.orlandocentro plex.com/bobcarr.shtml*

Orlando Broadway Dinner Theater
3376 Edgewater Dr, Orlando.
(407) 843-6275.
w *www. orlandobroadway.com*

Orlando International Fringe Festival
398 W Amelia St, Orlando.
(407) 648-0077.
w *www.orlandofringe. com*

Theatre Downtown
2113 N Orange Ave, Orlando.
(407) 841-0083.
w *www. theatredowntown.net*

UCF Conservatory Theatre
4000 Central Florida Blvd, Orlando.
(407) 823-1500.
w *www. cas.ucf.edu/theatre*

CLASSICAL MUSIC & DANCE

Festival of Orchestras
1353 Palmetto Ave, Suite 100, Winter Park.
(407) 539-0245.
w *www. festivalforchestras.com*

Orlando Ballet
1111 N Orange Ave, Orlando.
(407) 426-1739.

Orlando Chorale
PO Box 536968, Orlando.
(407) 896-8624.
w *www. theorlandochorale.org*

Orlando Philharmonic
812 E Rollins St, Suite 300, Orlando.
(407) 896-6700.
w *www.orlandophil.org*

Winter Park Bach Festival
1000 Holt Ave, Winter Park.
(407) 646-2182.
w *www. bachfestivalflorida.org*

DINNER SHOWS

Arabian Nights Dinner Attraction
6225 W Irlo Bronson Hwy, Kissimmee.
(407) 239-9223.
w *www. arabian-nights.com*

Dolly Parton's Dixie Stampede Dinner & Show
8251 Vineland Ave, Orlando.
(407) 238-4455.
w *www. dixiestampede.com*

Medieval Times Dinner & Tournament
4510 W Irlo Bronson Hwy, Kissimmee.
(407) 239-0214.
w *www.medievaltimes. com*

Pirates Dinner Adventure
6400 Carrier Dr, Orlando.
(407) 248-0590.
w *www.piratesdinner adventure.com*

NIGHTCLUBS & BARS

Alpha Bar
102 N Orange Ave, Orlando.
(407) 841-6544.

Central Station Bar
100 E Central Ave, Orlando.
(407) 426-8336.

The Club at Firestone
578 N Orange Ave, Orlando.
(407) 872-0066.

Parliament House
410 N Orange Blossom Trail, Orlando.
(407) 425-7571.

The Social
54 N Orange Ave, Orlando.
(407) 246-1419.
w *www. orlandosocial.com*

Southern Nights
375 S Bumby Ave, Orlando
(407) 898-0424.

LIVE MUSIC

Ballard & Corum
535 W New England Ave, Winter Park.
(407) 539-1711.

Bob Marley – A Tribute to Freedom
1000 Universal Studios Plaza, Orlando.
(407) 224-2690.

Café Annie
131 N Orange Ave, Orlando.
(407) 420-4041.

Chapters on Park
358 N Park Ave, Winter Park.
(407) 644-2880.

CityJazz
6000 Universal Blvd, Orlando.
(407) 224-2189 .

The Copper Rocket
106 Lake Ave, Maitland.
(407) 645-0069.

Hard Rock Live!
6050 Universal Blvd, Orlando.
(407) 351-5483.
w *www.hardrock.com*

House of Blues
1490 E Buena Vista Dr, Lake Buena Vista, Orlando.
(407) 934-2583.
w *www.hob.com*

Kate O'Brien's
42 W Central Blvd, Orlando.
(407) 649-7646.

Pleasure Island Jazz Company
3180 Buena Vista Dr, Lake Buena Vista, Orlando.
(407) 934-7781.

Red Fox Lounge
Best Western Mt. Vernon Hotel, 110 S Orlando Ave, Winter Park.
(407) 647-1166.

Scruffy Murphy's Irish Pub
9 W Washington St. Orlando.
(407) 648-5460.

Will's Pub
1850 N Mills Ave, Orlando.
(407) 898-5070.

CHILDREN'S ENTERTAINMENT

Central Florida Zoological Park
3755 NW Hwy 17-92 Sanford.
(407) 323-4450.
w *www. centralfloridazoo.org*

DisneyQuest
1486 E Buena Vista Dr, Lake Buena Vista, Orlando
(407) 828-4600.
w *www.disneyquest.com*

CRUISES & BOAT TRIPS

Aquatic Wonders Boat Tours
101 Lakeshore Blvd, Kissimmee.
(407) 846-2814.

All Orlando Day Tours & Excursions
119 N Kirkman Rd, Orlando.
(888) 609-5665.
w *www. allorlandotours.com*

Beresford Lady Boat Tours
244 S Woodland Blvd, DeLand.
(888) 740-7523.
w *www.beresfordlady. net*

WEDDINGS IN CENTRAL FLORIDA

APART FROM ITS fame as an immensely popular vacation spot, Central Florida is now widely recognized as one of the most sought-after wedding and honeymoon destinations. The region's picture-perfect weather is ideal for wedding ceremonies that range from simple, inexpensive backyard affairs to theme park extravaganzas that cost thousands of dollars. Themed weddings are extremely popular and organizers can create anything a couple desires. Private gardens, cruise ships,

Bridal bouquet

the Grand Staircase of *Titanic*, Cinderella's Castle, and several attractions from Hard Rock Café to SeaWorld and Walt Disney World are available as wedding locations to fulfil every fantasy – many a bride with a flowing train has been seen sporting Mickey Mouse ears. Orlando is also famous for its unusual weddings. Couples exchange vows while golfing, fishing, and even in a hot-air balloon. Many local planners offer ceremony and honeymoon packages to suit all budgets.

Wedding ceremony in progress at Disney's Wedding Pavilion

INDOOR SPECTACULARS

LIFE-SIZE replicas of certain rooms on the *Titanic* might seem an unusual place for a wedding, but **Titanic – The Exhibition** *(see p112)* offers just that. The stately surroundings of the ship are a compelling and romantic draw. The wedding package includes a ceremony on the Grand Staircase, photos in the parlor suite, and a tour of the exhibit.

TITANIC THE EXHIBITION

Logo of Titanic – The Exhibition

The **Medieval Times Dinner & Tournament** show allows couples to wed against a backdrop of 11th-century England. Arabian stallions, knights, and fair damsels form a part of the wedding party.

The marble halls of Orlando Museum of Art *(see p107)* provide an elegant backdrop for a wedding or a reception. The ceremony is conducted amid a prestigious collection of American artworks.

The Art Deco **Westin Grand Bohemian Hotel** offers a Bohemian-themed wedding with a stay at the upscale hotel. The ceremony is conducted at their rooftop garden. Located at the Universe Shrine Church, the Mary Queen Roman Catholic Chapel can seat a wedding party of up to 2,000 people. The chapel has exquisite stained-glass windows and presents a charming venue for a wedding.

The plush and impressive Grand Ballroom at **Adam's Mark** hotel holds up to 600 people. It is located within the Florida Mall and gives couples the opportunity to get married at the largest shopping center in Central Florida.

Couples can choose from a wide and exciting range of themed weddings at the **Central Florida Wedding Chapel**. Midnight services, Hawaiian ceremonies, pirate, gangster, and ghost-themed haunted weddings, and even a ceremony officiated by an Elvis impersonator – all these and many more options are available. It's hard to imagine a theme that organizers at the chapel won't attempt.

For a more intimate and exclusive gathering, **The Veranda** at Thornton Park is an ideal location. The B&B features a romantic courtyard hidden behind its five historic buildings, and has 12 rooms including a Bridal Suite with a king four-poster bed.

THEME PARKS

CALL IT ROMANTIC, child-like, or corny, a **Walt Disney World® Resort** wedding is always special. With more than 2,000 couples taking the plunge every year, Disney wedding packages start at around $3,000, while the custom wedding arrangements begin at about $7,500. For those not on a budget, a Disney wedding with 100 guests can cost up to $50,000.

A bride arriving in Cinderella's glass coach

Weddings at Magic Kingdom are private and expensive events that are held after the park closes. The bride arrives in Cinderella's glass coach and couples exchange vows in the scenic Rose Garden by Cinderella's Castle. Adding to the revelry are costumed footmen and trumpeters. Animal Kingdom offers a safari-themed affair, while a bride at the Disney-MGM Studios is driven around in a limousine and can leave her handprints in front of Mann's Chinese Theater. Celebrants at Epcot can choose the country pavilion they want to get married in. Disney's Wedding Pavilion, a Victorian chapel surrounded by palm trees, can accommodate 300 guests and as many as 12 weddings in a day. Details such as food,

flowers, photography, entertainment, and the honeymoon hotel are all taken care of by Disney planners.

Weddings are also held at the Yacht Club Resort, the Grand Floridian Resort & Spa, and BoardWalk Resort *(see p142)*. Of course, Disney characters are more than willing to attend the ceremony. **SeaWorld** not only has space, it also provides guests for your wedding. Ceremonies take place among dolphins, penguins, and a ring-bearing sea lion. The gardens at Ports of Call complex can entertain 750 guests.

OUTDOOR EXTRAVAGANZAS

LOCATED NEAR Downtown Orlando, **Harry P. Leu Gardens** *(see p108)* is a lush 50 acres (20 ha) of horticultural splendor. It offers several garden settings for weddings amid rose and camellia collections. The Rose Garden, the Edinburgh Floral Clock, and the Butterfly Garden here are very popular wedding venues. **Kraft Azalea Gardens** is a quiet spot on the banks of Lake Maitland in Winter Park. The garden has flowering trees from January to March and

provides a very romantic and beautiful setting for weddings and receptions. The secluded nature of the gardens lends an intimate quality to the event.

Wedding ceremonies at **Albin Polasek Museum & Sculpture Gardens** in Winter Park are performed on expansive grounds with Polasek's sculptures looking on. Couples can also get married in the garden's romantic chapel.

The **Rivership Romance**, a 100-ft (30-m) steel steamer ship, lives up to its name, creating a magical experience for couples who choose to get married aboard the ship. A party of up to 200 people can be accommodated on the ship and the package includes a cruise along the St. Johns River and an elaborate dinner, as well as dancing.

Offering 36 holes on two courses, the **Mission Inn Golf & Tennis Resort** combines sport and nuptials. Champagne breakfasts, bridal luncheons, and bachelor party golf outings are all available around the distinctive Spanish architecture. There's a 1930s yacht, *La Reina*, for cruises on Lake Harris.

Bok Tower Gardens *(see p123)* is one of the highest points in Florida and is a National Historic Landmark. Couples can exchange vows in a romantic setting of palm trees, flowering plants, and a 57-bell carillon.

Albin Polasek Museum & Sculpture Gardens

The romantic setting of Disney's Wedding Pavilion, a Victorian chapel surrounded by palm trees and a lake

Orange Blossom Balloons, which offers hot-air balloon weddings

The Unusual

Couples looking for a wedding ceremony that is out of the ordinary have a range of options to choose from. Companies such as **Orange Blossom Balloons** and **Blue Water Balloons** offer hot-air balloon weddings. The package includes transportation to the flight site, a ground-based ceremony that is followed by a one-hour balloon flight for two, and a congratulatory champagne toast at touchdown.

Brevard Zoo in Melbourne offers the use of its Serengeti Pavilion, Flamingo Pond, and Australian Aviary for weddings and receptions. As part of the event, zoo staff can conduct train rides through the park, and sometimes guide guests through a Native Florida Wetlands area by kayak. Biker couples get a slice of hog heaven at **Orlando Harley-Davidson**®. The bride and the groom, dressed in biker wedding garb, take a ride on prized Harley bikes, with the processional also following on Harleys. Those in search of even more speed can exchange vows at the

Daytona International Speedway. The ceremony is performed in the winner's circle and includes a victory lap. High-flying and airplane-loving couples will find antique aircraft from World War I and beyond at Kissimmee's **Flying Tigers Warbird Restoration Museum**. Aircraft-laden hangars and a private reception area are available for the ceremony.

Wedding Packages

Rather than leave for the honeymoon after the wedding, those getting married in Central Florida can choose from a wide range of wedding and vacation combination packages offered by most of the resorts and hotels.

The Westin Grand Bohemian in Downtown Orlando has three packages – ranging from a simple ceremony with live classical music to a three-course dinner for the couple and ten guests – all including a one-night stay in the Art Deco-inspired hotel. Prices range from $1,600 to more than $3,000.

Disney weddings are highly organized affairs, and offer

the celebrating couple many choices. Disney's Dream Maker plan includes admission to all four Walt Disney World theme parks, a horse-drawn carriage ride with champagne, dinner at one of Disney's restaurants, a spa treatment, admission to Cirque du Soleil *(see p75)*, and a three night stay at a Disney resort. Disney's ultimate package includes the private use of Magic Kingdom for as many as 400 guests, and a complimentary room for the honeymoon night. The cost for this kind of package starts at $42,000.

The **Wonderland Inn B & B** in Kissimmee is an excellent spot for a smaller, cosier wedding. The ceremony can be held in their garden gazebo under spreading oak trees. The package includes a champagne toast and wedding cake along with accommodations at the inn.

Wedding Details

There are entire books filled with lists of wedding planners, caterers, tuxedo rentals, coordinators, flower arrangers, and photographers. Invitations can be ordered from local print shops and office supply stores such as Kinkos. There's a wide variety of flower suppliers, from budget dealers such as 1-800-Flowers to boutique florists. Wedding gowns are a hot business, and stand-alone haute couture shops and stores in the high-end shopping malls supply designer dresses. Wedding planners usually take care of all these details.

Legalities

Marriage licenses are available at any courthouse in Florida, and some wedding organizers can obtain the license for you by mail. No blood test or waiting period is required for out-of-state residents. Florida residents, however, are required to undergo a three-day waiting period. If previously married, the date of divorce or date of spouse's death must be supplied.

DIRECTORY

FLORIDA COUNTY CLERK'S OFFICES

Clerk of the Court,
Orange County
425 N Orange Ave,
Suite 355,
Orlando.
(407) 836-2067.

Clerk of Circuit Court, Osceola County
2 Courthouse Square,
Suite 2000,
Kissimmee.
(407) 343-3530.

WEDDING PLANNERS

A Beautiful Wedding
6288 Indian Meadow,
Orlando.
(407) 876-6433.

Carolyn Allen's Bridals & Formals
5410 Central Florida Parkway,
Orlando.
(407) 238-2722.

Central Florida Wedding Locations
6288 Indian Meadow,
Orlando.
(407) 876-6433.
W www.orlandoweddinglocations.com

Just Marry! Just Celebrate!
222 W Comstock Ave,
Suite 202,
Winter Park.
(407) 629-2747.

Orlando Wedding Group
140 N Orlando Ave,
Orlando.
(407) 884-1809.
W www.orlandoweddinggroup.com

WEDDING SITES

Adam's Mark
1500 Sand Lake Rd,
Orlando.
(407) 859-1500.
W www.adamsmark.com/orlando

Albin Polasek Museum & Sculpture Gardens
633 Osceola Ave, Winter Park.
(407) 647-6294.

Blue Water Balloons
566 Buckminster Circle,
Orlando.
(407) 894-5040.
W www.bluewaterballoons.com

Bok Tower Gardens
1151 Tower Blvd,
Lake Wales.
(863) 676-1408.
W www.boktower.org

Brevard Zoo
8225 N Wickham Rd,
Melbourne.
(321) 254-9453.
W www.brevardzoo.org

Central Florida Wedding Chapel
5324 Central Florida Parkway,
Orlando.
(407) 238-9300.
W www.centralfloridaweddingchapel.com

Daytona International Speedway
1801 W International
Speedway Blvd,
Daytona Beach.
(386) 254-2700.
W www.daytona500.com

Flying Tigers Warbird Restoration Museum
231 N Hoagland Blvd,
Kissimmee.
(407) 933-1942.
W www.warbirdmuseum.com

Harry P. Leu Gardens
1920 N Forest Ave,
Orlando.
(407) 246-2620.
W www.leugardens.org

Kraft Azalea Gardens
Alabama Dr. off Palmer Ave,
Winter Park.
(407) 599-3334.

Medieval Times Dinner & Tournament
4510 W Irlo Bronson Hwy,
Kissimmee.
(407) 396-1518.
W www.medievaltimes.com

Mission Inn Golf & Tennis Resort
10400 County Rd 48,
Howey-In-The-Hills.
(800) 874-9053.
W www.missioninnresort.com

Orange Blossom Balloons
PO Box 22908,
Lake Buena Vista,
Orlando.
(407) 239-7677.
W www.orangeblossomballoons.com

Orlando Harley Davidson®
3770, 37th Street,
Orlando.
(877) 740-3770,
(877) 740-3221.
W www.orlandoharley.com/wedding

Rivership Romance
433 N Palmetto Ave,
Sanford.
(407) 321-5091.
W www.rivershipromance.com

Titanic – The Exhibition
8445 International Dr,
Orlando.
(407) 248-1166.

The Veranda
115 N Summerlin Ave,
Orlando.
(407) 849-0321.

Victorian Wedding Chapel
815 N Main St,
Kissimmee.
(407) 847-6775.
W www.flwedusa.com

Westin Grand Bohemian Hotel
325 S Orange Ave,
Orlando.
(407) 313-9000.
W www.grandbohemianhotel.com

Wonderland Inn B & B
3601 S Orange Blossom Trail,
Kissimmee.
(407) 847-2477.
W www.wonderlandinn.com

THEME PARK WEDDINGS

SeaWorld Orlando
(407) 363-2273.

Walt Disney World® Resort
(321) 939-4610.
W www.disneyweddings.disney.go.com/disneyworldweddings

SPORTS IN CENTRAL FLORIDA

HE AVERAGE temperature of Central Florida is 72°F (22°C). That alone should be enough incentive to think of the Sunshine State as a good sports-oriented vacation destination. The Great Outdoors in Central Florida means fishing, hiking, golf, and more golf. The region's miles of protected land can be explored on foot, bicycle, or boat. Central Florida is the spring training ground for several

Golfers in Orlando

Major League teams and of course, home of Orlando Magic basketball. Then there's car racing, with NASCAR and the Indy 500 an hour's drive away from Orlando. Indoor sports, water sports, and the odd horse-back ride are available year-round. Disney adds to the mix, not only with their Wide World of Sports athletic complex, but even a sports hotel, the All-Star Sports Resort.

---

sports are listed in the sports section of the *Orlando Sentinel (see p191)*. You can also contact local tourist offices for information about specific areas. Further sources of information are given in individual sections.

GOLF

IF GOLF IS YOUR passion, you may already know that Tiger Woods, Arnold Palmer, and 50 or so other PGA Tour players live in the Orlando area. There are over 130 courses within a 45-minute drive of downtown, and Orlando is home to six golf-instruction academies. The tourist comes first, and most of the best courses (several designed by Palmer and Jack Nicklaus) are open to the public.

In Walt Disney World, the **Palm & Magnolia Golf Clubs** challenge even seasoned pros, and host the PGA's Walt Disney World/Oldsmobile

Classic and the LPGA's Healthsouth Clinic. The Bay Hill Invitational is held every March at Palmer's **Bay Hill Golf Club & Lodge**, considered one of the fiercest courses in the country, while Nicklaus chips in with the **Grand Cypress Resort**'s 18-hole New Course, inspired by the Old Course at St. Andrews, Scotland. Other top-range courses include **The Oaks, Timacuan, Falcon's Fire Golf Club, Winter Pines Golf Course**, and **Dubsdread Golf Course**, all situated not more than a five-minute drive away from Downtown Orlando.

Combining vacation and golf is easy at resorts such as **Grande Pines Golf Club, Mission Inn Golf & Tennis Resort, Grenelefe Golf & Tennis Resort**, and the **Ventura Country Club. Kissimmee Bay Country Club** was nominated as one of America's best courses by *Golf Digest*.

Tiger Woods in action at a tournament at Bay Hill Golf Club

SOURCES OF INFORMATION

LOCATED IN Tallahassee, the **Florida Sports Foundation** is the clearing house for state-wide sporting events. The **Department of Environmental Protection** can provide information on outdoor activities. Spectator

---

A game in progress at Falcon's Fire Golf Club in Kissimmee

◁ A newly wedded couple against the romantic backdrop of Cinderella's Castle

TENNIS

ORLANDO SERVES up more than 800 tennis courts for visitors to raise a racquet everywhere, from public courts and clubs to resorts and apartment complexes. Walt Disney World has over 30 of the finest tennis courts in Central Florida, and most of the larger and not-so-large hotels have lit courts. The city of Orlando runs several public facilities, including the **Orlando Tennis Center** with 16 indoor courts and four outdoor lighted racquetball courts. On the West Coast, **Bollettieri Sports Academy** is the tennis school that produced Andre Agassi and Monica Seles. About a 90-minute drive from Orlando, it is the largest tennis training operation in the world. Many hotels have courts, and

Tennis court at Disney's Grand Floridian Resort & Spa

several resorts offer vacation packages that include tennis lessons. Contact the **United States Tennis Association (Florida Section)** for information on coaching, clubs, and competitions.

DRIVING SCHOOLS

CENTRAL FLORIDA is the home of the Daytona 500 and numerous other NASCAR, Indy, truck, motorcycle, and dirt bike races. The **FinishLine Racing School** offers a three-day program at the New Smyrna Speedway. The program is unique in the racing school industry in that it covers both aspects of race car involvement – stock and NASCAR driving. Drivetech teaches hands-on stock car racing at the USA International Speedway in Lakeland.

Racing fans can enjoy the thrill of the auto-racing experience at two Richard Petty Driving Experience centers *(see p73)* and Test Track *(see p46)* at FutureWorld in Epcot, which offers a 65-mph (104-km/h) simulation on a mile-long electric-car track.

DIRECTORY

SOURCES OF INFORMATION

Department of Environmental Protection
3319 Maguire Blvd,
Orlando, FL 32803.
☎ *(407) 894-7555.*

Florida Sports Foundation
2930 Kerry Forest Parkway,
Tallahassee, FL 32309.
☎ *(850) 488-8347.*
W www.flasports.com

GOLF

Bay Hill Golf Club & Lodge
9000 Bay Hill Blvd,
Orlando,
FL 32819.
☎ *(407) 876-2429.*
W www.bayhill.com

Disney's Palm & Magnolia Golf Clubs
1950 W Magnolia Palm Dr,
Lake Buena Vista,
FL 32830.
☎ *(407) 939-4653.*

Dubsdread Golf Course
549 W Par St,
Orlando, FL 32804.
☎ *(407) 246-2551.*

Falcon's Fire Golf Club
3200 Seralago Blvd,
Kissimmee,
FL 34746.
☎ *(407) 397-2777.*
W www.falconsfire.com

Grand Cypress Resort
1 N Jacaranda,
Orlando,
FL 32836.
☎ *(407) 239-4700.*
W www.grandcypress. com

Grande Pines Golf Club
6351 International Golf Club Rd, Orlando,
FL 32821.
☎ *(407) 239-6909.*
W www. grandpinesgolfclub.com

Grenelefe Golf & Tennis Resort
3200 State Rd 546,
Haines City,
FL 33844.
☎ *(863) 422-7511.*

Kissimmee Bay Country Club
2801 Kissimmee Bay Circle,
Kissimmee,
FL 34744.
☎ *(407) 348-4653.*

Mission Inn Golf & Tennis Resort
10400 County Rd 48,
Howey-in-the-Hills,
FL 34737.
☎ *(352) 324-3101.*
W www. missioninnresort.com

The Oaks
1500 Oaks Blvd,
Kissimmee,
FL 34746.
☎ *(407) 933-4055.*
W www. kissimmeeoaksgolf.com

Timacuan
550 Timacuan Blvd,
Lake Mary,
FL 32746.
☎ *(407) 321-0010.*
W www. golftimacuan.com

Ventura Country Club
3201 Woodgate Blvd,
Orlando, FL 32822.
☎ *(407) 277-2640.*

Winter Pines Golf Course
950 S Ranger Blvd,
Winter Park, FL 32792.
☎ *(407) 671-3172.*

TENNIS

Bollettieri Tennis Academy
5500 34th St,
W Bradenton, FL 34210.
☎ *(800) 872-6425.*

Orlando Tennis Center
649 W Livingston St,
Orlando, FL 32801.
☎ *(407) 246-2161.*

United States Tennis Association (Florida Section)
1280 SW 36th Ave,
Pompano Beach,
FL 33069.
☎ *(914) 696-7000.*

DRIVING SCHOOLS

FinishLine Racing School
3113 S Ridgewood Ave,
Edgewater, FL 32141.
☎ *(386) 427-8522.*
W www.finishlineracing. com

Spectator Sports

THOSE WHO PREFER SPORTS action from the stands can shout out while watching a home game of Orlando Magic basketball at the TD Waterhouse Center. Also in residence are the Arena Football League Orlando Predators and the Orlando Seals hockey team. The University of Central Florida Golden Knights football team plays at the Florida Citrus Bowl, where the famed New Year's Day championship is decided, along with the Florida Classic game pitting Bethune-Cookman and Florida A&M.

Unique to Florida is *jai-alai*, a fast-paced game brought to America by Cuban immigrants. Visitors can watch the game at Orlando-Seminole Jai Alai, a place where you can also wager on horseracing.

An Orlando Predators game in progress

A basketball player making a move at a game, Orlando

DISNEY'S WIDE WORLD OF SPORTS®

A JEWEL IN Disney's crown, Wide World of Sports is a world-class training and exhibition center for sports worldwide. It is the spring training home of the Atlanta Braves and the Tampa Bay Buccaneers and the permanent home of the Amateur Athletic Union, which holds more than 30 championship events a year. It also hosts the Pop Warner Super Bowl. There are almost too many pro and amateur events to list: USA Wrestling National Championships, the USA Judo Championships, and the US Men's Clay Court Championships are but a few.

The emphasis at DWWS is on baseball, with football or soccer taking a back seat. Baseball season runs from March to October, with basketball and football in the spring and summer

respectively, and golf and track and field events being held throughout the season.

Visitors can buy tickets to games, or take tours of the complex, which boasts four Major League-sized fields, two Little League fields, six NBA-sized basketball courts, an 11-court tennis complex, six beach-like volleyball courts, complete track and field facilities, and the interactive football "play-ground" called the NFL Experience. The new Hess Sports Fields include four multi-sport fields for soccer, football, lacrosse, and other sports, as well as four new diamonds for baseball and softball. Naturally, there are several sports-related Disney shops. The excellent All Star Café restaurant rounds out the experience.

BASEBALL

SINCE WORLD WAR I, Florida's warm climate has made it a favorite spring training site for Major League baseball teams. Each team returns to the same town every year, pumping millions of dollars into local economy and bringing much prestige. The towns identify strongly with their visitors.

In Central Florida, the training season is from mid-February through March. The Houston Astros spring-train at the **Osceola County Sports Stadium**, which is also home to the Kissimmee Cobras and the Senior Little League World Series. The Atlanta Braves work out the kinks at the expansive Disney's Wide World of Sports complex, accom-

The gigantic Disney's Wide World of Sports® complex

modating as many as 9,500 fans in the only double-decked baseball stadium set up for spring training in Florida; at 100-ft (30.5-m) high, this is also the tallest baseball stadium in the state. The AA Orlando Rays play a 70-game schedule at the stadium.

RODEOS

EVERY FEBRUARY and October since the 1920s, bull riders and cowboys from all over the country have been competing for big purses and top national rankings in Kissimmee's **Silver Spurs Rodeo**, which is billed as the largest in the Eastern United States. Echoing the time when Florida was one of the top cattle producers in the country, the event features competition in bull- and bronco-riding, steer-wrestling, and barrel-racing. There is year-round cowboy entertainment with the **Kissimmee Sports Arena & Rodeo**'s Friday night events, where riders and ropers from all over the Southeastern US compete for cash prizes for bareback riding, barrel-racing, and bull-riding.

Logo of Silver Spurs Rodeo

AUTO RACING

WORLD SPEED records were made and then broken on the hard, flat sand of Daytona Beach in the 1920s. Since then, Central Florida has been the center of American car racing.

Bronco-riding at Silver Spurs Rodeo, Kissimmee

Daytona International Speedway (see p118) is the home of NASCAR, the epitome of speed. In addition to 10 major weekends of racing activity, including the world-famous Daytona 500, the Speedweeks in February, and the motorcycle racing events in March and October, the speedway showcases 190-mph (305-km/h) stock cars, super-fast motorcycles, and souped-up, 125-mph (200-km/h) go-karts. Located just south of Daytona, **New Smyrna Speedway** offers various stock car racing events almost year-round, from the World Series of Asphalt in February to the Florida Governors Cup in November. Stock cars also roar west of Orlando at the **USA International Speedway** in Lakeland.

Race cars whizzing by at the internationally renowned Daytona 500

The Great Outdoors

CENTRAL FLORIDA IS A LAND of thousands of lakes and crystal-clear spring-fed rivers, punctuated by forests, as well as some of the most temperate climate in the country. A pristine beach is never more than a comfortable drive from any spot in the area; it's entirely possible to catch a sunrise surfing in Daytona, canoe down the St. Johns River, ride at a dude ranch, para- or hang-glide, bike a 20-mile (32-km) marathon, and still catch a glorious sunset in Melbourne Beach. With lush state parks and nature sanctuaries dotting the region, Central Florida is also a major ecotourism center, as well as prime hunting and fishing territory. Central Florida, in other words, is just as much fun for an active vacationer as it is for the theme-park lover.

Harry P. Leu Gardens, a lovely, serene park in bustling Orlando

A family enjoying a leisurely cycle ride in an Orlando park

BIKING & BIKE TRAILS

LAKE COUNTY, the only area that can be said to have hills, is the home of bicycling in Central Florida, with nine triathlons from May through October, and an annual 100-mile (160-km) Bicycle Festival in October. Clermont is the center of competition biking, including triathlons for kids over 7 and adults over 70.

Central Florida's "rails-to-trails" network affords hikers more than 220 miles (350 km) of reclaimed rail corridors for hiking. The 41-mile (66-km) stretch from Claremont is particularly impressive, running right through the Withlacoochee State Forest and paralleling the river of the same name.

Orange County alone has 22 miles (35 km) of trails, including 5 miles (8 km) across **Wekiwa Springs State Park**. The West Orange Trail extends 22 miles (35 km) along the borders of Lake Apopka and connects Oakland, Winter Garden, Ocoee, and Apopka. The trail features running routes, equestrian walkways, and paved paths for cyclists and skaters. The Cross-Florida Trail runs through the Little Big Econlockhatchee Forest, crossing Central Florida from the Gulf of Mexico to the St. Johns River, a 110-mile (177-km) corridor offering off-road biking opportunities as well as paddling along the Ocklawaha and With-lacoochee Rivers. The 12-mile (19-km) Rock Springs Run from the Wekiva River Basin to the Ocala National Forest is a designated mountain-biking trail.

PARKS & NATURE WALKS

THE CITY OF Orlando alone has 4,000 acres (1,618 ha) of parks, including the **Harry P. Leu Gardens** with the largest camellia collection and formal rose garden in Southern United States

A group of youngsters cycling along a scenic country trail near Orlando

Nature viewing the cowboy way in Central Florida

(see p108). Several nature preserves flourish within the city limits; these include the 7-acre (3-ha) Delaney Park, near Downtown Orlando, and the beautifully wild Dickson Azalea Park, to the southeast of downtown, surrounded by native ferns, palms, and oaks. Located in Apopka, a short distance from Orlando, **Kelly Park** features Rock Springs, naturally fed and bubbling into a meandering stream. Wekiwa Springs State Park, also in Apopka, is another oasis with beautiful waters and acres of land. **Blue Spring State Park** is a restful spot that wintering manatee call home from December through February *(see p116)*.

HORSEBACK RIDING

DOZENS OF riding academies and stables offer trails and lessons to tourists, and two "dude ranches" give a taste of Florida's cowboy past. Located on 750 acres (300 ha) in Kissimmee, **Horse World Riding Stables** offers trail rides and Western riding lessons. The Crescent J Cattle Drive re-creates 19th-century Florida for a three-day drive on horseback, complete with whip-cracking lessons and driving a herd. **Westgate River Ranch** provides not only day-long excursions into Wild Florida, but fishing, riverboat tours, and a rodeo.

HANG- & PARA-GLIDING

SEVERAL OUTFITTERS in Central Florida offer courses in hang- and para-gliding, as well as rides. For their hang- and para-gliding lessons, **Quest Air Soaring Center** takes you on flights of up to 60 miles (96 km). Located just north of Orlando in Coleman, **FreeFlight Skydiving School** offers simulated lessons in their "Vertical Wind Tunnel" and a full course of skydiving sessions. The largest glider teaching school in Florida, **Seminole-Lake Gliderport**, in Clermont, offers introductory sailplane rides for one or two people and sailplane rental. While at **Central Florida Flyers**,

Fountain in Harry P. Leu Garden

you can learn to hang-glide and skydive, take a hot-air balloon ride in the morning, and glide or jump in the afternoon.

SURFING & OTHER WATER SPORTS

AN HOUR'S drive from Downtown Orlando, the Space Coast offers 72 miles (115 km) of Atlantic shore and white sand beaches. The Easter Surfing Festival is one of the major stops along the professional surfing circuit. Most of the hotels on the beach at Daytona offer windsurfer rentals, and two large windsurfing schools operate within minutes of Downtown Orlando. To the east, area residents head for New Smyrna Beach, Cocoa Beach, Sebastian Inlet, and the pristine stretches of the Canaveral National Seashore. Located on the western coast, Clearwater is the prime spot for surfing.

Swimming is as natural as breathing to most residents of Florida. Many hotels have pools, but the real joy of Florida is the chance to swim in the ocean or in the lakes, springs, and rivers that abound throughout the state. The full range of water sports, from windsurfing to jet skiing, is offered at the region's resorts; waterskiing can also be enjoyed on freshwater lakes and inland waterways.

Jet skiers at a Buena Vista water sports complex

A couple enjoying brisk canoeing on an Orlando waterway

CANOEING

WITH MORE than 2,000 lakes and several connected chains, Orlando is prime boating territory. There are 17 miles (27 km) of natural springs leading from the clear, limpid waters of Wekiva Springs to the St. Johns River, with plenty of camping opportunities for the hardy and riverside restaurants and bars for the casual.

The Harris Chain of Lakes can take you, from the opposite end of the St. Johns, all the way to the Atlantic Ocean. The Econlockhatchee River runs through Orange and Seminole counties, affording ample opportunities to see undisturbed wilderness minutes from developed Florida. Blue Spring State Park's wonderfully clear water is as good for snorkeling and scuba diving as it is for boats. Many inland waterways are suitable for small boats. Houseboats can be rented from several marinas in Sanford on the St. Johns River, for example.

ECOTOURISM

WITH MORE SPECIES of plants and animals than any other state, Florida is a natural paradise, ranked 11th in the world for ecotourism. Just north of the Kennedy Space Center, the Merritt Island National Wildlife Refuge and the Canaveral National Seashore *(see p125)* is the largest wildlife preserve on the Eastern Seaboard, with more than 310 species of birds, best seen in winter. The Space Coast holds more than 220 sq miles (570 sq km) of protected wildlife refuges and 40 parks. Blue Spring State Park has a 72°F (22°C) spring, and is home to endangered manatees. It features camping, hiking, and canoeing. Speaking of the gentle giants, locally-run "manatee encounters" offer the chance for small groups to actually swim with them in crystal-clear springs.

Florida Eco-Safaris in St. Cloud is an assembly of nature preserves and the Crescent J Cattle ranch, which together makes up 4,700 acres (1,902 ha) of pristine Florida wilderness for trail rides and outdoor camping.

The **Enchanted Forest Nature Sanctuary** on the East Coast winds through the ancient Atlantic Coastal Ridge and 393 acres (160 ha) of coastal hardwood forest. **Camp Hammock** is a 7,000-acre (2,832-ha) working cattle ranch that offers Wildlife Tours Agriculture Tours as well as photographic tours to spot American bald eagles, Florida bobcats, and many other endangered species.

FISHING

FLORIDA'S MANY lakes and rivers provide lots of opportunities for freshwater fishing, but it is most famous for its deep-sea sport fishing for species such as the marlin. The Daytona Beach area features some of the best ocean fishing found anywhere. Marlins are found in the Gulf Stream, while grouper and red snapper can be caught from the reefs. Two dozen private charter boats sail daily from the docks at Ponce Inlet. Fishing on Lake Tohopekaliga and

Snowy egrets keeping a lookout for prey in Merritt Island National Wildlife Refuge

A quiet day's fishing in the calm waters of a lake in Kissimmee

the Kissimmee chain of lakes means largemouth bass, and this area produces more bass over 10 lb (4.5 kg) than any other place in the world. Lakes in the Greater Orlando area also offer catfish and bream, and Merritt Island, to the east, is known for sea trout, snook, and tarpon.

turkey, the **TM Ranch Hunting Preserve** has facilities for hunting jeeps; the preserve also provides trained bird dogs with every hunt.

HUNTING

ABOUT AN HOUR'S drive from Orlando, the Ocala National Forest *(see p120)* is the place for hunters, with whitetail deer and wild turkey in season. A private reserve where no license is needed to hunt game such as quail and

LICENSING & SEASONS

A SEPARATE FISHING license is required to fish on Florida lakes and rivers, or in saltwater. Proof of a success-fully completed hunter safety course is required before a license to hunt with a firearm or bow is issued. From May to September it's possible to hunt alligators; applicants are selected through a random drawing. December to January is licensed duck season. Antlered deer and wild hog season is November to January, as is wild turkey. The season for quail, turkey, and squirrel is November to March. Saltwater fish season is virtually year-round.

DIRECTORY

BIKING, BIKE TRAILS, NATURE WALKS & PARKS

Blue Spring State Park
2100 W French Ave,
Orange City,
FL 32763.
[(386) 775-3663.

City of Orlando Parks Department
w www.cityoforlando.net/public_works/parks

Florida Trails
w www.floridaconservation.org
w www.traillink.com

Florida Triathlon Events Sommer Sports, Inc.
838 W Desoto St,
Clermont,
FL 34711.
[(352) 394-1320.
w www.sommersports.com/home

Kelly Park
Kelly Park Dr,
Apopka, FL 32712.
[(407) 889-4179.

Wekiwa Springs State Park
1800 Wekiva Circle,
Apopka, FL 32712.
[(407) 884-2008.

HORSEBACK RIDING

Horse World Riding Stables
3705 Poinciana Blvd,
Kissimmee,
FL 34758.
[(407) 847-4343.
w www.horseworldstables.com

Westgate River Ranch
3600 River Ranch Blvd,
Lake Wales,
FL 33867.
[(866) 927-2624.
w www.westgateriverranch.com

HANG- & PARA-GLIDING

Central Florida Flyers
705 E Marks St,
Orlando, FL 32803.
[(407) 894-5715.
w www.centralfloridaflyers.com

Freeflight Skydiving School
1511 Taylor Ave,
Coleman, FL 33521.
[(352) 748-6596.
w www.freeflightskydiving.com

Quest Air Soaring Center
6548 Groveland Airport Rd,
Groveland, FL 34736.
[(352) 429-0213.
w www.questairforce.com

Seminole-Lake Gliderport
Clermont, FL 34712.
[(352) 394-5450.
w www.soarfl.com/main.htm

ECOTOURISM

Camp Hammock Ranch
Kenansville,
FL 34739.
[(407) 436-1081.

Enchanted Forest Sanctuary
444 Columbia Blvd,
Titusville, FL 32780.
[(321) 264-5192.

Florida Eco-Safaris
4755 N Kenansville Rd,
St. Cloud,
FL 34773.
[(866) 854-3837.
w www.floridaeco-safaris.com

FISHING & HUNTING

Florida Fishing Seasons
[(850) 245-2555.
w www.fishingfloridakeys.com/fish_seasons.htm

Florida Game & Fresh Water Fish Commission
3900 Commonwealth Blvd,
Tallahassee, FL 32399.
[(850) 245-2555;
1-888-HUNT-FLORIDA
(486-8356);
1-888-FISH-FLORIDA
(347-4356).
w www.floridaconservation.org/license

TM Ranch Hunting Preserve
15520 TM Ranch Rd,
Orlando, FL 32832.
[(407) 273-2026.

SURVIVAL
GUIDE

PRACTICAL INFORMATION

The State Seal of Florida

THEME PARKS, perennially gorgeous weather, and a location central to both Florida coasts brings 46 million people to the Orlando area every year, 26 times the number who live there. Not surprisingly, the main industry of Orlando is tourism. With four Disney theme parks, two at Universal, and two marine parks, the emphasis is on entertainment and creating the perfect family vacation. Mickey Mouse and other favorite characters attract children, while world-class museums, cultural events, and theaters appeal to parents. At peak tourist season, during the Thanksgiving, Christmas, and Easter holidays, airfare and hotel prices run high, while late winter and early fall bring heavy discounts, shorter lines, and readily available rooms. But there is much more to Orlando than just the theme parks. Central Florida is ranked as one of the best ecotourism destinations in the world, with miles of freshwater lakes, the magnificent St. Johns River, and pristine wildlife sanctuaries spreading to the East Coast. The warm weather also promises a range of sporting activities, such as swimming, horseback riding, para-sailing, waterskiing, and golf. It is impossible to take in everything that Central Florida has to offer in one or even two weeks.

Orlando/Orange County Convention & Visitors Bureau

TOURIST INFORMATION

SOME OF THE information booths at tourist and shopping areas in Orlando are really time-share dealers offering "half-price tickets" to theme parks in exchange for several bone-wearying hours of sales pitch. But there are genuinely helpful Orlando Tourist Center booths located downtown, on International Drive, and in many larger hotel lobbies.

Downtown's **Orlando City Hall** tourist office and the official Information Booth at Orlando International Airport are of particular help for brochures and discount coupons. Both these centers are open daily from 7am to 11pm. Concierge services are available at most hotels, and the customer service centers at the theme parks are an amiable information source. The Official Accommodations

Guide to Orlando, including a vacation planning kit, is available from the **Orlando/ Orange County Convention & Visitors Bureau**. Tourists can also call the **Florida State Tourism Board**'s toll-free number to order a visitor's guide to the state. The guest services at both Walt Disney World and Universal Studios are also extremely helpful. Interested callers can ask for vacation guides, which are mailed to them free of charge.

Both the daily **Orlando Sentinel** and the "alternative" **Orlando Weekly** newspapers publish calendar sections that apprise visitors of events in the area, which are duplicated on their websites. The *Sentinel* also hosts a new, hip online service called **Orlando**

CityBeat as a guide to trendy happenings in town. The monthly **Orlando Magazine** offers free advice on restaurants and cultural happenings. Free magazines, available at many coffee shops, bars, and restaurants, include *Industry*, *Watermark*, and *Axis*; these are a quick, easy way of keeping abreast of most events. Discount booklets, attraction guides, and hotel information pamphlets are easily available at popular chain restaurants such as Shoney's, Cracker Barrel, and IHOP.

ADMISSION CHARGES

MOST MUSEUMS, parks, and other attractions charge an admission fee. This can vary enormously, from $2 at

A hotel lobby in Orlando displaying tourist information brochures

◁ **Cabs waiting for passengers on an Orlando street**

A roadside tourist information center, Kissimmee

a small museum to almost $60 for a day pass at Walt Disney World's Magic Kingdom.

A family outing at a theme park is hence an expensive proposition. The two Universal Orlando parks are $54.75 per adult, while SeaWorld charges $53.95 for an adult one-day pass. Both Universal and SeaWorld admit children ages three to nine for $44.95. Walt Disney World tickets for adults are also $54.75 for a single day; kids' tickets are a relative bargain at $43.75. Multi-day tickets are available at all parks. At Disney they're called Park Hopper Tickets, allowing guests unlimited visits to all four Disney parks; the current price is $192 for four days ($152 for children). Universal Studios offers a "4-Park FlexTicket" that allows unlimited entry at Universal Studios, SeaWorld, Islands of Adventure, and Wet 'n' Wild for 14 days; the rate is just under $180 per adult and $145.95 for kids. Special rates are offered throughout the year, and there are "Florida Resident" passes during off-season, so it's a good idea to get to know a local. Note

that all the rates mentioned are liable to change.

Many sights of interest offer discounts to children, card-carrying students, and senior cititzens. The Orlando Museum of Art, for instance, charges $12 for adults, $10 for seniors and college students, and $5 for children aged seven to 18; there is no charge for children under six. Some institutions allow free admission on certain days or at particular times.

Reduce the admission price and buy budget meals in local restaurants by using coupons found in brochures available at tourist offices.

OPENING TIMES

MOST OF the attractions open daily. All the theme parks, for instance, are open 365 days in a year. Most of them open at 9am and close between 7pm and 11pm, depending on the season, with extended opening hours during the high season. State parks are usually open every day from sunrise to sunset, though the attached visitor centers may close earlier. Some sights close once a

week, often on Mondays. Many, including the Orlando Science Center, Orlando Museum of Art, Mennello Museum of American Folk Art, and Morse Museum of American Art *(see p107 & p114)*, have extended hours on Friday and Saturday, and are open only in the afternoon on Sunday. Some sights close on major national holidays: typically New Year, Thanksgiving, and Christmas.

WHEN TO GO

GIVEN ITS WARM climate, Central Florida is a favorite winter destination for most North Americans. Late fall and early winter are very crowded in Orlando, especially at the parks. Naturally, the busy season is also when hotels and airlines are the most crowded and most expensive, so it is to your advantage to book as early as possible. If you're determined to join the crowded tourist season at Disney, planning vacations around the New Year at Magic Kingdom or the Epcot International Flower and Garden Festival in April can make the trip more worthwhile.

Plan your family vacation for mid-January–February and September–October to avoid crowds and the summer heat. If you're willing to brave some high temperatures, May is a relatively quiet month at the parks. Theme parks often have off-season multi-day deals, and hotels offer discounted rates.

Visitors strolling along a street near Disney's Broadwalk Resort

A boy in a dolphin stroller, available on rent at SeaWorld

TRAVELING WITH CHILDREN

THE REASON most children come to Orlando is for the theme parks. However, some rides may be unsuitable for smaller children. Ask the park attendant for a description of the ride. Many so-called "thrill rides" are extremely scary for children, even ones that look safe at first view. New, technologically advanced rides that include 3-D, fog, and motion simulation, such as Men in Black – Alien Attack and the Amazing Adventures of Spider-Man *(see p92 & p96)*, can be a little frightening for young kids. Never put a crying child on a ride; every attraction has a rest area off to one side of the doors, and if the child gets too distressed there are medical stations nearby. Also scout out the "lost child" area, and rely on park personnel if your child wanders off.

The glare of Florida's sun can be damaging to young eyes, so remember to take sunglasses as well as sunblock and hats. Small wagons and strollers, even multiple seat strollers, can be rented from Visitor Services just inside the gates at the Disney, Universal, and SeaWorld parks. It's worth

remembering that Walt Disney World Resort guests are offered an "Extra Magic Hour" entry into the parks, one hour prior to the regularly scheduled park opening hours on specific dates. This helps families with small children avoid the massive early morning crowds.

Because of Orlando's dependence on tourists, most restaurants and hotels are child-friendly with special seats and menus as well as fun activities. Don't forget what may sound like a joke these days: the "early bird specials." Yes, they do exist. Some family-friendly restaurants in and around Orlando offer the punctual

guest heavy discounts for arriving for breakfast before 8am or between 4 and 6pm for dinner.

Theme parks, museums, and other attractions generally have special rates for children three to 18, while some allow free admission for those under three. One of the best child-friendly attractions is Kennedy Space Center *(see pp126–9)*, open every day of the year except December 25.

If you're driving, remember that Florida law requires all occupants of vehicles who are six years of age or older to wear seat belts, and they can ticket for seat belt violations alone. Children up to six years old must be secured in a crash-tested child restraint seat. Car rental agencies will have seats available.

SENIOR CITIZENS

FLORIDA HAS ALWAYS attracted senior citizens for recreation or permanent settlement. Hotels, car rental agencies, airlines, and many shopping venues offer seniors special discount rates, and it never hurts to ask for a discount where it might not be readily apparent that one is offered. The giant discount malls along International Drive make a point of slashing their already low prices for senior shoppers. Members of the **American Association of Retired Persons (AARP)** are offered many area discounts, including sports and cultural events, and the **National Council of Senior Citizens** *(see p191)* can provide hotel

A senior citizen enjoying a round at Disney's Magnolia Golf Course

Water fun for all at the Grand Floridian Resort & Spa, Orlando

and car rental discounts. Amtrak, Greyhound, and the LYNX bus system *(see p196)* have special rates for travelers aged 50 and over. The average theme park guest walks between 5 and 7 miles (8–11 km) a day, so it's important to know that standard and motorized wheelchair rentals are available from Visitor Services just inside the gates of all the theme parks.

TRAVELERS WITH DISABILITIES

Always be sure to make hotel management aware of any potentially serious health problems. Walt Disney World in particular has its own medical staff and facilities in case of an emergency. Always carry a list of medications. All of the resorts and the restaurants at the

Wheelchair access sign

theme parks have rooms that are wheelchair-accessible. Concierge services at major hotels can assist in getting handicapped parking placards for cars. At Universal, wheelchairs are available for rental at $7 per day and Electric Convenience Vehicles are available for rental at $35 per day. It is recommended that you call up at least 24 hours in advance to make a reservation. Universal Orlando puts great store in the "queue experience" as an important part of riding an attraction, and guests in wheelchairs are asked to join the line and wait in queue along with everyone else.

Disney has a limited number of wheelchairs available at the Guest Services Desk, at the entrances to Magic Kingdom, Epcot, Animal Kingdom, and Disney-MGM

Studios. Magic Kingdom and Epcot also have motorized wheelchairs. Disney offers a "Guidebook for Guests with Disabilities," which you can get by calling the main information number.

Sign language interpreting services are also available at Universal Studios Florida and Islands of Adventure at no extra charge.

COMMUNICATIONS

Online sources of Orlando information abound, from the websites of the *Orlando Sentinel* and *Orlando Weekly* newspapers, to city guides run by **CitySearch**, **icFlorida**, **Digital City Orlando**, and **MSN**. These not only give overviews of happenings and restaurants, but also offer bulletin board comments from local residents. The major television stations also have Internet calendars. There's a branch of business supply giant, Kinkos, or one of the major office supply stores – OfficeMax, Office Depot, and Staples – on practically every street corner, making fax and copying services readily available.

With the new push toward wireless Internet availability, there has been a mushrooming of access points in local Starbucks and Borders bookstore locations. Most major hotel chains, as well as the Orlando International Airport, also offer convenient Internet access. Downtown Orlando itself is a free Internet access zone. This includes the entire Lake Eola Park area.

Newspaper vending machines lined up in a row on a sidewalk in Orlando

Police officers on patrol, Florida-style

PERSONAL SECURITY

MOST CITIES IN the region, like elsewhere in the world, have "no-go" areas that should be avoided. The staff at the local tourist office or in your hotel should be able to advise. Note that downtown areas are generally unlike city centers elsewhere; they are first and foremost buisness districts, which are dead at night and often unsafe.

As beautiful as "The City Beautiful" may look, it also has the potential for less than secure situations. Certain areas of Orlando, such as the Orange Blossom Trail and areas surrounding the downtown main strip of Orange Avenue, should be avoided after dark, and even brightly lit sections of town shouldn't be navigated alone. If in doubt, take a taxi rather than walk. The downtown LYNX bus terminal is not a place to hang around in. Be aware of who is around you in the sprawling parking garages at the theme parks, and keep an eye on your belongings while enjoying the "party strips" of Downtown Disney's Pleasure Island as well as Universal CityWalk.

Carry as little money as possible when you go out. If you are attacked, hand your wallet over immediately; do not try to resist.

The major tourist centers of Central Florida are well policed. Given the region's eagerness to both attract and protect tourists, police officers are friendly and helpful to visitors. Orlando City police are visible in most high-traffic areas; the Mounted Police unit can be seen patroling downtown neighborhoods daily. The theme parks are fanatical about security and visitor service; Disney, for example, has its own fire and police departments and health personnel.

Even if you have only a slim chance of retrieving stolen property, you should report all lost or stolen items to the police. Most credit card companies have toll-free numbers for reporting a loss, as do **Thomas Cook** and **American Express** for lost traveler's checks.

A postcard from the "Sunshine State"

SAFETY FOR DRIVERS

CERTAIN AREAS OF Orlando are better avoided, and keeping alert to highway signs is a must. The well-traveled routes of major highways and main streets are the safest, but even the prominent thoroughfares can suddenly become illogical. The Florida State Police Department has a cellphone emergency 911 service in operation. The Automobile Association of America (*see p197*) places "Good Samaritan" vehicles on the highways to intercept emergencies of various kinds.

Keep some basic rules in mind while driving around the region. Local drivers change lanes frequently on expressways, so stick to the right and be alert near exits. Speed limits are rigorously enforced, and fines can be as much as $150. Avoid taking short cuts in urban areas. Stick to the main highways if possible. If you need to refer to a map in a city, don't stop until you are in a well-lit or busy area. Avoid sleeping in the car off the highway, although some rest areas on expressways have security patrols. Seat belts are mandatory for all under Florida law. The **Orlando City Hall** website lists road closures.

NATURAL HAZARDS

THE MAJOR cause of vacation injury in Orlando is the heat. Standing in long lines under the dazzling Florida sun can mean sunburn, rashes, heatstroke, and heat exhaustion. Bring hats, sunglasses, lots of bottled water, and a high SPF waterproof sunscreen – reapply this often, especially at water parks. Plan park visits early in the day or after 5pm.

The natural beauty of Florida can be dangerous. Orlando is riddled with 1,000 lakes, and chances are the larger ones might contain alligators. There are also several venomous snakes native to Florida. Don't forget to carry insect repellent for mosquitoes and summer gnats.

Florida's beaches are usually well-supervised by lifeguards, but do keep a close eye on young children. Riptides can be dangerous in some places.

A county sheriff, in the regulation dark uniform, and his patrol car

DIRECTORY

TOURIST INFORMATION

Florida State Tourism Board
☎ (888) 735-2872.
ⓦ www.flausa.com

Kissimmee/St. Cloud Convention & Visitors Bureau
☎ (407) 847-5000.

Orlando/Orange County Convention & Visitors Bureau
☎ (407) 363-5872.
ⓦ www.orlandoinfo.com

ONLINE INFORMATION

CitySearch
ⓦ http://orlando.citysearch.com/

Digital City Orlando
ⓦ www.digitalcity.com/orlando

icFlorida
ⓦ www.wftv.com/icflorida

MSN City Guide
ⓦ http://local.msn.com/Orlando

Orlando CityBeat
ⓦ www.orlandocitybeat.com

Orlando City Hall
☎ (407) 246-2121.
ⓦ www.cityoforlando.net

Orlando Downtown Wireless District
ⓦ www.cityaccess.pureconnection.net

MAGAZINES & NEWSPAPERS

El Sentinel (Spanish language edition)
ⓦ www.orlandosentinel.com/elsentinel

La Prensa
☎ (407) 767-0070.
ⓦ www.laprensaorlando.com

Orlando Business Journal
☎ (407) 649-8470.
ⓦ www.bizjournals.com/orlando

Orlando Leisure Magazine
☎ (407) 647-5557.
ⓦ www.orlandomagazine.com

Orlando Magazine
☎ (407) 767-8338.
ⓦ www.orlandomagazine.com

Orlando Sentinel
☎ (407) 420-5000.
ⓦ www.orlandosentinel.com

Orlando Weekly
☎ (407) 377-0400.
ⓦ www.orlandoweekly.com

The Wall Street Journal, Orlando office
☎ (407) 857-2600.

WHERE Orlando
☎ (407) 767-8338.
ⓦ www.where-orlando.com

TV & RADIO

ABC: WFTV-Channel 9
☎ (407) 841-9000.

CBS: WKMG-Channel 6
☎ (407) 291-6000.

Fox: WOFL-Channel 35
☎ (407) 644-3535.

NBC: WESH-Channel 2
☎ (407) 645-2222.

PBS: WMFE-Channel 24
☎ (407) 273-2300.

UPN: WRBW-Channel 65
☎ (407) 248-6500.

WB: WKCF-Channel 18
☎ (407) 645-1818.

WJRR (101.1 FM)
Rock/Alternative
☎ (407) 916-1011.

WLOQ (103.1 FM)
Smooth Jazz
☎ (407) 647-5557.

WMFE (90.7 FM)
Public radio/Classical
☎ (407) 273-2300.

WOMX (105.1 FM)
Adult contemporary
☎ (407) 919-1000.

WTKS (104.1 FM)
Talk radio
☎ (407) 916-7800.

WWKA (92.3 FM)
Country
☎ (407) 298-9292.

OTHER NUMBERS

American Association of Retired Persons
☎ (888) 687-2277.
ⓦ www.aarp.org

Mobility International
☎ (541) 343-1284.

National Council of Senior Citizens
☎ (301) 578-8800.

Orlando Weather
ⓦ www.orlandoweather.com

Seniors First
☎ (407) 292-0177.
ⓦ www.seniorsfirstinc.com

EMERGENCY NUMBERS

All Emergencies
☎ 911 to alert police, fire, or medical services.

Moneygram
☎ (800) 926-9400.

Orlando Police Information Desk
☎ (407) 246-2470.
ⓦ www.cityoforlando.net

Poison Control
☎ (407) 841-5222.

LOST CREDIT CARDS & TRAVELERS' CHECKS

American Express
☎ (888) 412-6945 (cards); (800) 221-7282 (checks).
ⓦ www.home.americanexpress.com

Diners Club
☎ (800) 234-6377.
ⓦ www.dinersclub.com

Discover
☎ (800) 347-2683.
ⓦ www.discovercard.com

MasterCard
☎ (800) 622-7747.
ⓦ www.mastercard.com

Thomas Cook
☎ (800) 223-7373 (checks).

VISA
☎ (800) 847-2911.
ⓦ www.visa.com

TRAVEL INFORMATION

MORE THAN 46 million visitors flock to the warmth and recreation of Central Florida each year, making it one of the most sought-after tourist destinations in the world. Orlando International is Florida's busiest airport, welcoming millions of visitors every year; and many more arrive by train and bus. The network of interstate highways

An American Airlines passenger jet

that converge in Orlando carry almost 200,000 cars a day through downtown. Amtrak offers daily service from points North and West, with sleeper cars, and even has room for the family car. Once there, almost all roads lead to the theme parks, with a celebrated public transit system taking some of the burden off the very busy highways.

The brightly illuminated terminal of Orlando International Airport

ARRIVING BY AIR

ORLANDO'S LOCAL airports are served by virtually all US domestic carriers and a wide selection of international airlines, including Orlando Native people-mover Airtrans, Aerolineas Argentinas, United Airlines and the British favorite Virgin Atlantic. A recent $1.2 billion expansion has made **Orlando International Airport** the third largest airport in the US, and the recent addition of discount carriers such as **Spirit Airlines**, **Song**, **JetBlue**, and United's new "low fare" service called **Ted**, is creating a flurry of cheaper flights to this vacation hub.

    Orlando-Sanford International Airport is undergoing a construction spurt of its own. This airport offers access from East Coast carriers such as Pan Am, Southeast, TransMeridian, and Vacation Express. **Daytona Beach International Airport** brings in daily flights from Atlanta on **Delta**,

Cleveland and Newark on Continental, and flights from the Bahamas on Vintage Airlines prop planes.

AIR FARES

TRAVEL COSTS TO the world's most popular vacation site depend very much on the season. Unfortunately for the vacationer, prime holiday time in Orlando is when fares are at the highest. The difference between late winter (February and March) airfares, when tourist traffic is low, and the

height of busy season (November and December) can more than double the price per ticket. The best deals can be found on midweek flights. Inexpensive fares can usually be found on the online travel websites, but they are geared toward larger carriers and do not include the more popular discount airlines such as JetBlue and **Southwest**. It is better to check online with these airlines directly, as they often have "cyberdeals" only available on the Internet. It can also be an advantage not to plan ahead, with some airlines offering last-minute specials on unsold seats.

AIRPORTS

ONE OF THE country's top airports for overall customer convenience, Orlando International Airport boasts state-of-the-art services. Fast intra-airport ransportation via monorail and moving walkways leads to shuttle buses, taxis, and public transportation to Downtown Orlando and the parks. Mutilingual tourist information centers by the

A taxi outside the Orlando International Airport

The shopping area at Orlando International Airport

security checkpoints are open from 7am to 11pm. The airport can also offer an evening's rest, with the Hyatt Regency Hotel and its 446 rooms right in the main concourse. Banks of rental car agencies are located on the baggage levels in both terminals and taxi and busstands are outside Level 1. Also to be added to the attractions at the airport are shopping and dining, with stores from Disney, Universal and SeaWorld right in the terminal. Much quieter than the main Orlando airport, the Orlando-Sanford International is about 30 minutes from Downtown Orlando. It is a major hub for charter flights from Britain and Canada, and is increasingly being used by smaller carriers such as Southeast and Pan Am as a low-pressure alternative.

Only ten years old, Daytona Beach International Airport offers direct flights from various East Coast cities to the world's most famous beach *(see p118)*.

GETTING TO TOWN

T HE LYNX BUS system *(see p196)* runs from Level 1 of the A side of the Main Terminal, departing every 30 minutes from 5:30am to 11:30pm. Travel time to Downtown Orlando is approximately 40 minutes, and to International Drive 60 minutes, at a cost of $1.25 for either destination. Make sure you have exact fare; the transfers to connecting buses are free. Many hotels have their own courtesy buses, but there are also shuttle buses *(see p196)*: the **Mears Transportation Group** *(see p197)* serves most destinations in the area. Shuttle vans, accommodating up to nine people, have posted rates running $14 to $16 per person for trips downtown or to Disney. Taxis *(see pp197)* from Orlando International to hotels and theme parks are available at both terminals A and B, just outside baggage claim on Level 1. To avoid costly metered fares, look for a yellow Mears cab for posted flat rate fares to downtown and Walt Disney World; they accept credit cards. Ground transportation at Orlando-Sanford International is conveniently found right outside the terminal.

Highway Patrol insignia

DIRECTORY

AIRLINE NUMBERS

American Airlines
📞 *(800) 433-7300.*
🌐 www.aa.com

Delta Airlines
📞 *(800) 221-1212.*
🌐 www.delta.com

JetBlue
📞 *(800) 538-2583.*
🌐 www.jetblue.com

Song
📞 *(800) 359-7664.*
🌐 www.flysong.com

Southwest Airlines
📞 *(800) 435-9792.*
🌐 www.southwest.com

Spirit Airlines
📞 *(800) 772-7117.*
🌐 www.spiritair.com

Ted (United Airlines)
📞 *(800) 225-5833.*
🌐 www.flyted.com

US Airways
📞 *(800) 428-4322.*
🌐 www.usair ways.com

TRAVEL SITES

🌐 www.expedia.com
🌐 www.travelocity.com
🌐 www.orbitz.com
🌐 www.priceline.com

AIRPORTS

Daytona Beach International Airport
📞 *(386) 248-8069.*
🌐 www.flydaytonafirst.com

Orlando International Airport
📞 *(407) 825-2352.*
🌐 www.orlandoairports.net

Orlando-Sanford International Airport
📞 *(407) 585-4000.*
🌐 www.
orlandosanfordairport.com

GETTING TO TOWN

Mears Transportation Group
📞 *(407) 423-5566.*

The People Mover monorail at Orlando International Airport

Getting Around

J UST ABOUT A century ago, Central Florida was mostly
dirt roads surrounded by orange groves. The present-
day convergence of highways, parkways, and six-lane
thoroughfares makes Orlando an automotive heaven.
Several major roads run through, across, or near
downtown, and almost all roads lead to the theme
parks. Walt Disney World and Universal Orlando resorts
have their own exits on Interstate 4 and the Central
Florida Greeneway. Local streets leading to the parks
are lined with restaurants and shopping malls.

You can get by without a car in Orlando, but life is
much easier with one. If you don't bring your own,
car rental rates are among the lowest in the US, and
gas is relatively inexpensive. In addition, Floridians
are generally courteous and considerate drivers.

Interstate Highway 4

City parking restrictions

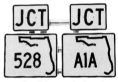

Speed limit (in mph)

Rest area, indicated off an interstate

RULES OF THE ROAD

O N A TWO-WAY street or
highway, all drivers
moving in either direction
must halt for a stopped
school bus. At intersections
with traffic lights, you may
turn right on red if the way
is clear and there is no sign
prohibiting the turn. Left
turns on red from a one-way
street into a one-way street
are also allowed. Passing is
allowed on both sides on any
multi-lane road, including
interstate highways.

According to Florida law,
wearing seat belts while traveling in vehicles is compulsory
for all (*see p188*). Driving
under the influence is treated
very seriously, so don't drink
even one beer. Violators can
be fined hundreds of dollars

or even be imprisoned for
a short period of time.

Most road signs are clear and
self-explanatory. If you are
caught disregrading instructions, you might be fined.
The speed limits in Florida
are as follows:
• 55–70 mph (90–105 km/h)
on highways.
• 20–30 mph (32–48 km/h)
in residential areas.
• 15 mph (24 km/h) near
schools.

Speed limits can vary every
few miles, so keep a sharp
eye out for the signs. On an
interstate you can be fined for
driving slower than 40 mph
(64 km/h). The speed limits
are rigorously enforced by
the Florida Highway Patrol,
whose representatives issue
tickets on the spot. A fine can
set you back as much as $150.

Overhead signs at the junction of two routes

HIGHWAYS & TOLLS

M ETROPOLITAN Orlando is
the crossroads of
Florida's busy highway
system, where the north–
south Florida's Turnpike
meets east-west Interstate 4.
The Bee Line Expressway
(State Road 528), which runs
east-west, the Central Florida
Greeneway (State Road 417)

An aerial view of Orlando, showing busy, merging highways

running south and east into Walt Disney World, and East-West Expressway (State Road 408) connecting Downtown Orlando to I-4, are toll roads. Tolls range between 50 cents and $1.50 per station. Toll roads also operate on an electronic system called SunPass; transmitters can be purchased locally. Florida toll booths do not take bills larger than a $20.

NAVIGATING

THE MAIN thoroughfare in Orlando is Interstate 4. Heavily trafficked, it connects all the theme parks and outlet shopping areas in the west with downtown and the bedroom communities to the east. During the morning and the evening rush hours, the highways slow to a virtual standstill, the worst being I-4 through downtown and the area around Walt Disney World, so time your trips accordingly. Be aware that the exit numbers on I-4 were changed in 2003, so older maps and directions will surely be incorrect.

Because of the expense, the toll roads are the least traveled, and while I-4 can sometimes become a parking lot during odd hours, roads such as State Roads 417 and 408 can appear blissfully empty.

Much has been done to improve roads heading west from downtown, and roads such as John Young Parkway can sometimes offer a slower but surer route to the theme parks. The Bee Line is the fastest way from Orlando International Airport to Universal Orlando and

Mears Taxicab dispatch fleet, which includes cars for rent

SeaWorld, while the Central Florida Greeneway leads directly west to Disney.

Visitors staying at any one of the massive hotels on International Drive will soon discover Sand Lake Road, which leads to the parks as well as to several enormous shopping malls.

CAR RENTAL

TO THE CHAGRIN of locals, rental car companies offer the best deals to out-of-towners, sometimes as low at $10 a day. Multi-day packages for weekend rentals are usually the best deals, and arranging those deals before you

Logo of the Hertz car rental company

leave home can often mean substantial savings. Check your existing car insurance for rental before you sign the contract. While a Collision Damage Waiver (CDW) is expensive, it sometimes covers damage to the vehicle that insurance will not, even if it was not your fault. Companies differ in their policies concerning gas; some charge for what you use while others ask that you fill the car before you return it.

The major companies (see p197) either have rental kiosks right in the airports – Orlando International's are right next to baggage claim; Orlando-

Sanford's rentals are right outside the terminal – or a short and free shuttle bus ride away. There are also several agencies in Orlando.

BIKE RENTAL

ORLANDO IS ideal for moving around on a bicycle with its 200 miles (322 km) of bike trails. The Disney resort hotels – Caribbean Beach Resort, Grand Floridian, and others – offer rentals on Disney property, while **David's World Cycle** rents mountain and road bikes.

If you prefer the motorized variety, **American V Twin Motorcycles** rents Harley Davidson motorcycles. **RELAY** in Winter Park and Celebration offers not only bicycles but also the self-balancing personal commuting devices known as Segway Human Transporters.

Bike riders on a trail in Walt Disney World® Resort

The dreaded rush hour in Orlando

An Amtrak train moving along a track at the Auto Train yard, Sanford

TRAINS

WITH A much-discussed light rail system still in the planning stage, rail travel through Central Florida means **Amtrak**. From an Art Deco-inspired station in the heart of the city, Amtrak offers a limited schedule of local travel, including stops in Downtown Orlando, Winter Park, Kissimmee, and points south to Miami. Fares run from $6 for a short hop to Winter Park, to around $30 to Miami, one way. Auto Train is very popular as it provides transport for family and vehicle from Washington, DC to Sanford. But do check for height restrictions on SUVs.

Of course, Amtrak connects across America and into Canada too, with Orlando being one of the more popular destinations. But cross-country rail travel is both time-consuming and expensive when compared to airlines. The 24-hour trip from New York can cost twice the comparable plane flight. A four-day trip from Los Angeles by rail will cost more than $1,100 per person, but that includes the comfort of a bedroom and meals.

LONG-DISTANCE BUSES

WHETHER YOU are traveling from other parts of the country or within Florida, Greyhound buses offer the cheapest way to get around. Some services are "express," with few stops en route, while others serve a greater number of destinations. A few routes have "flag stops," where a bus may stop to deposit or collect passengers in places without a bus station. Pay the driver directly, or, if you want to reserve in advance, go to the nearest Greyhound depot. Passes provide unlimited travel for set periods of time – from between four and 60 days – but are useful only if you have a very full itinerary.

PUBLIC TRANSPORT IN CITIES

THE AWARD-WINNING **LYNX** bus system, with more than 40 routes and 4,000 stops through three counties, makes getting around Central Florida inexpensive and easy. The brightly decorated buses fan out from the central station north to Lake Mary, east to Winter Park and Orlando International Airport, and south to Walt Disney World and Universal Orlando. The theme park routes in particular are probably the easiest way to the parks if you're staying downtown, with scheduled service from 7am to after 10pm. Look for the signs with pink paw prints denoting LYNX

Orlando's LYNX bus logo

bus stops. Standard, one-way fare throughout the system is only $1.25, and passes are available for unlimited travel. A Single-Day pass is $3, seven days of travel will cost $10, and a month-long pass is $36. Long-term passes can be purchased at Albertsons Supermarkets or online at the LYNX website, with Single-Day passes available from the driver of any LYNX bus.

Downtown visitors have the no-cost advantage of the free LYMMO service, which runs along its own traffic lane every 15 minutes between 6am and 10pm (midnight on Friday and Saturday). The service connects the Church Street entertainment area to the TD Waterhouse Sports Center, with stops including the Regional History Center and the Orange County Courthouse.

SHUTTLE BUSES

MOST MAJOR HOTELS offer free shuttle buses from the airports. Once you're at your destination, the same hotels usually have van transportation to Disney,

A hotel shuttle bus advertising the Orlando FlexTicket pass

Universal Orlando, and SeaWorld. If not, Mears Transportation *(see p193)* offers shuttle vans to various attractions in the area.

Shuttles from **AA Port Canaveral Transportation** and **Daytona Shuttle Service** can make a trip to the East Coast beaches easy, offering a 60-minute ride to the sand flats of Daytona Beach, fishing on the Atlantic Ocean, and the sights of the Kennedy Space Center. Round trip shuttle fare is approximately $50 (children 2–12, around $15 each way).

TAXIS

THE MOST READILY available taxis are at stands at the Orlando International and Orlando-Sanford airports, taxi-only lanes at most larger hotels, and those circling the theme parks, particularly at the main entrances to the various parks and at Universal CityWalk and Downtown Disney's Pleasure Island nightlife entertainment areas. Those operated by **Mears Taxi Dispatch**, with their bright orange paint, and Yellow Cab, are metered and thought to be the most

An I-Ride Trolley for the I Drive area

trustworthy – avoid hiring one of the many "gypsy" cabs, which may end up costing several times what the fare is worth. Reserving a taxi from the airport or by cell phone will give the option of paying by credit card.

Street sign of the I-Ride trolley service

OTHER MODES OF TRANSPORT

ONE OF Orlando's most popular tourist centers, International Drive provides special transportation for

visitors in the form of old-fashioned buses, called the **I-Ride Trolleys**. Trolleys run from the Major Boulevard area and Belz Factory Outlet shops to SeaWorld, with 83 stops in between; the frequency is 20–30 minutes year-round, seven days a week, from 8am to 10:30pm. Multi-day passes are available. Another old-fashioned way to travel around Orlando is by horse-drawn carriage. The **Orlando Carriage Company** runs quaint carriages from Church Street that ride through downtown, around Lake Eola and back, from 7:30pm until midnight. An even older form of transportation can be found in Orlando; **Why Walk Pedicab** and **Orlando Pedicab** both operate several free human-powered jitneys around downtown.

DIRECTORY

BREAKDOWNS

American Automobile Association (AAA)
℡ *(407) 444-7000.*
Ⓦ www.aaa.com

AAA General Breakdown Assistance
℡ *(800) 222-4357.*
NOTE: Rental companies provide 24-hour roadside assistance.

CAR RENTAL

Alamo® Rent a Car
℡ *(800) 327-9633.*
Ⓦ www.alamo.com

Avis Rent a Car
℡ *(800) 831-2847.*

Budget® Rent a Car
℡ *(800) 527-0700.*
Ⓦ www.budget.com

Dollar® Rent a Car
℡ *(800) 423-4704.*
Ⓦ www.dollar.com

Enterprise
℡ *(800) 736-8222.*

Hertz
℡ *(800) 654-3131.*

BIKE RENTAL

American V Twin Motorcycles
℡ *(407) 903-0058.*
Ⓦ www.amvtwin.com

David's World Cycle
℡ *(407) 422-2458.*
Ⓦ www.davidsworld.com

RELAY
℡ *(407) 645-3399.*
Ⓦ www.relaytogo.com

TRAINS

Amtrak
℡ *(800) 525-2550.*
Ⓦ www.amtrak.com

BUSES

AA Port Canaveral Transportation
℡ *(321) 231-3865.*

Daytona-Orlando Transit (DOTS)
℡ *(800) 231-1965;*
(386) 257-5411.

Daytona Shuttle Service
℡ *(800) 882-1127.*

LYNX Buses
℡ *(407) 841-5969.*
Ⓦ www.golynx.com

O&A Transport Airport Services
℡ *(407) 832-1342.*

TAXI RENTAL

Mears Taxicab Dispatch
℡ *(407) 422-2222.*

OTHER MODES OF TRANSPORT

I-Ride Trolley
℡ *(866) 243-7483.*
Ⓦ www.iridetrolley.com

Orlando Carriage Company
℡ *(407) 855-2900.*
Ⓦ www.
orlandohauntings.com/
carriage.html

Orlando Pedicab
℡ *(321) 217-2233.*

Why Walk Pedicab
℡ *(407) 740-8294.*
Ⓦ http://store.
bicyclerevolution.com/
whywalkpedicab.html

General Index

Acknowledgments

MAIN CONTRIBUTORS

PHYLLIS & ARVIN STEINBERG live in Florida. Phyllis writes about travel for US newspapers, magazines, and websites. She is also a food columnist for 24 newspapers in Florida and cruise editor for a popular travel website. Arvin writes travel articles for US newspapers, magazines, and websites, and is sports editor of a widely read travel website.

JOSEPH HAYES is a freelance writer for newspapers and magazines around the world, specializing in food, travel, and music. He is also an accomplished playwright, with productions in several countries.

CHARLES MARTIN is a Florida-based journalist and radio broadcaster who writes columns and articles on Florida events for numerous local, national, and international lifestyle magazines.

FACTCHECKER
Kia Bocko

PROOF READER
Bhavna Seth Ranjan

INDEXER
Shreya Arora

PHOTOGRAPHY
Dave King, Magnus Rew, Stephen Whitehorn, Linda Whitwam

ILLUSTRATIONS
Arun Pottirayil, Julian Baker

DK LONDON
PUBLISHER
Douglas Amrine

PUBLISHING MANAGERS
Jane Ewart, Fay Franklin

EDITORIAL & DESIGN ASSISTANCE
Brigitte Arora, Tessa Bindloss

SENIOR CARTOGRAPHIC EDITOR
Casper Morris

SENIOR DTP DESIGNER
Jason Little

DK PICTURE LIBRARY
Hayley Smith, Romaine Werblow
Gemma Woodward,

PRODUCTION CONTROLLER
Shane Higgins

SPECIAL ASSISTANCE
Many thanks for the invaluable help of the following individuals: Kelly Rote, Central Florida Visitors & Convention Bureau; Susan Mclain, Daytona Beach Convention & Visitors Bureau; Georgia Turner, Georgia Turner Group; Dave A. Wegman, Greater Orlando Aviation Authority; Danielle Courtenay, Julie Doyle, Julie A. Fernandez, Orlando/Orange County Convention & Visitors Bureau; Lita O'Neill, Polk County Natural Resources Division; Jacquelyn Wilson, SeaWorld Orlando & Discovery Cove; Susan L. Storey, NBC Universal, Orlando; Jason L. Lasecki, Walt Disney World Resort; Sandra Sciarrino, Wet 'n Wild.

PHOTOGRAPHY PERMISSIONS
Dorling Kindersley would like to thank the following for their assistance and kind permission to photograph at their establishments: Albin Polasek Museum & Sculpture Gardens, Audobon National Center for Birds of Prey, Buena Vista Watersports, Falcon's Fire Golf Club, Hard Rock Café Live, Holy Land Experience.

Placement Key – t=top; tl=top left; tlc=top left center; tc=top center; trc=top right center; tr=top right; cla=center left above; ca=center above; cra=center right above; cl=center left; c=center; cr=center right; clb=center left below; cb=center below; crb=center right below; bl=bottom left; b=bottom; bc=bottom center; bcl=bottom center left; br=bottom right; d=detail.

The publishers would like to thank the following individuals, companies, and picture libraries for their kind permission to reproduce their photographs:

ALAMY: Mark J. Barrett 119cla, Randa Bishop 107bl; ANTIQUE & CLASSIC BOAT SOCIETY: 23tl.

CENTRAL FLORIDA FAIR: 22 tc; CENTRAL FLORIDA VISITORS & CONVENTION BUREAU: 18tr; CORBIS: 19bcr, 131 (inset), 170tc; Archivo Iconografico, S.A 11b; James L. Amos 182b, Tony Arruza 18bl, 103b, 119cra; Yann Arthus-Bertrand 194b; Bettmann 192tc; Gary Braash 19crb; Duomo 118tr; Raymond Gehman 26-27, 102; Martin Harvey 19tr; Lake County Museum 7(inset), 116tl, 185 (inset), 190c; David Muench 19cla, Marc Muench 119bl; James Randkley 10; Phil Schermeister 15b, 19cr; George Teidmann/ Newsport 25b,179bl; Partrick Ward 22cla; Nick Wheeler 132cl; RAIMUND CRAMM: 125cla; MARTY CSERCSEVETIS: 158bc; CYPRESS GARDENS: 123tr.

© DISNEY: 1c, 2–3, 3 (inset), 5tl, 8cl, 13t, 16tr, 16cla, 16clb, 16br, 28, 29b, 30tr, 30clb, 30bcr, 31tl, "The Twilight Zone™ is a registered trademark of CBS, Inc. and is used pursuant to a license from CBS, Inc." 31cra, *La Nouba* by Cirque du Soleil ® 31br, 32–33, 34bl, 36tr, 36br, 37tr, 37br, 38tr, 38bl, 39br, 40tl, 40br, 41tl, 42cla, 43tl, 44b, 46bl, 47tr, 48-49, 50tl, 50br, 51tl, 52tl, 52b, 53tl, 54bl, 55tl, "The Twilight Zone™ is a registered trademark of CBS, Inc. and is used pursuant to a license from CBS, Inc." 56, 58-59, "TM & (c) 2003 The Jim Henson Company. JIM HENSON'S mark & logo, BEAR IN THE BIG BLUE HOUSE mark & logo, characters and elements are trademarks of The Jim Henson Company. All Rights Reserved. From the television series Bear in the Big Blue House created by Mitchell Kriegman" 60tl, 61b, 62tl, 62b, 64cl, "It's Tough to be a Bug!" based upon the Disney/Pixar film "A Bug's Life" © Disney/Pixar 64br, 65tl, 65br, 66tr, 66b, 67tr, 68-69, 70tr, 70cl, 70bl, 71tr, 71bl, 72tr, 72cla, 72bl, 73tr, 73cl, 74cl, 74br, 75tl, *La Nouba* by Cirque du Soleil ® 75c, © LEGO 75br, 132bc, 133tr, 133b, 136tr, "Woody" from the Disney/Pixar film "Toy Story" ©Disney 136cl, 136br, 138cl, 149br, 163tl, 170cl, 171tl, 171b, 174-75, 177tc, 178br, 187b, 188br, 189tl, 195br.

ENZIAN THEATER/FLORIDA FILM FESTIVAL: 13c, 22crb, 166tc, 166bc; FLORIDA DEPARTMENT OF ENVIRONMENTAL PROTECTION DIVISION OF RECREATION & PARKS: 117b; FLORIDA MALL: 159tl, 160cl; FLORIDA STATE ARCHIVE: 15c; FRANK LANE PICTURE LIBRARY: © David Hosking 180tr.

GENESIS SPACE PHOTO LIBRARY: 20tl, 20c, 20clb, 128bc, 128br, 129bl, 129br; SEAN GILLIAM: 196t; GREATER ORLANDO AVIATION AUTHORITY: 134tl, 162b, 192cl, 193tl.

HARD ROCK CAFÉ: 113c, 132tc, 133tl; ©HEIDI TARGEE: 112crb; HIGGINS HOUSE: 134cr; HOLIDAY INN FAMILY SUITES RESORT, ORLANDO, FLORIDA: 135bl, 137tl.

INDEX STOCK PHOTOGRAPHY. INC., New York: 125cra; INSTITUTE OF SYSTEMIC BOTANY, UNIVERSITY OF SOUTH FLORIDA: Guy Anglin 19clb

KENNEDY SPACE CENTER – VISITORS CENTER, Cape Canaveral: 21c, 126tr, 127cr, 127ca, 128tr; KISSIMMEE ST-CLOUD CONVENTION & VISITORS' BUREAU/Doug Dukane: 180b, 183tl.

MAD COW THEATRE: 109tl; MARINE SCIENCE CENTER, PONCE INLET: 19tl; MARY EVANS PICTURE LIBRARY: 27(inset); FRED MAWER: 126clb; MEARS TRANSPORTATION GROUP: 195tr.

©NASA: 13br, 20tr, 21tr.

ORANGE BLOSSOM BALLOONS: 172 tl; ORLANDO & ORANGE COUNTY CONVENTION & VISITORS BUREAU: 12ca, 25tl, 106br, 108tl, 109br, 114br, 160tr, 160b, 161tc, 162cl, 164cl, 164br, 165tr, 166cl, 167tl, 167b, 168br, 176tc, 178tr, 178cl, 179tc, 180tr, 180cl, 181tl, 182tl, 186cl, 197tc; ORLANDO TOURISM BUREAU: 138bl; ORONOZ, Madrid: 11tc.

PHOTOLIBRARY: Wendell Metzen 110-111; PLANET EARTH PICTURES: 125cra.

REUTERS: Charles W. Luzier 176cl; MARIAN RYAN: 18cl, 18cr.

© SEAWORLD ORLANDO: 4br, 6-7, 12bl, 17cr, 24tl, 78, 79b, 80bl, 83cb, 84ca, 84bl, 85tl, 86cl, 87tl, 87br; SILVER SPURS RODEO: 179c; STARWOOD: 135tl; ARVIN STEINBERG: 18cb,18bcr, 19bcl; PHYLLIS STEINBERG: 118c.

THE MENNELLO MUSEUM OF AMERICAN FOLK ART: *Bird*, Paul Marco 107tr.

PHOTOS COURTESY OF UNIVERSAL ORLANDO: 4tr, 17tr, 81tr, 88c, 88b, 89cla, 89cb, 89br, 90tl, 90b, 91tl, 91br, 92tl, 92b, 93tr, 94-95, 96tl, 96br, 97tl, 97br, 98tl, 98bl, 99br, 137br, 148br, 168tl.

VILLAS OF GRAND CYPRESS: 14bl.

WET 'N WILD ORLANDO: 17cr, 23br, 81br, 100tr, 100cla, 100clb, 100bl, 101tl, 101cra, 101crb, 101br, 101bl.

©ZORA NEALE HURSTON NATIONAL MUSEUM OF FINE ARTS: *Festival Girl*, Jane Turner 106cl.

Front endpaper: © DISNEY: cla; SEAWORLD ORLANDO: tc; CORBIS: Raymond Gehman br.

JACKET
Front – CORBIS: Darrell Gulin c; DK IMAGES: Dave King crb; © SEAWORLD ORLANDO: Kraken® bl; © DISNEY: Epcot®, Spaceship Earth main image. Back – DK Images: Stephen Whitehorne br; © DISNEY: Kali River Rapids® tl. Spine – © DISNEY: Epcot®, Spaceship Earth.

All other images © Dorling Kindersley. See www.DKimages.com for further information.

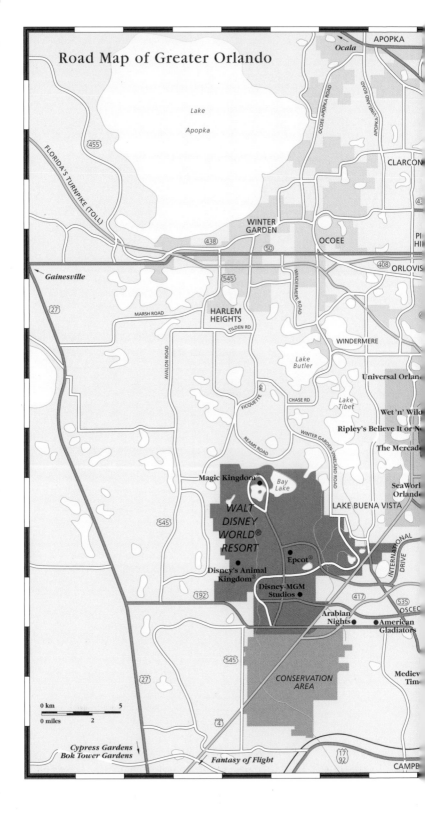